THE AUTHORS Tim Boatswain has degrees in Ancient History and Archaeology and Social Anthropology and has worked in the fields of Byzantine Studies and numismatics. He is at present Dean of the Faculty of Humanities, the University of Luton, England.

Colin Nicolson graduated with First Class Honours in Medieval and Modern History from the University of Birmingham. At present he teaches Modern European History at the University of North London. His publications include books and articles on Africa, immigration, and the origins of the First World War. He has written travel articles on India and South East Asia, and has, for many years, been a frequent visitor to Greece, Turkey and Cyprus.

SERIES EDITOR Professor Denis Judd is a Fellow of the Royal Historical Society and Professor of History at the University of North London. He has published over 20 books including biographies of Joseph Chamberlain, Prince Philip, George VI and Alison Uttley, historical and military studies, stories for children and two novels. He has reviewed extensively in the national press and in journals, and has written several radio programmes.

The front cover shows a detail from the sixteenth century icon of St Demetrios. By kind permission of the Greek Ministry of Culture, Byzantine Museum, Athens.

Other Titles in the Series

A Traveller's History of France
A Traveller's History of Paris
A Traveller's History of Spain
A Traveller's History of Italy
A Traveller's History of Russia
A Traveller's History of Scotland
A Traveller's History of England
A Traveller's History of London
A Traveller's History of Ireland
A Traveller's History of Turkey
A Traveller's History of Japan
A Traveller's History of India
A Traveller's History of China

A Note on Transliteration, Spelling and Pronunciation

Greek names have tended to be spelt according to their Greek forms rather than the Latinized: *k* rather than *c*, *-os*, *-on* rather than *-us*, *-um* (eg. Khalkidike and not Chalcidice, Kypselos and not Cypselus). To avoid irritation to readers accustomed to the tradition of Latin transliteration, and at the risk of being inconsistent, some familiar names, like Herodotus, Socrates and Thucydides, have been left in ther Latin form; as have non-Greek names. It is thought that Greek vowels were probably pronounced as in modern Italian, but modern Greek pronunciation is, unfortunately, no guide to the ancient Greek.

A Traveller's History of Greece

THE TRAVELLER'S HISTORY *SERIES*

'Ideal before-you-go reading' *The Daily Telegraph*

'An excellent series of brief histories' *New York Times*

'I want to compliment you . . . on the brilliantly concise contents of your books.' *Shirley Conran*

Reviews of Individual Titles

A Traveller's History of France

'Undoubtedly the best way to prepare for a trip to France is to bone up on some history. *The Traveller's History of France* by Robert Cole is concise and gives the essential facts in a very readable form.' *The Independent*

A Traveller's History of China

'The author manages to get 2 million years into 300 pages. An excellent addition to a series which is already invaluable, whether you're travelling or not.' *The Guardian*

A Traveller's History of India

'For anyone . . . planning a trip to India, the latest in the excellent Traveller's History series . . . provides a useful grounding for those whose curiosity exceeds the time available for research' *The London Evening Standard*

A Traveller's History of Japan

'It succeeds admirably in its goal of making the present country comprehensible through a narrative of its past, with asides on everything from bonsai to *zazen*, in a brisk, highly readable style . . . you could easily read it on the flight over, if you skip the movie.' *The Washington Post*

A Traveller's History of Ireland

'For independent, inquisitive travellers traversing the green roads of Ireland, there is no better guide than *A Traveller's History of Ireland. Small Press*

A Traveller's History of Greece

THIRD EDITION

TIMOTHY BOATSWAIN and COLIN NICOLSON

Series Editor DENIS JUDD
Line drawings *ALISON HEPBURN*

Interlink Books
An imprint of Interlink Publishing Group, Inc.
New York • Northampton

First American edition published 2001 by

INTERLINK BOOKS
An imprint of Interlink Publishing Group, Inc.
99 Seventh Avenue, Brooklyn, New York 11215 and
46 Crosby Street, Northampton, Massachusetts 01060
www.interlinkbooks.com

Library of Congress Cataloging-in-Publication Data
    A traveller's history of Greece/Timothy Boatswain and Colin Nicolson:
series editor, Denis Judd: line drawings, Hepburn - 1st American ed.
        p.   cm.
    Bibliography. p.
    ISBN 1-56656-366-6
    1. Greece-History.   I. Nicolson, Colin.   II. Judd, Denis, 1938-
    III. Title.
    DF757.B63   2001
    949.5-dc20   89-15341
                                                              CIP

Printed and bound in Canada

To request a free copy of our 48-page full-color catalog, please call
1-800-238-LINK, visit our web site at **www.interlinkbooks.com**,
or write to us at: **Interlink Publishing**
46 Crosby Street, Northampton, Massachusetts 01060

Table of Contents

PART II **Greece from 1453 to the Twentieth Century:**
Colin Nicolson

Preface

Modern Greece presents the traveller with many images, some of them stereotyped, even tawdry; some of them as fresh and unexpected as flowers in a desert; others contradictory, and perhaps confusing. The glories of Classical Greek art and architecture are instantly and universally recognizable, despite the ravages of both time and pillaging barbarians. The broken Doric columns and the noseless naked gods have each survived their despoliation and neglect with the dignity associated with high birth and noble purpose. The plays of Euripides and Aeschylus still hold modern audiences spell-bound. Homer's epic verse has been translated into countless tongues. Above all, the magic and myths of the Olympian deities, their foes, lackeys, lovers and mentors, maintain their archetypal primacy in Western culture and the Western psyche.

But Greece means many other things. A language with a dauntingly different alphabet from that of the West, and words, lacking Latin or Germanic roots, upon which the traveller can get no easy purchase. How easy it is to sympathize with Casca's complaint in *Julius Caesar* that 'it was Greek to me'. Modern travellers will associate Greece with uninhibited dancing, inexpensive tavernas, the tang of retsina, blistering heat, a leisurely approach to life, and reasonably priced package holidays. And who, in the end, is to say that Zorba the Greek is any less a figure than Herakles in the long progress of Western civilization?

There are also the contradictions. How can so democratic, generous and friendly a people fall so regularly under the control of right-wing military regimes? How is it possible to reconcile the Greek genius for trading and personal profit-making with the vigorous Communist and Socialist sympathies of so many citizens of Greece? Why did the civilized nation that built the Parthenon tolerate for so long such poverty among large numbers of its citizens? Above all, what became of the Ancient Greeks? Are these quick, noisy, dark-haired Mediterranean people really the descendants of those graceful, clear-browed athletes and warriors of antiquity? Then there is the final puzzle. What happened to the Greek people between the passing of the Classical Age and the emergence of Modern Greece? How did the philosopher Aristotle beget, metaphorically, Aristotle Onassis? Was Perikles somehow the spiritual sire of Philip of Greece, now Duke of Edinburgh and consort to Queen Elizabeth II? Is the goddess Aphrodite connected, in some mysterious way, with the actress and singer Melina Mercouri?

It is one of the triumphs of this clearly written and unfailingly informative book that the reader can readily discover how the major themes of Greek history have unfolded over the centuries. Not merely are the obvious gaps filled in, but the apparently safe verdicts of popular tradition are often reinterpreted and given a sharper perspective. This traveller's history does not peter out when the old gods were overthrown and disregarded, and the flame of Greek democracy extinguished for centuries. As a result, the visitor to Greece now has a historical guide that will make sense of the present as well as of the past.

Denis Judd
London

PART I

Early Greece to Byzantium

TIMOTHY BOATSWAIN

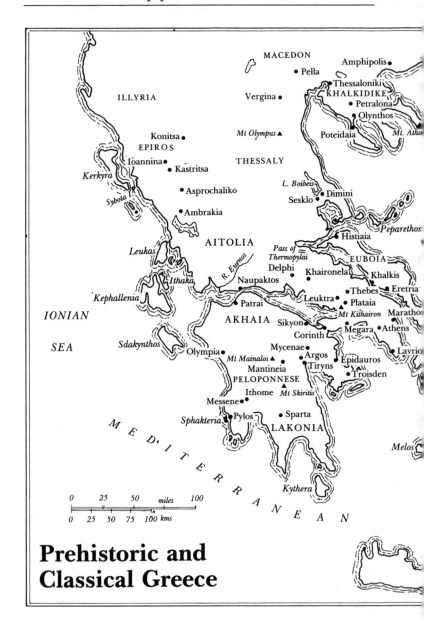

MACEDON

Amphipolis •

• Pella

Thessaloniki

ILLYRIA   Vergina •   KHALKIDIKE

• Petralona

Olynthos

Mt Olympus ▲   Poteidaia   Mt Athos

Konitsa •

EPIROS

Ioannina •   • Kastritsa   THESSALY

Kerkyra   L. Boibeis

Sybota   • Asprochaliko   Sesklo • • Dimini

•Ambrakia

Peparethos

AITOLIA   • Histiaia

Leukas   Pass of

Thermopylai   EUBOIA

R. Euenos   Delphi   Khaironela   Khalkis

Ithaka   Naupaktos

Kephallenia   • Patrai   Leuktra • •Thebes   Eretria

• Plataia

IONIAN   AKHAIA   Sikyon •   ▲ Mt Kithairon   Marathon

Corinth   Megara   •Athens

SEA   *Sdakynthos*   Mycenae •   • Lavrio

Olympia •   Mt Mainalos ▲   •Argos   Epidauros

Mantineia   Tiryns   • Troisden

PELOPONNESE   ▲

Ithome   Mt Skiritis

Messene •

• Sparta

Sphakteria • Pylos   LAKONIA

Melos

M E D I T E R R A N E A N

0   25   50   *miles*   100

0   25   50   75   100   *kms*

Kythera

Prehistoric and
Classical Greece

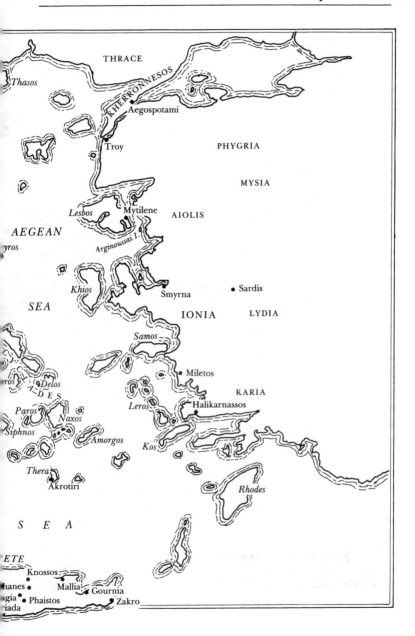

CHAPTER ONE

Early Greece

Prehistoric Greece

Greece (Hellas as it was called by the Greeks) is a land of many different countries, often quite distinct from each other and separated by the difficulties of a rough and spectacular terrain. Prehistoric people must have made adaptations to the local habitats just as their descendants in the ancient and modern periods have, but the first attempts to live in Greece seem to have been made in the north where there were well-watered forests and grazing lands. At Petralona cave, some sixty kilometres from Thessaloniki in northern Greece, archaeologists have found a human skull, the remains of human activity and the evidence of fire which date back as far as 500,000 years ago. It is possible that these remains represent the earliest inhabitants of Europe, and there is now enough evidence to suggest that human occupation in Greece covers all the sequences of the Palaeolithic (Old Stone Age) down to the end of the Neolithic period (New Stone Age), about 3000 BC. At Epiros in the west of northern Greece there are palaeolithic sites (Asprokhaliko and Kastritsa on Lake Ioannina, and Klidi, in the Vikos Gorge near Konitsa) which suggest that the colourful Sarakatsani shepherds of today may still be treading in the footsteps of palaeolithic hunters who pursued the migrating herds of red deer that roamed Epiros some 100,000 years ago. The Sarakatsani drive their flocks over quite long distances from summer pastures on the Pindos mountains to winter grazing on the coastal lowlands, apparently following the trails of those stone age hunters of prehistory.

Homo sapiens, from whom we are descended, seems first to have

1

appeared in Greece about 40–30,000 years ago. Although it is not known for certain where homo sapiens originated, the evidence would suggest 'modern man' moved into Europe in two main waves of immigration, from Africa. With mankind's development of agriculture and pastoralism Neolithic settlers began to establish a sedentary village life in Greece in about the seventh millennium BC. This settlement happened in a very piecemeal fashion and, in some areas, the Stone Age way of life continued down into the Bronze Age. Penetration into southern Greece, where the plains with deeper soil and large rivers are to be found, was not easy because of high mountain barriers and lack of good harbours.

The phases of the Neolithic have tended to be identified by their archaeological sites, for example Sesklo and Dhimeni in Thessaly, and their cultural affinities appear to have been with Anatolia (the central plateau of Turkey) and the Levant in the early stages, and Anatolia and the Balkans in the later. These were a pre-Greek people whose old languages, which do not appear to have all been alike, were often referred to in classical times as Pelasgian. The survival of numbers of female figurines in either clay or stone at various sites perhaps gives us an insight into an important aspect of Neolithic culture. The figurines are highly stylized, emphasizing the reproductive parts of the female anatomy which has led to the assumption that they are idols, revealing that the nature of Neolithic religion was associated with the concerns of procreation and fertility; the main needs of Neolithic society being the continuance of the community, the reproduction of domesticated animals, and fruitful harvests.

Cycladic Culture

When the metallurgy of copper and tin began to be developed in those areas of natural resource east of Greece, like Mesopotamia (Iraq), Anatolia and Cyprus, communication and trade rapidly increased around the Aegean Sea. By the third millennium BC the Neolithic culture of Greece was gradually replaced by the Bronze Age. The central islands of the Aegean, the Cyclades (literally meaning 'a circle' as the islands appear to form a circle in the sea), developed a culture which depended upon the skills of their people as seafarers. A few scattered settlements, usually near the sea, and almost 2000 graves have been identified throughout the islands, and at Khalandriani on Syros and Phylakopi on Melos quite sophisticated walled citadels were excavated.

Among the Cycladic artefacts found, both in houses at the settlements and within graves, are human figurines sculptured in the excellent island marble (in particular that from Naxos and Paros). The size of the figures varies from a few inches each to over two feet tall. They are mainly representations of naked women whose arms are folded across their chests, below their breasts, and whose legs are pressed closely together. The heads of the figurines are very stylized so that on the face often only the nose has been carved. As they have survived, pristine white, smoothly polished, symmetrical and beautifully balanced, the figurines display a sureness of touch and a fundamental character which has been much admired and copied by modern artists, like Brancusi, Epstein and Modigliani, who have drawn inspiration from their line and form;

Cycladic marble figurine

Henry Moore, who had such a feeling for natural shapes and mass, declared, 'I love and admire Cycladic Sculpture. It has such great elemental simplicity.'

Scholars have been able to identify different groupings by the location and morphology (study of the changing shapes) of the styles, but it is not completely clear to what extent the differences in the figurines are chronological or regional. An interesting group, the Keros–Syros Culture (named after two of the islands) *c.* 2800–2300 BC, has some remarkable shapes, including musicians who seem to be playing pipes and a lyre. Recent research has suggested that the figurines were painted so that, for example, the faces would have had eyes, mouth and hair painted in. It is unlikely the figurines had a purely aesthetic function but as there is no documentary evidence their purpose can only be inferred from their provenance, site context and the objects themselves. The dominance of the female form has led to a comparison with those from the Neolithic period and to the assumption that they are associated with some form of fertility cult, so the figurines are often referred to as Cycladic Idols. In the end, however, neither the sculptures themselves nor the archaeological contexts within which they have been found, point to any certain purpose.

Minoan Crete

There is evidence to show that the island of Crete to the south of the mainland was in contact with the Cyclades, and it was at about the time when the Keros–Syros Culture was coming to an end that Crete began to achieve a prosperous economic and artistic life with the building of the first palaces. Though there appears to be a Bronze Age town at Gournia and isolated villas have been found, the focus of Cretan society seems to have been centred on royal palaces. The Cretans, perhaps through contact with Egypt, developed advanced techniques of metalwork and building. They were also literate and developed a syllabic script, which is an intermediate stage between the hieroglyphic system (found, for example, in Egypt) and an alphabet. Confined to Crete and found mainly on clay tablets, this script, known as Linear A, has so far not been deciphered. The wide distribution of Cretan pottery and the influence of Minoan (the name given to their culture by the archaeologist Arthur Evans, after Crete's mythical King Minos) motifs throughout the Aegean, and even as far afield as Sicily and Spain, suggests the Cretans of the Bronze Age were expert seamen.

The first palaces were destroyed by an earthquake *c.* 1730 BC, but new palaces were built heralding the zenith of Cretan power in the periods designated Middle Minoan III and Late Minoan I (1750–1450 BC). The excavations at the palace sites at Knossos, Phaistos, Hagia Triada, Mallia and Zakro testify to the complex level of organization and prosperity achieved. The palaces were built on several levels with large numbers of rooms of varying sizes: reception halls, groups of rooms that formed apartments, bathrooms with extensive drainage systems, workshops and, at the lower levels, storage rooms (magazines) with large pottery containers (*pithoi*) for storing oil and corn (many still *in situ*). Fluent and brightly-coloured frescoes of plants, animals and humans decorated the walls. Although the naturalistic style of Minoan painting has affinites with Egyptian, Minoan artists work with a freedom of line and colour which is quite unique.

Arthur Evans, who had started excavating at Knossos in 1900, noted that Minoan art generally had a lightness which lacked the foreboding solemnity that so often infused the images of other early societies. In contrast to warlike Mycenae, on the mainland of Greece, the Minoan sites also appeared to lack any type of fortification. Minoan culture seemed to be the creation of a much more peaceful and balanced society, which led Evans to represent Minoan civilization as some sort of 'golden age'. The more recent discoveries of human sacrifice at a shrine at Arkhanes and the possibility of cannibalism at a house near Knossos, where the butchered bones of children have been found, suggest a picture much more in keeping with the story of Theseus and the Minotaur.

According to the legend the Athenians were required to make a payment to Crete by sending seven youths and seven maidens who were devoured by the Minotaur (the half-man, half-bull, son of King Minos' queen, Pasiphaë). The Athenian hero, Theseus, with the help of Minos' daughter Ariadne, killed the Minotaur and was able to escape out of the labyrinth (a maze constructed for Minos by the craftsman Daedalos).

'Bull-leaping' fresco from Knossos

Minoan religion has a snake goddess and also appears to have had a bull cult. The discovery at Knossos of a fresco depicting a bull-leaping scene with young men and girls has created speculation about the Theseus story and the apparent Athenian subservience to Crete. If the Cretan navy was totally dominant in the Aegean this might explain why the palaces required no fortifications, and the payment of tribute as the demand of an imperial power. The connection between Athens and Crete appears to have been confirmed by recent isotope analysis of Minoan copper which suggests that it was originally mined at Lavrion near Athens. Was the historical truth that Athens paid tribute to Crete in ingots of copper?

According to vulcanologists, the volcano on the island of Thera (Santorini) erupted in 1500 BC. The force of the eruption was far greater than the celebrated explosion of Krakatoa in AD 1883 and blew off the top of the volcano at Thera, leaving approximately 135 sq. km of the island submerged beneath the sea. In 1967 excavations began, and are still continuing, at a site near Akrotiri in the south of the island. A whole town with streets and houses is emerging from the layers of volcanic ash. The pottery and wall paintings found at the settlement, and now in the National Museum at Athens, are Minoan in character, although the original population may have been Cycladic. It seems from the lack of skeletons that the people managed to escape from the town before it was totally destroyed; this suggests perhaps there were some earthquakes or minor volcanic activity before the mighty explosion. The eruption of Thera must have had tremendous consequences for the whole of the Aegean (for example, there would have been colossal waves), and Crete, which is less than 100 kilometres to the south, would most certainly have suffered damage. The archaeological evidence has shown that the 'new' palaces on Crete were also destroyed by some natural disaster *c*. 1450 BC. The disparity between the date of the eruption of Thera and the destruction of the palaces, some fifty years, has caused much scholarly debate which has yet to be fully resolved. Although Arthur Evans resisted the idea, it does now seem certain that after this second destruction of the palaces the dominance of the Aegean shifted from Crete to the mainland of Greece.

Mycenaean Civilization

On the mainland, during the change from the periods usually called the Early and Middle Helladic, *c*. 2100–1900 BC, the archaeological evidence testifies to the arrival of a new people causing violent upheaval and disruption to the existing cultural pattern. These invaders belonged to the group of people known as Indo-European (one branch is sometimes referred to as Aryan), whom philologists believe to have a common root to their language (take, for example, the word 'one' which is *eka* in Sanskrit, *aina* in Old Persian, *unus* in Latin and *eis*, *en* in Greek). The Indo-Europeans settled down in India, Iran and Europe. In Greece they mixed with the previous inhabitants and absorbed words from the older, non-European languages, developing the language which we now know as Greek. Greek words that end in *inthos* or *indos*, *ssos* or *itos* and *enai* appear to have a non-Indo-European origin, for example the place names *Korinthos* (Corinth), *Knossos* (the Minoan palace), *Athenai* (Athens). Strangely, the Greek word for sea, *thalassa*, also seems to have been borrowed from the earlier inhabitants, which might suggest that the Indo-Europeans settling in Greece has no previous experience of the sea.

From about 1600 BC (Middle Helladic) the Bronze Age people of Greece began to develop an elaborate culture centred around monarchies, which displayed considerable material prosperity, a complex bureaucracy and a warlike nature. These people built large palace sites, usually with a citadel fortified by 'cyclopian' walls (constructed with huge irregular stones – later Greeks thought they must have been erected by the race of giants known as the Cyclops). This early Greek civilization is mainly referred to as Mycenaean after the citadel at Mycenae in the southern part of Greece, the Peloponnese. Mycenae was the alleged locus of the murder of Agamemnon by his wife Klytemnestra. After the sack of Troy, the story goes, he returned to his royal seat bringing with him the Trojan priestess Kassandra as concubine, and was overpowered and slain by his wife and Aegistheos, her lover. The archaeologist Heinrich Schliemann, following Homer, believed he had discovered Agamemnon's grave, but the burial treasures, including the famous golden death mask, belong to an earlier age. Other important sites are at Pylos and Tiryns, and evidence of Mycenaean occupation has also been found at Athens and Thebes. It appears that it was after the second destruction of the Minoan palaces (after 1500 BC) that the Mycenaeans took over some of the palaces in Crete, and having learnt the art of writing produced the first Greek script, Linear B. Tablets of the syllabic Linear B have turned up in large quantities at Knossos and other sites on the mainland of Greece. In 1952 they were deciphered by Michael Ventris, but they have proved to be rather unexciting and mainly consist of lists of commodities; they are most likely archives, recording the produce stored in the palaces.

Though of Indo-European stock, the Mycenaeans drew more upon their contacts with the Near East and Crete: for example, Mycenaean art often showed a strong dependency upon Minoan forms and iconography. Fine examples of Minoan naturalism can be seen on the inlaid dagger blades discovered in Shaft Grave V at Mycenae: one shows leopards hunting wild duck on the edge of a papyrus swamp; the most famous depicts a lion hunt in progress with an archer and four Mycenaean spearmen carrying huge shields. The mastery of the sea must have been the means whereby these cultural influences became available to Greece. Mycenaean artefacts, in particular pottery, from Cyprus and Syria confirm the contact the Greeks had established with the east. There is also evidence from the Hittite archives of the late fourteenth and thirteenth centuries (the Hittites established a powerful empire centred in Anatolia – the central plateau of Turkey) which seems to refer to the king of *Ahhiyawa*, whom scholars have identified with the king of the Mycenaeans, as a neighbour; this suggests Mycenae had reached a level of some importance to be mentioned by one of the leading powers of the Near East.

Dark Age Greece

Mycenaean civilization flourished until about 1200 BC when catastrophe overwhelmed the whole of the east Mediterranean. According to the Egyptian records of the time the chaos and destruction was caused by the 'Sea Peoples', but the picture is far from clear and it is uncertain whether there was an external invasion or just internal disruption. Whatever the cause, the entire economic system, trade, the kingship and centralized bureaucracy, the art and craftsmanship, and literacy collapsed and disappeared. In Greece, the palace sites were burned and widespread emigration from the mainland across the Aegean seems to have taken place. The splendour of palace life is followed by a dark age where shadowy sub-Mycenaeans reoccupy the sites for about 150 years. In about 1050 BC another wave of Greek-speaking people (the so-called 'Dorian Invasion'), who brought iron metallurgy with them, came down from the north to settle in the south as the remnants of Mycenaean civilization petered out.

THE DORIANS

These new Greeks, the Dorians, who spoke a dialect in common with the north-western Greeks, soon settled the mainland, apart from Athens, and formed the new ruling class. This 'invasion' by the Dorians may well have caused another migration across the Aegean to the islands and the west coast of Asia Minor (Turkey), where the later Greeks spoke dialects which represented the language of the Mycenaeans: Ionic, Aeolic, and Arcado-Cypriot. Associated with these so-called East Greek dialects is Attic, the language of the Athenians, who were thought of as being related to the Ionians, the main colonists of Asia Minor. The Dorians themselves also continued their migration by crossing the Aegean and settling in Crete, Rhodes and Lycia (the south-west of Turkey). The distinction between the Dorians and the other Greeks, as preserved in their language, was to have important consequences for the Greeks by maintaining ethnic antagonisms and rivalries into the period when history began to be recorded.

For 300 years (1050–750 BC) after the collapse of the civilization of the Mycenaeans, our knowledge of Greek history is restricted to scanty archaeological evidence. Large-scale building ceased and often all that has survived is the pottery. In the religious sphere, however, there does appear to have been continuity with the survival of the myths and legends of an earlier age. It was the Mycenaean royal houses which provided material for the remarkable legends surrounding the sack of Troy and the destruction of Thebes upon which both the poet Homer, perhaps in the eighth century BC, and then the Athenian tragedians, Aeschylus, Sophocles and Euripides, drew in the fifth century BC.

CHAPTER TWO

Archaic Greece

During the eighth century the Dark Age in Greece came to an end with a rapid development in Greek culture. Important factors in the revival of Greek civilization were the restoration of trading contacts with the advanced eastern societies of Anatolia and the Levant, and another era of colonization in both the west and east Mediterranean. Some of the consequences which followed the re-establishment of contact with the east were, for example, the development of the Greek alphabet by adapting Phoenician script; the improvement of metal technology; Greek artists, whose output had been virtually reduced to geometric patterns on pottery, borrowed and developed the more sophisticated oriental forms and designs; and the Greek diet was improved by the introduction of the chicken. The chief cause of the new wave of colonization was the economic one of land shortage. The evidence of burials suggests a big increase in population on the mainland, which sent colonists seeking land in the accessible parts of southern Italy and Sicily, as well as in the eastern Aegean. The origin of the name 'Greek' was apparently a consequence of Greek colonists meeting the Romans in southern Italy. During the Dark Age the Greeks had adopted the name 'Hellenes' (Hellas for Greece) and 'Greek' followed from a misunderstanding: when asked where they came from the colonists replied Graia, a small city in Boiotia, and so in Latin they all became 'Graeci', 'the people of Graia'.

The village, which seemed to have replaced the palace centres of Mycenaean civilization as the Greek social and political unit, was in turn superseded in many places by the city-state (*polis*, from which the English word 'politics' is derived). The city-state was an independent community, small by modern standards but self-governing, and which consisted essentially of a city and its surrounding countryside. Once it had evolved, some time near the end of the Dark Age, it became the characteristic form of the political and social organization of the Greeks for the remainder of antiquity.

The City-State

The origin of the *polis* is a matter of scholastic debate. One view has attributed the development of the city-state to the geographical characteristics of Greece, where narrow valleys and plains surrounded by high mountains might be expected to encourage regional communities to coalesce around a dominant centre. Another argument, while accepting that the physical geography of Greece might have facilitated the formation of city-states, holds that the configuration of the *polis* is more likely to be the consequence of the needs of co-operative defence against the hostile migrating settlers of the eleventh century BC. The territory of each city-state was defined by natural geographical barriers, and each could pursue an essentially independent existence, being self-sufficient in food by relying on the so-called 'Mediterranean triad' of the olive, vine and grain. The city provided a fortified site for resistance against attack which then became the political and administrative centre for the territory. A less historical hypothesis suggests that the Greeks had an innate tendency to live in a *polis*; indeed, Aristotle had described man (i.e. civilized man = a Greek) as 'by nature an animal of the *polis*'. Whatever the truth behind these different theories, the city-state was the prime political unit in shaping ancient Greek history.

The political structure of the Mycenaean world had been centred around monarchy but, although the institution did not completely disappear during the Dark Age, it was a rarity among the city-states. Power at the beginning of the new era, which historians have labelled the Archaic Period (*c.* 700–500 BC), appears to have been in the hands of the aristocracy (literally 'the rule of the best'). In Greece the main measure of wealth was land and property, and during the Dark Age social stratification and the initial formation of an aristocracy seems to have been based upon the ownership of land as well as birth. Overpopulation and a shortage of land brought about tensions between the aristocracy and the people which erupted into social turmoil. The Archaic Period was a literate age and we can read about the resentment felt against the ruling landowners; for example, in his *Works and Days* the poet Hesiod complains about the hard life of a Boiotian farmer, who is constantly oppressed by the local aristocracy. The social order, however, was to be challenged as a consequence of some fundamental economic changes. The revival of trade and the development of commerce brought a different kind of wealth to the city-states which, along with an influx of new cultural influences from abroad, must have unsettled the economic supremacy, and therefore the political control, of the nobility.

The Tyrants

In the seventh century BC, as a consequence of the political and social conflict between the aristocracy and the people, a series of usurpers came to power in the city-states whom the Greeks labelled tyrants. Later writers, like Aristotle, were to see tyranny as one of the worst types of government, representing absolute autocracy, which, unlike kingship, did not recognize customary law but subjected people to arbitrary rule – *tyrannos* (tyrant) is not a Greek word but seems to have been Levantine (for a Greek such an origin is a measure of the odium in which the title was held). Tyrants appear to have gained their support from the ordinary people in opposition to the aristocracy. Although the evidence is rather scanty for this early historical period, it seems a tyrant was likely to be an aristocrat himself who initially used autocratic power to defend the people against the oppression of the rich. Once the misuse of power by the nobles had been suppressed the tyrant found his popular support waning, and eventually the unconstitutional rule of tyranny became resented by all, so that the people and the aristocrats combined together to oust the tyrant.

The phenomenon of tyranny arose in several city-states, for example at Corinth where Kypselos, who was thought to be the first tyrant in Greece, and his son Periander ruled from 655 to 585 BC. During this time Corinth became the dominant port and the most prosperous city in Greece. Its geographical position enabled it to exploit trade routes both to the west and east. Among the archaeological evidence which demonstrates its wide trading contacts is Corinth's ubiquitous pottery – mostly small vases, highly decorated in orientalizing designs (for example, heraldic mythical beasts), containing scented oils. Corinth's architects and artists also made important advances in the building and decorating of temples, eventually shifting from the materials of wood and terracotta into stone, although at Corinth itself, (probably as a consequence of the Roman sack in 146 BC) all that survives to testify to these advances are the monolithic columns (single stone shafts) of the Temple of Apollo, built about forty years after the end of the rule of the tyrants.

Hoplites

The arrival of the city-state, along with the advances in metal technology, also led to new methods of warfare which were to have a profound effect upon the political development of Greece. Fighting in the Dark Age had probably been focused around individual combat between champions – nobles who could afford the equipment and the time to train. Though there is no evidence of cavalry engagements at this time, it appears the aristocracy rode to war either in chariots or mounted on horseback, which would have helped their ability to attack and withdraw from a fight. While the metal available for weaponry was scarce and society relatively fragmented, the nobility could maintain their military superiority. The formation of the city-state and the general increase in prosperity brought about change which led to the creation of the heavily-armed soldier (*hoplite*) who fought in mass formation (*phalanx*). The training and discipline that such co-operative action demanded produced an army that generally proved far superior to the individual champions of the Homeric age. The need for city-states to be able to put in the field such a well-equipped, highly-trained body of men had, beside military implications, important social, political and moral ones.

City-states were too small to afford standing armies, so their soldiers were essentially amateurs who were called up in times of war, and the number of fighting men available to a city-state would depend upon its size. (Individual city-states seem to have usually been able to field between three and ten thousand hoplites.) In peacetime the young men were kept fit and trained through athletic contests whose forms were related to warlike activities. (The modern Olympics has certainly maintained the contestants' psychological state of hostility even if the form of the games aims to conform with a more peace-loving perception.)

In Homer, the prime moral obligation of an individual had been to his family. The hero fought for his own and his kin's honour. In the *Iliad*, when Achilles is aggrieved by Agamemnon, it is his personal sense of insult that determines his resolve not to fight for the Greeks, and it is his own emotional feelings at the death of Patroklos that motivate his return to the battlefield. The Trojan hero, Hector, was of course fighting for his homeland, but when he is killed by Achilles the emphasis is on the personal tragedy for his family, and it is the obligations of a father that drive Priam, putting aside his kingship, to seek the return of his son's body from Achilles. Although it has to be remembered that Homer's work is literature and not history, nevertheless, the *Iliad* and the *Odyssey* seem to paint a believable picture of an heroic society.

The coming of the city-state shifted the focus from the honour of the individual and the ties of kinship to the duties of the citizen: patriotism to one's city-state can be seen as a reflection of the need for co-operation and equality in the battlefield. Without an ethical system that endorsed a sense of duty to fellow citizen and state, the very mode of hoplite fighting would have failed. The Athenian tragedian Aeschylus, writing in the fifth century BC, dramatizes the overthrow of the values of the herioc society in his trilogy, the *Oresteia*, where in the final play the ethic of a blood-feud between and within families is replaced by the concept of independent justice (*dike*): Orestes, driven across the known world by the fearsome Erinyes (Furies) who pursue the revenge of his murdered mother, seeks sanctuary with Apollo and is finally adjudged guiltless by Athena, whereupon the Furies are transformed into 'The Kindly Ones' (*Eumenides*). In more general terms kinship and the honour of an individual are no longer the sole arbiters of morality but society now mediates human relations on the basis of equity among all its members.

As status in the city-state tended to be based upon wealth, and as

A statue of a Spartan hoplite

wealth, as we have seen, depended upon ownership of property, political power was organized in accordance with property qualifications. It was now the social group who could afford both to be away from work during the campaigning season and the armour of the hoplite – usually an independent land-owning farmer class – that gained the upper hand in the government of the city-state. When tyrannies were overthrown the political supremacy of the hoplites became manifest, establishing *oligarchy* ('the rule of the few'). The sovereignty of a city-state depended upon the two main elements of government: decision-making and then the implementation of policy. In most Greek city-states there were three main bodies that formed the government: an assembly (usually called an *ekklesia*) of citizens which deliberated and decided policy; a council (*boule*) which prepared and organized government business and administration; and executives who actually carried out the decisions. In oligarchies the ability to formulate policy resided very much with the council, who determined what motions could be put before the assembly. Membership of the council and the executive was limited on the basis of property qualifications, so that the ordinary people were excluded. The executive posts (often referred to as magistracies) were normally limited to the duration of one year and, usually only being open to the wealthy, would be elected by the assembly, although in some oligarchies selection was carried out by the council.

Sparta

One city-state had never had to overthrow tyranny and consequently became the byword for the ideal form of hoplite government. The Athenian philosopher Plato based his ideal *Republic* on an interpretation of its constitution. The city-state was Sparta. Lakedaimonia or Lakonia (Laconia, hence 'laconic'), the land of the Spartans, and had been settled by the Dorians *c.* 1050 BC. Sparta itself, in the plain of the Eurotas river, was not a true city but a collection of four villages (*obai*). The spartan constitution was based upon a hoplite assembly (called the *apella* rather than *ekklesia*) and a council (*gerousia* rather than *boule*). The main peculiarity of the Spartan political system, which has never been adequately explained, was that there were two kings. They were chosen from two royal families, who claimed common descent back to the hero Herakles (more commonly known by his Roman name, Hercules). The duality of the kingship demonstrates that they were, in fact, never true monarchs, and the real political power in Sparta rested much more with the five executive officers, known as the *ephoroi*, who were elected annually. The essential flavour of Spartan government was conservative: the *gerousia* was chosen from men over sixty and the ephors used their immense powers to check any radicalism, in particular any moves by the monarchy or senior generals towards autocracy.

The development of Lakonian society was strongly related to its military activity and the successive conquests it had achieved in the Peloponnese. Spartan society was organized into a rigidly hierarchical state with an élite of Spartan citizens (*Spartiatai*), who alone had full political rights, and groups of dependants. Those Dorians who were not Spartiatai (or as they often called themselves *Lakedaimonioi* – inhabitants of Lakedaimonia) but dwelt near Sparta were known as *perioikoi* ('dwellers around') and they were bound to give military service to Sparta. As Sparta expanded towards the sea, a second group, probably non-Dorians, were brought under subjugation, the *helots* (the meaning of the name is uncertain – it might mean 'marsh dwellers'), who seem to have been treated like slaves. In the eighth century BC the Spartans expanded westward and subdued the Messenians. It is difficult to differentiate between the status of the Messenians and helots. The land of both was divided up and an allotment (*kleros*) given to each Spartiate; the Messenians were forced to work the land, giving half the produce to their Spartiate masters.

The whole Spartan constitution, the social and military system, was geared to producing a hoplite army which could sustain the superiority of the Spartiatai. The traditional founder of Spartan *eunomia* ('good order') was Lykourgos, but the historical evidence suggests that much of the Spartan way of life was based upon earlier tribal customs which evolved in response to the peculiar needs of her élite society. The state took a strong hand in attempting to shape a powerful military élite; from an early age Spartan youths were given a communal and rigorous upbringing and at the age of twenty the men became eligible for election to dining clubs or messes which dominated their lives. The emphasis was on physical training, discipline and loyalty to the state in order to create what was effectively a professional army. The harsh demands of Spartan life are well illustrated by some of the male initiation ceremonies: one involved the ritual stealing of cheese from an altar, which was defended by youths with whips and sticks. This ceremony later turned into an endurance test where initiates were sometimes whipped to death. Another vicious institution was the *krypteia* (secret society), a picked body of youths who lived hidden in the countryside and at night killed any helots they came across. The life style of the Spartans was so restrictive and harsh that it is perhaps not surprising that Spartans abroad were often seduced by the freedom and luxuries available in other societies.

Family life was deliberately devalued and the distinctions between the sexes attenuated; female activities basically imitated that of the men – for example, although women were not expected to fight, girls did undergo rigorous physical exercise along with the boys (both sexes performing athletics naked). Even though Spartan women had a good deal more freedom than other Greek women, who were under severe male control (ancient societies were all essentially patriarchal – where the male dominates), they were made to conform to the male ethos. The Spartan attitude to marriage is indicative of the social values instilled into Spartans: marriage was a clandestine affair and a man did not expect to establish a household until after he was thirty, monogamy was not strictly observed and adultery was unremarkable. The marriage ceremony itself is revealing in that the bride underwent a ritual capture, was then masculinized by having her head shaved and being dressed as a man, and finally awaited the bridegroom in a darkened room.

Because of the depreciation of family life, the rigours of a tough physical existence, the separation of the sexes and the demand for perfect offspring, it is understandable that procreation among Spartans seems to have been a problem: the citizen-body which made up the army was very small for the military role it had to perform in maintaining its own supremacy (the only evidence we have of a full military levy comes from the battle of Plataia in 479 BC when only 5000 Spartiatai could be put into the field). As a result of a dwindling population the situation grew worse so that Sparta suffered from a severe shortage of manpower and thus the very system that had been instituted to sustain her supremacy became instrumental in incapacitating her ability to survive.

Athens

The social tensions which had initiated the move towards tyranny in many Greek cities also existed at Athens. According to tradition, after the rule of the legendary Theseus, there was a continuation of monarchy at Athens. By the seventh century, however, the king (*basileus*) had lost most of his powers and the office had been subsumed into an annually-appointed executive of nine *arkhontes*. An archon after his term went on to become a life member of the council (called the Areopagus, because they met on the Hill of Ares). An aristocratic group, known as the *Eupatridai* ('sons of good fathers'), had an exclusive right to hold these posts. In 640 BC an Athenian noble named Kylon won an event at the

Olympic games and, some years later, with the aid of his father-in-law Theagenes, the tyrant of Megara, he attempted to overthrow the aristocracy and seize power in Athens but the coup failed.

SOLON

Perhaps as an aristocratic reaction to the fear that their political supremacy was under threat, in 621/0 BC (the Athenian year ran from June to to June) Drakon introduced his code of laws, by tradition the first at Athens. Far from addressing the new political demands of the hoplites or the social inequality that existed at Athens in a spirit of moderation, Drakon's code became proverbial for its harshness (hence 'Draconian'): for example, from the evidence that survives, capital punishment was a common penalty for a wide variety of crimes.

In 594/3 Solon was appointed an archon and introduced a new code which, in contrast to Drakon's, attempted to address the many problems facing Athens. Major grievances were the system of land tenure and the payment of one-sixth of all produce to the landowners, which often forced peasants into debt and then enslavement. In an attempt to avoid the danger of a tyranny, Solon alleviated the burden of debt and reorganized the Athenian state by breaking the exclusive power of the aristocracy. He established four classes of Athenian society based upon agricultural wealth, reserving the archonship for the wealthy (not just the Eupatridai), and established a new council, the Boule of 400 representatives, alongside the Areopagus. (According to tradition Solon was the founder of the Athenian state and some of his poetry survives, quoted in later sources.)

PEISISTRATOS

Many of Solon's reforms, however failed, and bitter disputes arose over the archonship so that eventually a military leader, Peisistratos, seized power as tyrant. Although he was twice expelled he established a regime which lasted from 546 BC to the expulsion of his son Hippias in 510. Under his rule Athens flourished both materially and culturally. During this period the tyrant's patronage of the arts is evidenced by magnificent building projects, rapid advances in sculpture, the emergence of Athenian black-figure vases and the new work of poets at Athens.

After the death of Peisistratos, however, political opposition to his son increased and in 514 an assassination attempt was made. Hippias survived, although his brother Hipparkhos was slain, but the two assassins, Harmodios and Aristogeiton, became important political heroes ('the tyrannicides') for future generations of Athenians. In the end, a leading member of the aristocratic family of Alkmaionidai, Kleisthenes, gained the support of the priesthood at Delphi, who used the oracle to persuade the Spartans to drive Hippias out of Athens in 510.

KLEISTHENES

The Spartans had hoped for a return to a conservative oligarchic form of government, but after a couple of years Kleisthenes allied himself with the ordinary people (*demos*) and began the process of establishing a democracy. He created ten new tribes based on an artificial geographical basis to avoid the old political ties of kinship that had existed. Each tribe was composed of *demoi* (village units), which had their own political apparatus and provided a sense of grass-root democratic involvement. The assembly now became the focus of political decision-making. Kleisthenes' reforms paved the way for the introduction of radical democracy which was to characterize Athenian history in the fifth century.

The Arts

Among sculptures of the Archaic period are the first Greek monumental standing male and female figures, known in the singular as a *kouros* ('youth') and *kore* ('maiden'). Influenced, it seems, by Egyptian sculpture, these figures (the males nude, the females clothed) were erected, perhaps as dedications, in Ionia, the mainland and islands of Greece at sanctuary sites or cemeteries. A fine pair of *kouroi*, carved in limestone and dated to the beginning of the sixth century BC, were found at the oracular sanctuary of Delphi. On the bases of these over-life-sized sculptures were inscribed the names Kleobis and Biton. The historian Herodotus tells us the story of these two young men: when the fabulously wealthy king of Lydia, Croesus, was entertaining Solon, who happened to be visiting his kingdom, the monarch took the opportunity to ask the wise

Athenian, 'Who is the most fortunate man in the world?'. Croesus, fully expecting to be named himself, was surprised to be given the name of an obscure Athenian, a father who had died in battle defending his city. Croesus thought he would at least receive second place, but Solon named Kleobis and Biton. These two young men, when their mother, a priestess of Hera, wished to attend a festival of the goddess in the city of Argos, had pulled her carriage themselves to the temple, since the draught animals were working in the fields. Their mother had prayed to Hera to grant her sons the greatest gift possible for mortals. Later she found her sons had died while sleeping in the temple. The validity of Solon's choice was confirmed when Croesus was defeated and captured by the Persian king Cyrus and the Lydian kingdom came to an abrupt end. Croesus was about to be executed by being burnt on a pyre when he cried out affirming the truth of Solon's answer, that no man could be called truly

One of a pair of marble statues from Delphi

fortunate until dead, and Cyrus immediately asked for an account of Croesus' exclamation. After hearing his story the Persian king was overwhelmed by a desire to be merciful but the fire had already been started and the attendants were unable to quench the flames. When all seemed lost the god Apollo, in answer to prayer, sent a downpour of rain which put out the fire and saved Croesus' life.

Although early sculptures like Kleobis and Biton are in limestone, Greek artists soon preferred to sculpt in the harder marbles of the islands and mainland, with their beautiful colours and tightly-packed crystals which give such a fine finish. It is perhaps surprising for modern taste, which is still influenced by the Renaissance concept of purity of material, to realize that Archaic Greek statues were originally painted in bright colours. It also has to be remembered when assessing the quality of Greek art that much of the ancient sculpture we see in European museums today are Roman copies, which seem to lack the vitality of the Greek originals.

It was during the Archaic period that Greek architects began to develop the conventional structure of the temple, which was probably based upon the central and sacred room of the Mycenaean palace, the *megaron*. The Greek temple's primary function was to house the cult statue of the god or goddess, which was placed in the main room (*naos* or *cella*), and around the outside of the room's walls were rows of columns (peristyle). It is probable that the introduction of stone columns and much of the decoration on the façade of a Greek temple were translations from the earlier building materials of wood and terracotta. (The traveller Pausanias, who wrote a guide book to Greece in the second century AD, records seeing a wooden column at the Temple of Hera on his visit to Olympia.) The decoration of Greek temples evolved into three main 'orders', the Doric, the Ionic and, rather later, the Corinthian. Ever since their development these orders have had a profound effect, observable all around us, upon architects and designers, and even a visit to the humble British pillar post-box demonstrates Greek influence; around the edge of the mushroom-shaped dome the decorative 'dentals' (teeth) have been borrowed from a Greek temple.

Other Greek artistic and intellectual pursuits like literature, philosophy and science also developed rapidly in this period. The eastern

Greeks of Ionia, probably through their greater contact with the well-established cultures of the Near East, made important contributions to Greek civilization. Thinkers like Thales, Anaximander, Pythagoras and others attempted to grapple with the problems of the universe. Lyric poetry began to make its appearance, and it was during this period that Homer, who is believed to have come from Ionia, composed the *Iliad* and the *Odyssey*, epic poems which demonstrated a strong poetic tradition. The account of the Trojan war and Odysseus' subsequent adventures, although concerned with a long-lost heroic past, so reflected Greek perceptions of their own customs and ethics that Homer became the basis of Greek education, and this remained true for Greek-speaking peoples down into the era of Byzantium in the Middle Ages.

CHAPTER THREE

The Persian Wars

Oligarchy and Democracy

The Classical period in Greece (approximately the fifth century BC) can be characterized as the age of the city-state. It represented the epitome of civilized life for the political and moral thinkers of the age. Greek citizens measured their quality of life not only against their individual liberty within the *polis*, but also by the autonomy – the political independence and freedom from outside interference – of their own city-state.

The autocracy of the tyrants of the Archaic period had been rejected in favour of more pluralistic forms of government. The majority of city-states were governed by oligarchies. These 'few' were the better off in the community whose role as hoplites gave them status and political power. Athens, after the expulsion of the Peisistratid family, had rejected both tyranny and oligarchy in favour of democracy. It was a version of democracy which would not be recognized today as it excluded from the political process both women and those not born of Athenian parents (slaves, of course, also had no political rights). All adult male citizens were enabled to speak and vote for, or against, motions put before the Assembly. Citizens not only took part in legislation but were also required to serve their term on the executive of the government. During the heyday of the democracy all the government posts were chosen by sortition – by lot – except for the office of general (*strategos*): there were ten generals who were elected annually by the citizens. (Presumably it was thought too important a post to allow anyone, regardless of merit or ability, to command Athenian forces. As a consequence of its elective nature the office of general was the most powerful in the government.)

Fierce political debate arose within the Greek city-states as to the merits of oligarchy as opposed to democracy. The vigour with which the argument was conducted often led to apparently irreconcilable factionalism and subsequent instability of government. This state of affairs, combined with the continual demand of each city-state for its complete autonomy, was to have a profound effect upon the political development of Greece: it was not only difficult for city-states to unite their citizen body when concerted action was required, but Greek political unity was hampered, alliances between city-states often foundering on the requirement of autonomy, even when Greece was threatened by external enemies.

The Ionian Revolt

An example of the difficulties of organizing united action occurred at the beginning of the fifth century BC. The dominant and expanding power in the Near East at the end of the sixth century was Persia. Under the rule of the Achaemenid dynasty, the Persians had rapidly absorbed the established kingdoms of the east Mediterranean: Media, Lydia, Babylonia and Egypt. The defeat of the legendary Croesus, the last king of the Lydians, had brought the Persians into contact with the Greek colonies of the western seaboard of Asia Minor (modern Turkey). Most of these colonies had been founded by the Ionians and consequently this area tended to be known as Ionia. Although it was under the suzerainty of Lydia, the Greek cities appeared to have had reasonably amicable relations with their powerful neighbour, and as long as they paid tribute to the Lydian court the cities were granted autonomy to run their own affairs.

The Ionians now incorporated into the Persian Empire, took a less docile view of their subject status and in 499 organized a revolt. The precise causes and conduct of the Ionian Revolt are not well understood. Our main source is Herodotus, who has been referred to both as 'the father of history' and 'the father of lies'. Herodotus was himself an eastern Greek from the city of Halikarnassos (modern Bodrum in

Turkey). Exiled from his home town, he travelled to Athens and wrote an account of the conflict between the Greeks and the Persians. At the time there was virtually no tradition of recording history, so he was breaking new ground. He had little idea of researching evidence and had to rely on the oral and hearsay accounts of witnesses, recalling events thirty years later. Apart from inevitably giving an essentially Greek perspective of the conflict, he also reveals a prejudice against the Ionians and a bias in favour of the Athenians, so that his account of the Ionian Revolt cannot be considered satisfactory.

The rebellion was unsuccessful, and in his need to apologize for the failure, Herodotus, perhaps following a common human tendency to find a scapegoat, implausibly fixed the motives for the revolt upon the personal foibles of Aristagoras, the leader of the most powerful Ionian city, Miletos, and the cause of its failure on the ineffectiveness of the Ionian people. As there are no other contemporary Greek accounts or Persian records, it is not easy to reconstruct an explanation for the rebellion. Herodotus hints at some financial difficulties; perhaps the burden of tribute payable by the Ionians to Persia and a restriction on previous trading with the hinterland was exacerbated by the Persian authorities imposing their own Greek nominees as tyrants over the Ionian cities.

At the beginning of the revolt, the Ionians appealed to the mainland Greeks for aid against the Persians. Sparta, the leading military city-state refused to send help. According to Herodotus the Spartan king, Kleomenes, turned down the Ionian request when Aristagoras revealed that the Persian capital of Susa was three months' journey from the sea; the Spartans, whose foreign policy was consistently determined by the need to maintain a strong military presence, which meant the bulk of her citizens, near home, could not contemplate engaging in a war with such a distant enemy. Sparta was primarily concerned with inhibiting, or repressing, any threat of insurrection from her subservient peoples, the helots and *perioikoi* of Lakonia and Messenia, who formed the majority of the population. She also had to ensure her continued leadership, or hegemony, of the Peloponnesian League lest any neighbouring city-state incited or supported her slave population to revolt.

The Ionians, however, did receive support from Athens and Eretria (a modest twenty-five ships). Eretria, a small city on the island of Euboia, had in a previous dispute received aid from Miletos and now thought herself honour bound to reciprocate. Athens considered herself the senior Ionian city and had founded Miletos, but when the Athenian Assembly voted to send help there were probably other motives besides the emotional call of kith and kin which persuaded the people to support the revolt. With the largest population of any city-state on the mainland, Athens was no longer self-sufficient in food and relied upon imports from the Black Sea. If her corn ships were to be able to keep her supplied, she required access to the cities of the Sea of Marmara and the Bosporos. In those days ships needed to sail close to land for navigation, to shelter from the unpredictable weather of the Aegean, and to take on water and food supplies, so it was necessary to make frequent stops and the existence of friendly ports was vitally important.

Persia had already threatened Athens' trade route when in 514 BC King Darius had invaded Europe and brought under his control the Greek coastal cities which were important staging-posts for Athenian ships travelling to the Black Sea. We do not know exactly what was Persia's imperial strategy but it seems highly probable that Darius was attempting, with this expedition, to secure a land route into Europe to facilitate further Persian expansion. Persia's rise to power had been rapid and unremitting and it is likely that there were political and social forces within the court and among the aristocracy that demanded continual imperial success from its monarchs. Fortunately for Greece Darius' expedition ended in failure and any plans for further expansion westward were shelved for the moment.

If it seems clear to us now, with the advantage of hindsight, that Persian ambitions to expand into Europe would eventually end in the subjugation of Greece, the Greek city-states at the beginning of the Ionian revolt seemed wholly unaware that this might be the consequence of Persian imperialism. For apart from the slight aid from Athens and Eretria, the mainland ignored the struggle of the Ionians.

The first major operation of the Ionian rebels was to march on the city of Sardis. This city had been the capital of the Lydian kings and it now served as the Persian administrative centre for the region. Although the Persian garrison held out in the citadel, the Ionians burnt the rest of the city to the ground, including the temples and sacred places – an act in contradiction to the code of war, as it was considered never wise to alienate any gods to whomever they belonged. The Ionians then withdrew and were subsequently defeated by Persian forces near Ephesos. At this point the Athenians and Eretrians, who had joined the march inland to Sardis, perhaps disillusioned with the conduct of the rebels, decided to withdraw and returned home. The Ionians continued the revolt until in 494 they were defeated in a major sea battle at Lade, off the coast of Asia Minor, by the Persian fleet which was mainly comprised of Phoenician and Egyptian warships. In the following year Miletos was forced to capitulate and, as was normal practice in the ancient world, the young men were massacred and the women and children sold into slavery. The fall of Miletos signalled the end of the revolt.

The consequences of the Ionian Revolt for mainland Greece were to be manifold. The Athenians were embarrassed by the disastrous conclusion of the revolt, presumably because their support had been so small; and when Phrynichos produced, probably in the summer of 493 BC at the Dionysia (an important part of this festival to the god Dionysios was the performance of plays), a tragedy based on the fall of Miletos, the audience was so distressed that the play was banned and the playwright fined. Darius had learnt a political lesson from the revolt and Herodotus tells us that he replaced the old system of tyrants in the Ionian cities with democracies, though what Herodotus means by the term in this context is uncertain. But Darius also, according to Herodotus, could not forgive the Athenian and Eretrian complicity in the revolt and swore to be revenged. It is difficult for us now to know how significant the theme of revenge might be in Persian thinking. Herodotus tends to construct his history as if it were a drama, but we should be wary of applying modern perceptions to the motives and actions of the ancient world. Certainly Darius used the Athenian and Eretrian involvement in the Ionian revolt as a *casus belli* – a cause for war – even if the proposed punishment of these city-states disguised a greater desire for the conquest of Greece. The Persians also probably realized that, as long as the mainland of Greece was free, the Ionians, looking at the autonomy of their fellow Greeks, would remain recalcitrant to Persian rule.

Marathon

In 492 BC Darius appointed his son-in-law Mardonios to resecure the land route to Europe. It may have been within Mardonios' brief to advance into Greece but his fleet was destroyed in a storm off Mount Athos. It was not until two years later that an expedition was mounted against Eretria and Athens. Under the command of Datis and Artaphernes, an amphibious force set sail from southern Asia Minor. After reducing some of the Cycladic islands the Persians arrived at Eretria. The Eretrians resisted for six days but were then betrayed by some of their own number. Not only was there no united resistance to the Persian threat between the factions within cities but several city-states, like the island of Aegina, had already yielded by submitting to the traditional Persian demand for 'earth and water' (which symbolized surrender to Persian rule).

Having sacked Eretria, the Persians sailed across from Euboia to the mainland, landing at the bay of Marathon. They were probably taken to this landing-place by Hippias, the ex-tyrant of Athens, who was

Fragment from a grave relief

accompanying the Persian forces and, would, no doubt, had Athens been conquered, have been installed as a Persian puppet ruler. It was possibly in Hippias' mind that his father, Peisistratos, had once successfully deployed Thessalian cavalry against the Athenians at Marathon and, since Persian military strength also lay in their cavalry, the bay could be thought an excellent location for engaging the Athenians.

Athens, having watched impotently the fate of Eretria, knew that she would be next to feel the might of the Persians and now appealed to Sparta to send her military support. The messenger Pheidippides ran the journey to Sparta, but the Spartans declared themselves unable to march because they were in the middle of a religious festival. Cynics might well see this as remarkably convenient for the Spartans but we must be careful not to apply a modern gloss to the ancient view of the sacred. Athens, then, was on her own apart from the aid of the small city of Plataia. Plataia had in the past been protected by Athens from her powerful neighbour Thebes, who constantly sought to end Plataia's autonomy. Despite the magnitude of the crisis facing Athens the Plataians determined to remain loyal to their ally and dispatched all their citizens who could bear arms, perhaps a thousand strong, to the aid of their neighbour.

According to Herodotus, the Athenian hero of the hour was Miltiades, an Athenian colonial who had been acting as tyrant in the region of the Kherronnesos (Chersonese, better known during World War I as the Gallipoli peninsula). He had been forced to flee to Athens when the Persians advanced into Europe and on arriving there had been elected general. He now advised the Athenians to march out and do battle with the Persians. The walls of Athens were probably not in a fit state to withstand a prolonged siege and perhaps Miltiades did not trust the resolve of the Athenians to defend the city; there are enough hints in Herodotus' account to suggest that there were those Athenians who were prepared to compromise with the invader, possibly supporters of Hippias – the spectre of factionalism appears once more.

The whole Athenian army marched out from the city to Marathon – the twenty-five miles or thereabouts which has given its name to the long-distance race. Once there it made camp (the exact location is not known) on the hills above the bay, no doubt blocking the road to Athens.

It consisted of 10,000 hoplites – infantry soldiers drawn from the citizen body, armed with javelins and a sword and protected by a helmet, breastplate, greaves (leg armour) and a large circular shield. The heavy armour of the hoplite resulted in poor visibility and mobility but this was compensated for by fighting in a tight formation: in the battle-line the shields were held so that they not only protected each soldier's left side but also overlapped his neighbour's right flank; the enemy were presented with an impenetrable 'wall of steel' and when the hoplites charged they relied on the sheer weight of their impact to smash through their opponent's line.

The Persian force would have been made up of various contingents from the subject peoples, stiffened by crack Persian regiments. The exact size of the Persian army is not known, but it is generally accepted that they heavily outnumbered the Athenians; of the various computations that have been made the figure of 30,000 – three times the size of the Athenian army – does not seem wildly unreasonable. The Persian soldiers were lightly armed, protected only by a helmet or cap, a wicker shield and a leather jerkin; they fought as light mobile soldiers, mainly attacking the enemy with arrows, javelins and darts. The cavalry was traditionally the strongest wing of any Persian army; it would, however, have been difficult to transport a large number of horses across the Aegean so that there may only have been a relatively small force of cavalry with the expedition.

Herodotus was not a military man and his account of the battle provides a rather confused picture of events. After some delay, and apparently upon the advice of Miltiades, the Athenians decided to attack the Persian force camped below in the bay. Although technically not the commander-in-chief (who was Kallimakhos), it was Miltiades who apparently led the attack. The Athenian phalanx of hoplites charged at the double, although Herodotus' claim that they ran for over a mile is incredible because of the weight of their armour. The strength of the Athenians lay in the wings of their battle-line and, although their centre was checked and was forced to give ground, the flanks swept the Persian opposition before them. They then turned on the exposed rear of the Persian centre. The battle was won and the surviving Persians fled to their ships.

In ancient set-piece battles, victory was often obtained by being able to break through, or outflank a battle-line and attack the enemy from behind. The issue was rarely decided while the two lines were locked in face-to-face combat but if one side's vulnerable rear was exposed then the contest would soon be settled. The defeated side's casualties, even allowing for the deliberate exaggeration of the victors, were always dramatically larger than the winner's. This is probably because most deaths occurred when the vanquished were attempting to flee and so exposed their unprotected backs. Herodotus gives the Persian dead at Marathon as 6400 and the Athenian as only 192. Although the Athenian figure looks remarkably low it is likely to be correct, since the winning side would take care to account for its own casualties, and in the relatively small community of Athens the people would be very much aware of those who had died and the precise figure would become well known.

The Athenian dead (including Kallimakhos) were cremated and placed beneath a conical mound (*soros*) on the plain of Marathon. The mound is still to be seen today and has been excavated in part to reveal the remains of charred bones and weaponry from the battle. It is worth noting here a theory that has gained some currency with regard to the purpose of the sculptured frieze which ran round the upper part of the wall of the Parthenon temple on the Acropolis in Athens. (Most of the sculptured panels of the frieze, part of the Elgin marbles, are now on display in the Duveen Gallery in the British Museum. They are a matter of some controversy as the Greek government would like them returned to Athens.) The Parthenon was built after 447 BC and has a commemorative aspect as part of a restoration programme to celebrate the Greek victory over the Persians. The frieze itself appears to represent the procession of the Panathenaic festival – the most important religious ceremony when the ancient olive-wood cult statue of Athena was dressed in a new saffron-coloured robe. There are some difficulties with identifying the frieze as an exact representation of the procession but, as John Boardman has pointed out, the number of horsemen who are shown on the frieze might represent the 192 killed at Marathon.

Herodotus' account of the battle raises some intriguing questions. It is puzzling that there is no mention of the Persian cavalry; a Byzantine source states that the Ionian Greeks who were forced to accompany the Persians advised the Greeks when the 'horses were away'. If there is any validity in the claim it may mean the cavalry had been embarked on the ships. If most of the Persian ships had already been launched this would certainly help explain why only seven ships were captured by the Athenians. The Persian fleet would have been beached and it would have needed organization and considerable manpower to launch the ships, something that could not easily be accomplished in the midst of a battle. It is reasonable to suggest, though it is, of course, only speculation, that when the Athenians attacked the Persians were already in the process of embarking, having abandoned hope of drawing the Athenians into battle, and that Artaphernes and Datis were intent on sailing around the cape at Sounion to attack Athens itself. If this is true the horses, because they would naturally be difficult to load, would have been embarked first. The idea that some of the Persian fleet was already at sea and heading for Athens before the battle started is given weight by Herodotus noting that the Persians stopped at a small island to pick up Eretrian prisoners – not something they would have been likely to do if they were trying to race the Athenian army back to the city. Herodotus also reports that some Athenians flashed a signal to the Persians. Was this perhaps a pro-Persian faction in Athens advising the enemy that the city was ripe for capture? It is unlikely we shall ever solve all the problems Herodotus' account of the battle presents.

For the Athenians the victory was a remarkable demonstration of the prowess of her citizens and it reinforced the people's confidence in the government of democracy. The Spartans had arrived the day after the battle and were impressed by the Athenians' achievement; Athens now took her place as a leading city of Greece. When the German (Archaeological) Institute excavated the stadium at Olympia they found many votive offerings (a thanksgiving, often the result of a vow), which had been deliberately buried in the seating banks. Among the many pieces of armour there was not only an oriental helmet, booty from Marathon, but also a Greek helmet, the crown badly squashed, with on the side the inscription: 'Miltiades dedicated this to Zeus'. The type (Corinthian) and style of the helmet confirm that this must have been the very helmet that Miltiades had worn at the battle of Marathon.

Xerxes' Invasion of Greece

The Persians had suffered a severe blow to their prestige and it is possible that the Athenian victory inspired a revolt from the empire by Egypt. A decade later it was left to Darius' successor, Xerxes, after he had suppressed Egypt, to attempt to avenge Marathon. A Persian force advanced by both land and sea and the scale of the invasion reveals that Xerxes did not just intend to punish Athens but to conquer the whole of Greece. The Persians had made careful preparations: supply dumps were organized along the route, a canal was dug at the peninsula of Athos (a shallow depression still remains) to avoid the dangerous promontory, and a bridge of boats was prepared for crossing the Bosporos from Asia into Europe.

While the Persians were making these extensive preparations the Greeks showed little sign of being aware of the impending danger. Only perhaps at Athens was there a statesman who understood the threat that

Themistokles

was facing Greece. Miltiades, the hero of Marathon, had fallen from favour as he had urged the Athenians into an unsuccessful assault against the island of Paros. Despite receiving a mortal wound in the attack, he had been convicted of corruption and died in an Athenian prison. His fate was not untypical of the way the Greeks reacted to the failure of their leaders (imagine Montgomery receiving such treatment for his failure at Arnhem in World War II). An explanation for this apparent fickleness may well be found in the continual fear among Greeks that powerful individuals might seek tyranny unless curbed, and the fierce competition of political rivals who were always ready to exploit a leader's failings to bring him down.

At Athens a new leader had arisen in Themistokles, who showed his foresight and political adeptness when a new vein of silver was discovered (483/2 BC) at the Athenian mine at Laurion (Lavrion). One view among the Athenians was that this windfall should be equally distributed among all the citizens but Themistokles managed to persuade the Assembly to allocate the additional funds for a ship-building programme. Athens was able to increase the size of her navy to 200 triremes, which were to play a vital part in resisting Xerxes' invasion. The trireme was the principal warship of the Greek world; it was a long narrow craft mainly propelled by three banks of oarsmen on each side of the boat. At the prow of the ship on the water-line was a ram which was driven against an enemy ship. (The Greek navy has recently taken delivery of a replica of such a ship – designed by two Britons – which has proved to be both fast and manoeuvrable.)

The rest of Greece seemed ill-prepared to meet the Persian menace and it was not until 481 that a congress of Greek states met at the Isthmus of Corinth to consider some joint action. Most of northern Greece felt unable to resist the Persian invasion, but thirty-one states formed an alliance – known to modern historians as the Hellenic League. Sparta, as the dominant military force, was elected leader. An interesting monument to this rare demonstration of Greek unity has survived in Istanbul. After the Greeks' victory the members of the League erected, as a votive offering, a golden tripod to Apollo at the sanctuary at Delphi. A tripod usually consisted of a bowl, into which libations could be poured, supported on three legs. In this particular case it was a golden bowl balanced on the heads of three serpents whose bodies were entwined into a single bronze column. On the base of the column were inscribed the names of the thirty-one states that formed the alliance. The bowl was looted during antiquity but in AD 330 the base was taken by the Roman emperor Constantine the Great from Delphi to his new Christian capital, Constantinople (Istanbul) in order to decorate the hippodrome where the chariot races took place. The column still stands in the centre of the remains of the hippodrome, although none of the serpent heads remain on the column (one head is in the Archaeological Museum – it was knocked off during a polo match).

Thermopylai

The Hellenic League was divided about the strategy they should adopt in attempting to stop the Persian invasion. Sparta and her Peloponnesian allies wished to defend a wall at the Isthmus of Corinth, but this would have meant abandoning the cities of central Greece to the Persians and Athens urged the allies to confront the enemy as far north as possible. In the end it was agreed in 480 BC to send a force to the Vale of Tempe which divides Thessaly from Macedonia to the north. However, when the allied army reached Tempe it was realized that they could easily be outflanked by the superior numbers of the Persians (Herodotus puts the whole Persian force at over five million, which is clearly inconceivable; a figure over 200,000 would have been remarkable). The Greeks abandoned Tempe but sent another force into Boiotia in order to block the road south. With an army of only about 7000 the Spartan king, Leonidas, held the narrow pass at Thermopylai while the combined navies attempted to check the Persian fleet at Artemision.

For two days Leonidas' army resisted the Persian attack but eventually a Greek traitor, said to be Ephialtes of Malis, led the Persian royal guard, the Immortals, along a secret path which outflanked the pass. When Leonidas realized the Persians would soon be at his rear he dismissed his army but determined to remain with his 300 Spartans, 400 Thebans (who were not trusted by the allies as they were thought to be prepared to go over to the Persians) and 700 Thespians who refused to leave. Spartan ideology did not countenance retreat or surrender but expected each man to fight to the death. After a fierce and prolonged battle Leonidas, the Spartans and the Thespians were annihilated (only some Thebans surrendered). While the battle raged at Thermopylai a hard-fought naval engagement took place. Both sides received heavy casualties but on the news of Leonidas' death the Greeks decided to withdraw.

Salamis

Nothing now stood between Athens and the Persian army but the Athenians acted without yielding to panic. Themistokles, who is consistently represented by Herodotus as the crafty and intelligent schemer (perhaps in imitation of Odysseus in Homer), persuaded the people, aided by a subtle interpretation of the Delphic oracle, to evacuate the city as indefensible and seek refuge in neighbouring friendly states. The Persians arrived at Athens to find the city deserted apart from a few who defended the weakly fortified Acropolis ('the upper city = citadel'). Athens was sacked and the temples on the Acropolis destroyed.

Themistokles is credited by Herodotus with tricking Xerxes into risking a naval battle in the narrow waters between the island of Salamis and the mainland. The Peloponnesian Greeks wanted once more to withdraw behind the Isthmus of Corinth but it is likely that the Athenians put pressure on them, perhaps by threatening to abandon resistance to the Persians, to maintain the fleet off the coast of Athens. In fact, Xerxes himself would have been anxious to force the issue with a battle as it was already September and the campaigning season was drawing to an end. In the ancient world it was really only possible to campaign in the summer as the winter created problems of food supply and communication. The Persian fleet had suffered storm damage on more than one occasion and its commanders would be anxious to avoid the vagaries of the winter weather in the Aegean. So it was probably the shortage of time which persuaded the Persians to attack the Greek fleet in the unfavourable waters at Salamis. While the battle raged Xerxes apparently looked on from the mainland, seated on a golden throne. The narrow waters did not allow the Persians' superior numbers to tell and the warships became jammed against each other so that the excellent fighting qualities of the Greek hoplites, who were acting as marines, carried the day.

Plataia

The defeat at Salamis was a major blow to the Persian invasion plans and Xerxes returned to Asia with a portion of his army, but he left a powerful force behind to winter in Thessaly under the command of Mardonios. Mardonios hoped to detach the Athenians from the Greek alliance by promising to spare Athens from a second attack if they agreed to submit to Persia. The proposal was rejected by Athens but perhaps Themistokles used the offer as a bargaining counter to demand that the allies take some action in central Greece. Whatever the case the League put a large army into the field the following year.

In 479 Mardonios moved his army south into Boiotia and dominated the plain with his cavalry so that the Greek force, under the command of the Spartan Pausanias, who was regent to the young king Pleistarkhos, clung to the northern slopes of Mount Kithairon. Pausanias had a force of over 37,000 hoplites (including as many as 5000 Spartan citizens – a large number by Spartan standards) and Mardonios probably had an army of much the same size. The two sides opposed each other near the city of Plataia (Plataea), each general waiting for some tactical advantage. The Persian cavalry constantly made probing attacks against the Greek positions and eventually after several weeks, having fouled the Spartans' water supply, forced Pausanias to organize a retreat. The Greek army got broken up in the confusion of the move and Mardonios seized his chance and ordered his infantry to attack, but the training and fearsome bravery of the Spartan hoplites destroyed the Persian attack and in the mêlée Mardonios was slain. Resistance crumbled and the Greeks stormed the Persian camp; no prisoners were taken and only a small Persian contingent were able to flee to the north.

The victory at the battle of Plataia, as it became known, had driven the Persian invader permanently from Greek soil. Despite Mardonios' competent generalship and the weakness of the Greeks' tactical position, Greek unity and the fighting ability of the hoplite had defeated a powerful enemy. Around the same time as the victory at Plataia (on precisely the same day according to Greek tradition) a Greek naval expedition destroyed the Persian fleet, which had been beached at Mykale on the coast of Asia Minor. Once more the main factor in the Greek victory was the superiority of the Greek soldier, man for man, over the Persian. The threat to Greece was over, the war was won and the freedom of the Greek states preserved.

For Herodotus the outstanding moral truth of the Greek victory over the Persian Empire was that the Greek political system, and in particular the democracy of Athens, which promoted the freedom and autonomy of man, had triumphed over the oriental despotism of the Persian monarchy. The tyranny of autocracy was only fit for aliens, barbarians (non-Greeks, who when they spoke made 'bar bar' sounds), not 'civilized' men (those who lived within the *polis* and were fully engaged in its government). It was the free citizen who had vanquished the enslaved subject.

A Persian horseman attacking a Greek soldier from an engraving on a Chalcedony gemstone

CHAPTER FOUR

The Athenian Empire

After the defeat of Persia the League of Greek states decided to maintain the alliance in order to exact revenge (the acquisition of booty would have been a significant motive – booty was often an important part of a state's income) and liberate those city-states in the Aegean and Ionia still under Persian rule. Operations against Persia now had to be conducted by the allies' navy. Although Sparta only had a few ships (her military needs at home gave priority to the army and her lack of a cash economy meant she could neither purchase the necessary materials such as timber and sail-cloth, nor pay for the oarsmen to man a large fleet), she still led the allies. Spartan mentality, however, was ill-suited to conducting campaigns abroad: rigid conservatism inhibited her ability to adapt to foreign circumstances. Her constant concern with her internal security – the need to suppress the subject peoples – had spawned an insularity which rejected outside contacts (for example, she did not have a trading economy) and hampered any ventures outside the Peloponnese.

The allies were soon expressing dissatisfaction with Spartan leadership. Pausanias had been entrusted with the command of the main allied enterprise but he revealed himself to be tyrannical and corrupt. Herodotus tells us he was accused not only of corresponding with the Persian court in the hope of preferment from the Great King but also of aping oriental despotism and extravagance in his actions and clothes. Whatever the truth of these allegations, and some seem unlikely, the Spartan government feared his behaviour. Sparta was always suspicious of its successful generals lest they used their authority and power to overthrow the government and establish autocracy. The stern discipline and the narrow existence at home, along with the Spartan ideology of their own superiority over other Greeks, apparently warped their attitude so that, when they has access to power and the relative luxury of life abroad, they became avaricious and susceptible to megalomania – at least, that is how the Spartans were often perceived. Pausanias was recalled to Sparta and eventually executed by being walled up in a temple – yet another example of a successful Greek general coming to grief at the hands of his own side. The allies were now alienated and reluctant to accept another Spartan commander and so turned to Athens to assume the leadership of the League.

The Delian League

Athens' power and influence in the Greek world had grown enormously as a consequence of her major role in the defeat of the Persian invasion. Themistokles, in the face of protests from the Spartans who wished to keep Athens weak, had made sure that not only the city, after the Persian sack, but also the new port of the Piraeus were well fortified. (Like many Athenian leaders, Themistokles soon lost popularity with the people and finally fled to the Persian court where the Great King made him tyrant of the city of Magnesia in Asia Minor.) Apart from her association with the Ionian cities, it was Athens who provided the majority of ships for the allied navy and so she was now seen as the natural protectress of the island and maritime city-states. Athens eagerly accepted the role of leader and a new alliance was formed; the members swore their allegiance to Athens by dropping pieces of metal into the sea, symbolizing the perpetual nature of the alliance. Each ally paid tribute, either in cash or in contributions of ships and men, and the treasury was kept on Delos, the sacred island of Apollo's birth – the alliance is sometimes referred to as the 'Delian League'. Athens provided the treasurers and the amount of the contribution was assessed by the Athenian Aristides, known because of his scrupulous fairness as 'the Just'. There is a story that Aristides was once on his way to the Athenian Assembly when he saw a poor man struggling to scratch a name on a broken piece of pot – an ostrakon – which was used as a voting ballot when it was proposed to ostracize a citizen (banishment for ten years without loss of rights or property). Aristides stopped and, recognizing that the man was illiterate, offered to help write the name. 'Whose name shall I write?' 'Aristides,' the man replied. 'Why do you want Aristides ostracized?' 'Because I am tired of hearing him called "the Just".' Aristides, it is said, characteristically obliged and scratched his own name on the potsherd.

THUCYDIDES

Herodotus concludes his account of Greek history at this point and we now have to turn to the Athenian, Thucydides, to take up the narrative. Although as a historian he inevitably has things in common with Herodotus, Thucydides denies an interest in the past and sets out to write about contemporary events. His concern is with the prolonged war between Athens and Sparta, known as 'The Peloponnesian War'. As an Athenian general, he had experience of action and, when he himself was exiled for military failure, he had access to witnesses from both sides of the war. He claims both to have carefully researched his material, although he rarely acknowledges his sources, and to have spurned the tales (*mythoi*) he found in other histories (perhaps a criticism of Herodotus' apparent gullibility). He eschewed the easy, fluent and anecdotal narrative of Herodotus, ruthlessly applying a rational analysis to his reconstruction of events. Thucydides also believed in the primacy of the motivation of individuals and he is constantly providing psychological insights into the protagonists of his account. In the end, however, as with Herodotus, Thucydides was a moralist who perceived a teleology (a final purpose) in history that was determined by Nemesis (the goddess of retribution): he argued that the ultimate downfall of Athens in the Peloponnesian War was a consequence of the Athenians' misuse of power.

The Melian Dialogue

Athens, having acquired the hegemony of the Delian League, gradually, through the use of force and political controls, converted the alliance into an empire and the allies into subject peoples. It is unclear how the League determined policy at the beginning: one view is that the alliance was governed bicamerally, with a council, consisting of representatives from each ally, sharing decision-making with the Athenian Assembly. But whatever the initial constitution may have been, the reality became that Athens solely decided policy for the allies.

The crucial factor in Athens' ability to control the League was her naval superiority: the maritime city-states of the alliance were vulnerable to the powerful fleet of the Athenians and recalcitrant allies could be coerced into obedience. Athens was also quite prepared to use force to compel some cities to join the alliance: soon after the formation of the League, the island of Skyros and the city of Karystos, on Euboia were forcibly enrolled. Later there was the notorious attack on the Cycladic island of Melos. The Melians were Dorians, whereas most of the islands had been settled by Ionians, and they had resisted joining the League; epigraphic – inscriptional – evidence has also suggested that the Melians, during the Peloponnesian War, were paying contributions to Sparta. After one abortive attempt to subdue the island, the Athenians besieged and eventually captured it in 416. The Melians were to suffer the punishment often considered the normal for a defeated enemy in the ancient world: all the males were executed and the women and children

A silver coin from Athens

sold into slavery. The playwright Euripides, noted for his dramatic criticisms of contemporary life, is thought to have written his compelling and moving play *The Trojan Women* as a comment on the action of the Athenians.

The Melian episode is interesting, not only because its tragic outcome represents one of the worst aspects of Athenian imperialism and provides a salutary counterbalance to the often over-romanticized accounts of Athenian democracy, but also because Thucydides records a dialogue which took place between the Athenians and the Melians before the siege got under way. In his *History*, Thucydides used speeches on several occasions in order to provide insight into the thinking of the participants. He did not claim to reproduce actual verbatim records but he aimed to provide the essence and sense of what was being said. In this practice he was following a tradition, used also by Herodotus, but he created highly-developed set-pieces through speeches, debates and dialogues. (It should be remembered that in the ancient world, where an author's work was often recited before a public audience, history tended to have a dramatic quality, suitable for performance, which many modern historians might think out of place in a 'scientific' reconstruction of the facts. Speeches could, clearly, be very useful vehicles for enlivening drier historical narratives.)

In the Melian dialogue, the Athenian delegates attempt to justify their imperialism by making an analogy between their behaviour and natural law: in nature the strong prevail over the weak, and as it is with animals so it must be with man. The Melians should submit because the Athenians are stronger. This may seem a remarkably crude argument but, regardless of the accuracy of Thucydides' reporting, it does reveal the apparent truth that force lay at the basis of Greek politics. In Thucydides' judgement, as we have already seen, it was the misuse of power by Athens which was to lead to her downfall, and here, in the Melian dialogue, we have a glaring example of the failure of Athens to recognize an ethical standard which raises man above animal behaviour.

The Mytilenian Debate

Besides coercing city-states into the Delian League, Athens did not allow existing members to withdraw from the alliance. When Naxos (*c.* 470 BC) and Thasos (465) attempted to secede they were both reduced into submission and harshly punished. While the war was being actively pursued against Persia, Athens might have been able to argue that the solidarity of the alliance, and the permanent nature of the oaths the allies had taken, prohibited secession. However, after the failure of an expedition against Persian-controlled Egypt (454), the League's operations against Persia ceased and it is possible (though the evidence is not certain) that a few years later a formal peace was concluded between Athens and the Great King, Artaxerxes. Despite the end of hostilities, however, Athens maintained the League, denying any ally the opportunity to leave. She had converted a voluntary alliance into an empire based on her thalassocracy (mastery of the sea). Defections were considered treacherous rebellions which were savagely repressed: for example, when the oligarchs of the city of Mytilene on the island of Lesbos revolted, Athens threatened to mete out a fierce punishment on the whole people, not just the rebels. After the revolt was suppressed the Athenian Assembly met to decide the fate of the Mytilenians. In their anger, the Athenians decreed that all the men should be executed and the women and children sold into slavery.

The next day the Athenians began to regret their decision and another meeting of the Assembly was held. Thucydides recorded the speeches of the two main speakers in the debate (again, he is rendering the sense of the arguments rather than an accurate record). The proponent for the execution of the total male population was Kleon, whom Thucydides loathed and labelled as a demagogue – a populist politician who persuades the people to behave irrationally by appealing to their baser motives. Kleon rehearsed the view that a harsh punishment would act as a deterrent against other city-states that might be contemplating rebellion. He was opposed by Diodotos, who argued that, on the contrary, not only would those who were opposed to Athens be made more desperate rather than deterred by the example of Mytilene, but Athens' friends would also be likely to be alienated by this savage treatment, since such a blanket reaction to the rebellion did not discriminate between friend and foe. It is noteworthy that both speakers assumed the political and moral appropriateness of the Athenian empire:

what was at issue was the way the empire should be managed, not whether imperialism was right. In the end Diodotos' argument carried the day in the Assembly and a fast ship was sent in pursuit of the state trireme which had set off the previous day with the order for the executions to be carried out. The rowers of the second ship were offered additional financial incentives by the Mytilenian envoys, who had come to Athens to plead their city's case, in order to encourage them to overhaul the first ship. Fortunately for Mytilene, the second ship arrived just in time to stop the awful punishment being carried out.

Athenian Imperialism

Alongside the use of bare force, Athens employed a variety of measures and controls to ensure the compliance of her erstwhile allies. It has been possible, mainly because of the survival of inscriptions, often in a very fragmentary state, to reconstruct the methods by which she imposed her dominance throughout the Aegean. When the Delian League had been formed it was Athens who had determined and collected the tribute from each member. After 454 Athens had moved the treasury from the island of Delos to the Acropolis at Athens. The pretext for the transfer had been the loss of the expeditionary force in Egypt and the fear that the Phoenician fleet, operating for the Persians, might threaten Delos. A sceptical response to this excuse is fully justified as there is no evidence that the Persians were in any position to take the initiative in the Aegean again. Once the treasury was re-located the Athenians took a quota (one-sixtieth) of each member's tribute and donated it to the goddess Athena. Lists carved in stone were set up recording each year's contributions. The lists have partly survived, and although the inscriptions have required considerable reconstruction, it has been possible to deduce the annual contributions of the member states: the fluctuations and omissions in the amounts paid give indications of when cities had rebelled or been punished.

Athens was happy to encourage members to convert contributions of men and ships into cash donations, because it gave her greater control over the navy as it was almost entirely commanded and crewed by her own citizens; in fact, most small states aided this process, preferring to pay in cash rather than lose precious manpower. Athens not only spent the tribute on maintaining the navy but, besides giving a quota to Athena, also used the money for her own benefit: new building works on the Acropolis were financed by the tribute. After the sack of Athens by the Persians it had been decided to leave the destroyed temples on the Acropolis as a lasting memorial to the suffering and the contribution of the Athenian people to the Persian Wars. Later the Athenians changed their minds and began a building programme, not to restore the buildings destroyed but to construct new and grand temples worthy of an imperial power. These buildings – the Parthenon, Erekhtheion, and the Propylaia – became the pride of Athens and today still illustrate the magnificence of classical architecture.

At some point during the growth of the empire, Athens decreed that all members of the alliance should use the Athenian system of weights and measures, and that only Athenian coins would be valid currency within the League. As each city-state had tended to employ its own system of weights and measures and minted its own coins, such an imposition of a universal standard might be thought, on the face of it, not only more convenient but a step to a more rational commerce between the Greek cities. However, the autonomy of each city was symbolized by its own weights and measures and its particular emblem stamped upon its coinage; the Athenian dictate was just another instance of gross interference and infringement of freedom by Athens. It is probably also true that Athens used her command of the sea to her own commercial advantage and controlled the trading activity in the Aegean.

Athens felt at liberty to intervene in the internal politics of the allies, consistently promoting the cause of the democrats against the oligarchs. Epigraphic evidence indicates that some cities had to adopt an Athenian type of constitution and democracies were imposed along with garrisons and Athenian officials to ensure there was no backsliding. Throughout the cities, individual democrats were appointed to act on behalf of Athens – in Greece representatives who acted for another state were known as *proxenoi* (literally meaning 'on behalf of strangers'), and were rather like modern consuls. Athens' *proxenoi* often acted like spies and were even, on occasion, instrumental in promoting revolution in the cause of democracy. The reward for the *proxenoi* was that they were made honorary Athenian citizens – a significant prize as Athenian citizens now claimed a privileged status over the subject members.

Citizenship in the ancient world gave an individual political and legal rights, and Athens now ascribed a superior rank to her own citizens in comparison to the citizens of other cities within the empire. In any dispute Athenians were in a predominant position and all the major jurisdiction of the member cities was shifted to the law courts at Athens to be tried before Athenian judges and juries. When Rome became the leading political power in the Mediterranean her citizens had a similar privileged position, but the Roman government was inclined to grant citizenship to the upper classes of her conquered peoples as a means of acquiring their loyalty and Romanizing the empire. Athens, far from extending the privilege of her citizenship, became more jealous of its privileges and restricted holders only to those who had been born of both an Athenian father and mother, whereas before only one Athenian parent had been necessary.

Athens, then, was disposed to treat her allies as her property and in an imperial fashion even settled her own citizens on allied land. In the ancient world, where societies were essentially agrarian, land was the most important measure of wealth. Athens annexed land from recalcitrant allies, thus depriving them of sovereignty over their own territory and of a share of their wealth, and Athenian colonists, known as cleruchs (*klerouchoi*), were then settled on the land in place of the natives. The colonists were chosen from Athens' own landless and were therefore the poorest citizens, so not only was this a method of alleviating poverty and reducing the numbers in an overcrowded city, but it also provided Athens with a loyal garrison (the colonists retained the rights of their Athenian citizenship) to guard a possibly dissident ally. It also seems clear that the Athenian rich benefited by being able to purchase, on favourable terms, land and property among the allies. The exploitation of the allies' land and the settling of colonists by Athens became one of the most hated features of her imperialism.

PERIKLES

The main architect of Athenian imperialism is often seen as Perikles who, although his background was aristocratic, was so popular with the

Pericles

people that the held the office of general for eleven consecutive years. Thucydides admired Perikles and believed he wielded a calming influence over the worst excesses of the democracy: when he was at the helm sound, rational judgements were made concerning policy; but after his death demagogues like Kleon used emotional appeals which persuaded the Assembly to act rashly.

Perikles' perception of the Athenian empire can be best appreciated from the speech Thucydides put in his mouth at the funeral of those Athenians who were killed at the beginning of the Peloponnesian War. This oration is one of the most famous in antiquity and it has been influential in forming in modern minds a rather idealized picture of the democracy at Athens. Perikles, although he praised the degree of liberty available to the Athenian citizen so that each individual could exercise his talents and potential, believed in the dominance of Athens over her former allies and he encouraged the imperial ambitions of her citizens.

It was this ambition which eventually brought about a long and damaging war that ended in Athens' downfall and destroyed any hope of the Greek city-states creating some sort of long-lasting unity.

The Arts

The fifth century was the zenith of classical Greece, and Athens became the foremost intellectual and artistic centre. The new-found wealth she had acquired through her empire not only enabled Perikles to initiate the magnificent building programme on the Acropolis but other beautiful temples were erected, like the Hephaisteion (Temple of Hephaistos, usually known as the Theseion because of an erroneous attribution to Theseus) in the city, or the Temple of Poseidon on the promontory of Sounion (where Byron was to carve his name on a column). Although Athens was the most ambitious builder, many fine temples were constructed throughout Greece: for example, at Aigina (Aegina), Bassai, and the great Temple of Zeus at Olympia.

Greek sculptors abandoned the rather stiff conventions of the Archaic style and through their observations of the human body began to develop an ideal type of form based upon the realities of nature. The development of bronze-casting techniques freed them, from the restrictions of stone so that much more active and natural poses could be attempted. Polykleitos from Argos perfected the male nude through a mathematical formula, which became known as his Canon. Although his writings and his original sculptures have been lost, a few Roman copies in stone, like the Doryphoros (the Spear-bearer), are extant and reveal his subtle use of symmetry and balance. Where the original bronzes have survived we can glimpse the sculptor's powerful aesthetic and amazing technical control: for example, the Charioteer of Delphi, the Zeus (or Poseidon – it is not possible to identify the god with certainty) from Artemision (in the National Museum in Athens), and the two remarkable bronzes found off the coast of southern Italy at Riace (in Calabria).

Marble architectural sculpture reveals quite clearly the growing confidence of the Greek sculptor in handling naturalistic forms: for example, the rigidness of the Archaic can still be seen in figures from the Temple of Aphaia on Aigina, more flexibility is shown on the pedimental figures of the Temple of Zeus at Olympia, whereas the sculptures from the Parthenon seem to have been completely freed from the constraints of their material. The artist in charge of the Parthenon sculptures was the Athenian Pheidias, who had previously created the colossal statue of Zeus for the temple at Olympia. (When the archaeologists were excavating the site of Olympia they found Pheidias' workshop beneath a later Christian basilica – the identification was made partly on the basis of a pottery cup which had his name scratched upon the base.)

It was also during the early fifth century that Attic red-figure pottery (many of the shapes associated with wine-drinking) reached its fully-developed form and was much prized throughout the Greek world. A complex firing technique enabled artists to reproduce acutely observed everyday scenes and grand mythological set-pieces which exploited the contrast between the rich red of the clay and a dark lustrous slip (a diluted form of clay which could be turned black when firing).

Literary activity in the fifth century reflected the confidence and spirit of enquiry that pervaded the age. We have already noted the prose writing of Herodotus and Thucydides; lyric poetry reached new heights in the skilful hands of the Theban poet, Pindar. It was at this time also that Athens contributed uniquely to western culture through its development of Attic tragedy. Its origins are obscure but drama formed a crucial part of the religious celebrations of the god Dionysios. The great tragedians of the age were Aeschylus, Sophocles and Euripides, whose surviving plays mainly deal with traditional mythological tales and were written for the annual drama competition which constituted the Dionysiac festival. Comedies were also performed in competition, and some of the plays of Aristophanes, the greatest of the comic dramatists, are extant.

CHAPTER FIVE

The Peloponnesian War

The Causes

The long war between Athens and Sparta, which lasted from 431 to 404 BC, dominated the political history of Greece in the second part of the fifth century as it involved nearly all the major city-states as allies of one side or the other. Known as the Peloponnesian War not because much of the fighting took place in the Peloponnese but because Sparta's allies were mainly the city-states of the Peloponnesian League, it is one of the best-known episodes in ancient history since Thucydides has left us an extremely detailed account of the events. His claim to be the first scientific historian, demonstrated by his apparent concern with objectivity, detail and chronology, offered a model of historiography which became an influential example to subsequent historians.

At the beginning of his account Thucydides, displaying a subtle understanding of human motivation, gave his analysis of the causes of the war. While he recognized that there were a series of immediate events which triggered the outbreak of hostilities between Athens and Sparta, he understood that there was a deeper, more fundamental cause which was a consequence of the psychological state of the combatants – that the 'real' cause of the war was Sparta's fear of Athens' expanding imperialism. As we have already seen, Sparta was continually concerned with maintaining her dominance on the mainland of Greece in order to check any incitement to rebellion of her subject peoples in Lakonia and Messenia. Such a rebellion would most probably end in the overthrow of the Spartan government and the end of the rule of the Spartiatai. Unless Athenian imperialism was halted it might well pose a threat to Spartan dominance.

This dominance over mainland Greece was maintained by keeping the other city-states in a relative condition of weakness. This could not be done entirely through Spartan military power, as the exclusive nature of her system of citizenship meant that she only had a small population of Spartiatai for her army; however superior they might be to other Greeks as hoplites, there were too few Spartiatai physically to control the whole of mainland Greece. Sparta therefore maintained her hegemony by balancing her most powerful rivals against each other, her reputation for invincibility on the battlefield enabling her to keep this precarious balance in operation. If any city-state appeared to threaten her dominance she used military force, both her own and allied hoplites (mainly the Peloponnesian League), to coerce and weaken them. Her most dangerous rival in the Peloponnese itself was the city of Argos, and on several occasions when Argos appeared to be growing too powerful Sparta defeated her, imposing a treaty which curtailed her rival's influence.

The Affairs of Kerkyra, Poteidaia and Megara

While Athens was pursuing expansion in the Aegean there was no threat to Spartan hegemony in mainland Greece, but the rewards of imperialism had created a desire, among all classes of Athenian citizens, for further acquisitions beyond the Aegean. Under Perikles' leadership, Athens began to exercise imperialistic ambitions towards both the Greek cities of Magna Graecia (southern Italy and Sicily) and the Greek mainland. Sparta could not allow Athens to prosecute such a policy if it upset the balance of power in mainland Greece. Nevertheless, Sparta seemed reluctant initially to enter a war with Athens, but in the end her own allies, in particular Corinth and Thebes, forced the outbreak of hostilities.

Corinth had been sorely provoked by Athenian interference in her own spheres of influence. One of the leading city-states of Greece, with a large navy operating in the Ionian Sea, she had, through her colonies, important political and trading contacts with southern Italy and Sicily. Although Athens may have challenged Corinth's trading interests in the west – the archaeological evidence reveals that the export of Corinthian tableware (fine pottery) had been already superseded by the ubiquitous Athenian black-figure pottery in the sixth century BC – it seems probable that it was mainly Athens' political activity which fuelled Corinth's resentment.

In 432 Corinth became embroiled in a dispute with her former colony Kerkyra (Corcyra, the island of Corfu). Kerkyra became anatagonistic because Corinth had interfered in the politics of Epidamnos (now Durrës in Albania), a small city on the north-west coast of Greece which was a colony of Kerkyra. A typical dispute had arisen between the democrats and the oligarchs of Epidamnos which soon spilled over into a war between Kerkyra and Corinth. Kerkyra was the most powerful of the west coast islands and she maintained a large navy, although ultimately her resources could not match those of her mother city, Corinth. Faced with the superior strength of Corinth the Kerkyraeans appealed to Athens for aid. Athens, apart from her natural desire to support democrats against oligarchs, was also looking for opportunities for new acquisitions in the west. To safeguard her sea passage to the west it was in her interest, on the one hand to have an alliance with Kerkyra, and on the other not to allow Kerkyra's powerful navy to fall into Corinthian hands. However, she was cautious about an alliance with Kerkyra lest it infringe an existing treaty she had with Sparta which only allowed each side to make new alliances with neutrals – those not already allied either to Athens or Sparta. As Kerkyra was a colony of Corinth and Corinth was an ally of Sparta, it was a moot point as to whether Kerkyra was neutral or not. Athens finally agreed to the alliance but only sent a few ships in support. This small fleet proved enough to embarrass Corinth's naval operations and she demanded support from her ally Sparta.

At the same time, Athens and Corinth came into conflict in the north of the Aegean over the Corinthian colony of Poteidaia in the Khalkidike. Although a colony of Corinth, she was also a member of the Delian League and therefore part of the Athenian empire. The trade in raw materials from the Khalkidike was important to Athens and she closely controlled the politics of the region. Poteidaia had traditionally received its magistrates – the governing executive – annually from Corinth; such an arrangement helped avoid partisanship within the city's executive. Athens, however, became suspicious of Poteidaia's loyalty and demanded that not only should this practice cease but that the city should dismantle her walls. Poteidaia refused and appealed to the Spartans for aid. No help was forthcoming from Sparta, however; Athens besieged the city and eventually captured it.

Thucydides also refers to some legislation against the Megareans as being one of the immediate causes of the Peloponnesian War. Megara was Attica's neighbour to the west and was traditionally allied with Corinth. She was not powerful, but was strategically important as she controlled the eastern approaches to the Isthmus of Corinth and access to the eastern end of the Corinthian Gulf. On several occasions Athens had supported democratic movements against her traditionally oligarchic government in an attempt to gain control. In 432 the Athenians passed legislation – known as the Megarean Decrees – the exact nature of which is not clear but which imposed some commercial or political sanction on Megara. Whatever the impact of these measures, Corinth, as Megara's main ally, would have seen Athens' action as provocative.

Thucydides records a meeting of the Peloponnesian League where Corinth put forward her complaints against Athens. Thebes too, as Athens' traditional enemy, rebuked Sparta as tardy for not declaring war. The *casus belli* that Sparta's allies advanced was that Athens had broken the existing treaty but their claim was arguable. Thucydides' account of the Corinthian delegate's speech to the Spartans hints that the Corinthians were threatening to leave the League if Sparta refused their demand. The Spartans might have found this threat irresistible as the loss of Corinth's allegiance would have dramatically upset the balance of power in the Peloponnese.

The First Stage of the War 431–421 BC

Sparta and her allies had an enormous advantage over Athens in resources on land, with a far larger hoplite army than Athens and her empire could put into the field. Athens' navy, however, ruled the seas, and the city of Athens, because of the forethought of Themistokles, was not only protected by sound fortifications but was also linked to the Piraeus by 'the long walls' – parallel defensive walls stretching from the city to her port. The Spartans had no aptitude for siege warfare, but even if Athens were to be besieged the city could still be supplied from the sea, so it was with great reluctance that Sparta went to war.

Athens' reaction to the Spartan declaration of war is presented by Thucydides through the person of Perikles. Athens was apparently not in search of war with Sparta but Perikles was confident that, as long as she did not risk a pitched land battle but remained behind her long walls, kept her empire intact (providing her with financial resources), and controlled the seas with her navy, she could wear Sparta down into seeking peace. There is a suspicion that Perikles' war strategy, as presented by Thucydides, had only been fully developed with the advantage of Thucydides' hindsight. He seems to have believed that Athens' defeat was not only a consequence of her misuse of power but also a result of the abandonment of Perikles' policy. Once Perikles was dead, in his view, the Athenian democracy lost its moderating hand and demagogues, merely pursuing their own political purposes, persuaded the people to abandon Perikles' cautious counsel against taking risks and to engage in new, and ultimately fatal, enterprises. Thucydides was a moderate democrat himself and this analysis is perhaps as much a reflection of his own view as it is that of the reality.

Perikles' strategy, as Thucydides has described it, was not a recipe for winning the war, and the defensive posture of remaining behind the protection of their walls was to have an immediate unforeseen and devastating effect upon the Athenians. Sparta and her allies took the initiative in the first phase of the war by annually invading Attica and systematically cutting down the olive groves, Attica's main agricultural product (an olive takes between fourteen and eighteen years before it yields any fruit). The country people of Attica fled to the safety of Athens, and Athenian morale naturally suffered at seeing their land fall into enemy hands without a blow of resistance being struck at the invaders. The city soon became overcrowded, and the deterioration of conditions within the walls led to an outbreak of plague. Many died, and not only did Athens suffer a serious loss of manpower but in the second year of the war Perikles himself was carried off by the disease.

KLEON AT SPHAKTERIA

Despite her plight Athens managed to hold on and the resulting stalemate reflected the comparative strengths of the combatants – Athens dominating the sea and Sparta unassailable on land. Both sides were becoming exhausted, and the situation only changed when each scored a military success and the occasion was used to negotiate a truce with honour.

In 425 Athens, almost fortuitously, captured 120 Spartiatai. Such a small number might not seem very significant in comparison to the large numbers of soldiers who fought in the battles of the ancient world, but to capture a single Spartiate, who was sworn to die rather than fall into enemy hands, was a notable achievement which undermined the Spartan reputation for invincibility. An Athenian squadron of ships, sailing around and up the west coast of the Peloponnese, had landed on and fortified the promontory of Pylos at the north end of the bay of Sphakteria. Leaving a garrison the ships sailed on and the Spartans, fearing raids into their territory and the danger of the Messenians being incited to revolt, brought up a force to besiege the Athenians. In an attempt to isolate Pylos the Spartans landed hoplites, including some Spartiatai, on the island of Sphakteria immediately to the south. Another Athenian fleet then arrived and cut them off from the mainland. The besiegers found themselves besieged and despite many heroic efforts to supply them, the luckless Spartans on the island were completely trapped.

The Athenian generals on the spot were reluctant to face the besieged Spartans in a fight but eventually Kleon, Thucydides' hated demagogue who had succeeded Perikles, promised the Athenian Assembly that he would bring the affair to a successful conclusion. Thucydides remarks, with a good deal of prejudice, that the people felt that they would win whatever happened: if Kleon was successful it would be a great victory; if he failed the Athenians would be rid of him. He was successful, and after a sterling resistance against superior odds the thirsty, famished and exhausted Spartans, including the 120 Spartiatai, were forced to surrender. The news of this defeat greatly dented the morale of the Spartans, who now eagerly sought an opportunity to recover their citizens. (The attitude the Spartans had to any of their citizens taken as prisoners of war might be seen as analogous to that of the modern state of Israel.)

BRASIDAS AND THE PEACE OF NIKIAS

While Sparta suffered this setback at Sphakteria, one of her generals, Brasidas, was inflicting severe damage on Athens in the north of the Aegean. Brasidas had marched overland through Greece and, in a mixture of diplomacy and warfare, had won over much of the Khalkidike. Even the Athenian colony of Amphipolis on the river Strymon, an important trade depot for timber and minerals, had fallen to him. It was for his failure to save Amphipolis from Brasidas that Thucydides, the Athenian general charged with its defence, was exiled. (His punishment was in all probability a blessing for future generations for perhaps without his banishment he might not have written his history.)

Following his victory at Sphakteria Kleon attempted to check Brasidas' success. In an engagement fought before the walls of Amphipolis the Spartans were once more victorious, but in the battle both Kleon and Brasidas were killed. It seems that the Spartans, always suspicious of how their own generals might use their power, had come to fear Brasidas' success, and his death offered them an opportunity to negotiate a halt to hostilities and regain the 120 Spartiatai held prisoner at Athens. Similarly, the losses in the north and the death of Kleon provided the Athenians with a motive for seeking peace, and so in 421 BC, after a decade of exhausting warfare, a treaty was agreed which returned the map to its pre-war formation. Thucydides, however, recognized that this peace, named the Peace of Nikias after the chief Athenian negotiator, could not be a lasting one as it failed to resolve the issue of Athenian imperialism.

Neither side fully honoured the treaty, and Athens soon sought an alliance with Argos, Sparta's main rival in the Peloponnese. Up to this point Argos had not taken sides in the war as she had been bound by a treaty of neutrality previously imposed upon her by Sparta. With the expiry of the treaty Argos hoped to reassert her power, and in 418, near the city of Mantineia in the Peloponnese, the Argives and the Spartans, and their respective allies, met in battle. Despite some tactical difficulties, the superior fighting qualities of the Spartans once more carried the day and Sparta was able to impose a peace on Argos which ended her participation in the war.

Alkibiades and the Sicilian Expedition

Athens, thwarted in her attempts to use Argos to challenge Sparta in the Peloponnese, sought new ways of increasing her power. Among the politicians at Athens there was a young and unconventional aristocrat named Alkibiades. Although enormously talented, his intelligence was matched by a disdainful irreverence. The Athenians were attracted by his exciting and magnetic personality but fearful of his flamboyance and ambition. Alkibiades opposed the conservative Nikias, the general who had negotiated the peace with Sparta, and urged the Athenians to pursue further imperialistic ventures. A plea for military help from the Sicilian city of Segesta, which was in dispute with a neighbour, provided an opportunity to interfere in the politics of Sicily and expand her empire in the west, and she planned a major expedition.

Perhaps in the hope of controlling the mercurial Alkibiades, the Assembly appointed Nikias as one of the expedition's leaders, along with Alkibiades and Lamachos. The appointment of Nikias, who was opposed to the enterprise from the start, was symptomatic of the Athenian democracy's inability to adopt a consistent position in the second part of the war. In this particular instance, the joint leadership of the expedition did not provide a useful balance to the high command but compromised the conduct of the campaign from the beginning. Nikias was ever unwilling to make a firm decision and when quick action and resolution were demanded always havered.

The night before the armada was due to sail from Athens a religious desecration occurred in the city which was to have significant consequences. Along the streets and before the doors of many properties in Athens were sculptures of the head of the god Hermes set upon ithyphallic pillars (Herms). Hermes was not only the messenger of the Olympian gods but was also the protector of thresholds, and as a guardian symbol of good fortune the phallus was much favoured as an *apotropaic* (warding off evil) talisman. During the night the Herms throughout the city had been wilfully damaged. A rumour soon spread that the perpetrator of this sacrilege was none other than Alkibiades. A pupil of the philosopher Socrates, who was regarded as atheistic and corrupting, he was thought to have once parodied the sacred rites of the

Eleusinian Mysteries (part of the cult of Demeter, the mother of Persephone and the goddess of the harvest), and it was now generally accepted that he was the most likely culprit.

Perhaps with proper reflection common sense would have informed the Athenians that as the main advocate for the Sicilian expedition, Alkibiades was most unlikely to jeopardize either the venture or his own opportunity for achieving success by flouting public religious susceptibility with such a sacrilegious prank. Despite the allegations the Assembly decided to let him sail with the expedition, but in his absence his political enemies persuaded the people there was a charge to answer and a state trireme was dispatched to bring him back to Athens for trial. On the return journey, however, Alkibiades was able to jump ship and he then defected to Sparta.

The magnitude of the legend that accrued around the figure of

Silver decadrachm from Syracuse

Alkibiades is plainly apparent in the pages of Thucydides. Although he was a moderate democrat and was suspicious of Alkibiades' flamboyancy and ambition, Thucydides also acknowledged his brilliance, but it is possible that he overestimated both Alkibiades' ability to influence affairs and his historical significance. Thucydides believed that Sparta's opportunities to win the war were mainly a consequence of the information and advice that Alkibiades gave. In Sicily the Athenians' military expedition was aimed primarily against Syracuse, the largest and most powerful city on the island. A Dorian colony, her natural sympathies were with the oligarchies of Sparta and the Peloponnese, and the Athenians believed that if Syracuse could be captured the rest of the island would then ally itself with Athens. So the city was invested by Nikias and Lamachos. But Alkibiades supposedly advised the Spartans to send one of their own commanders, Gylippus, to conduct the defence of the city for the Syracusans. This move was seen by Thucydides to be crucial to Syracuse's success.

Thucydides also credits Alkibiades with advising the Spartans to fortify a strongpoint in Attica, Dekeleia. The Spartans garrisoned this rocky position, which overlooked the plain of Attica, and were able not only to harass the countryside continually but to inhibit any movement by Athenians outside the city – so much so, for example, that the Athenians were no longer able to work the silver mines at Lavrion. Dekeleia also became a sanctuary for runaway slaves and dissidents and Thucydides claimed that while it was held by the Spartans as many as 20,000 runaways fled from Athens (thereby reducing the manpower available) and sought refuge there. Finally, Thucydides was convinced it was Alkibiades who redirected the Spartan war effort towards Athens' empire in the Aegean, encouraging them to support defecting Athenian allies, and seeking an alliance with Persia so as to build a fleet that could effectively challenge Athenian naval supremacy. Whether Alkibiades really did play such a crucial role cannot be corroborated, but that Thucydides, and no doubt many other Athenians, believed that this was so demonstrates his extraordinary reputation.

The Athenian attack on Syracuse did not prosper and Nikias, who had always been ill-suited for the enterprise, became ill and asked to be relieved of the command, but the Athenians insisted that he remain at his post. After four years of siege, with Lamachos killed in action and despite considerable Athenian reinforcements, the Syracusans began to gain the upper hand. In a passage of great pathos Thucydides describes how the Athenian expeditionary force, demoralized by disease, with its navy defeated and no hope of returning to Greece, retreated blindly away from Syracuse into the hinterland of Sicily. Harried by the Syracusans, exhausted, deprived of food and water, they were butchered at a river crossing as the soldiers rushed to quench their thirst. Nikias and his fellow commanders were put to death and the remaining prisoners were thrown into the Syracusan stone quarries. The non-Athenians were eventually sold as slaves; the Athenians, crowded together in the most terrible conditions, without food or water or shade from the burning sun, were left to die and rot.

The Spartan Alliance with Persia

It is a testimony to the courage and determination of the Athenian people that, although they had handled the Sicilian expedition with vacillation and foolishness, now, when faced with the catastrophe of their defeat, the democracy stood firm and refused to capitulate. The tide of war, however, had turned against them; they had lost, according to Thucydides, over 40,000 Athenian and allied troops and as many as 200 ships in Sicily and were now desperately short of resources. Thus, in the final phase of the war, it was mainly a matter of trying to hold the empire together to survive. Sparta, for her part, now not only exploited her strategic advantage but also assumed a moral superiority over Athens, proclaiming that she was engaged in a war of liberation of the Greeks, with the object of freeing subject states from the tyranny of Athenian imperialism. The emptiness of this claim would be demonstrated when a victorious Sparta slipped neatly into the imperialistic role wrested from Athens.

The rhetoric of a war of liberation and the immediate weakness of Athens were exploited by Sparta in an effort to persuade Athens' subject states to rebel and so erode the financial basis of the empire. Those subjects where the oligarchs had the upper hand welcomed the opportunity to revolt, but without outside support they were not strong enough to resist Athens. If Sparta's policy was to be successful she had to be able to offer military support to the rebels, and this meant she would have to confront Athens at sea. With virtually no navy, and with her economy, which was not based upon a monetary system, unable to provide her with the resources to build a fleet, she had to rely on the ships of her allies to furnish one. Thucydides believed that it was once more Alkibiades who advised the Spartans on what to do, suggesting that they negotiate with the Persians, who had ample resources, to provide the necessary cash for building a fleet and paying for the rowers.

The Persian king, Darius II, must have derived some satisfaction from watching Greece divided in war, particularly as he wanted to regain the Ionian cities. He was presumably content to see Athens engaged in an exhausting struggle as her maritime empire was the most threatening to Persian interests in Ionia. He agreed to give financial support to Sparta on condition that those Greek cities which had formerly been his subjects were returned to Persian rule. It is a measure of the parochialism of Greek politics that both Sparta and subsequently Athens were prepared to abandon the Ionian Greek city-states in order to enlist Persia's aid. With Persian money financing the building of a fleet, Sparta was able for the first time in the war to confront Athens in the Aegean.

Oligarchic Revolution at Athens

By this time Alkibiades had fallen foul of his Spartan hosts. It was claimed that he had seduced the wife of King Agis, and he now sought refuge with the Persians. In the hope of returning to Athens, he began negotiations with some Athenian oligarchs, promising to gain Persian support for Athens if he was recalled. The oligarchs in Athens were growing stronger as, after the Sicilian disaster and the consequent ferment among her subjects, many Athenians had lost confidence in the democratic government. In 411 there was an attempt to establish a moderate oligarchy, but the Athenian navy, which was based at the island of Samos, refused their support and in the end forced the restoration of democracy. (The rowers of the triremes were recruited from the poorer citizens and were resolutely committed to the democracy.)

The democrats now enlisted the support of Alkibiades, who readily changed sides in return for a pardon. He was elected a general and immediately demonstrated his military brilliance by defeating the Spartan fleet and capturing the city of Kyzikos in the Hellespont. After four years of campaigning in which he systematically re-established Athenian control throughout the Aegean, he returned to Athens in triumph and led the religious procession to Eleusis, the first time it had taken place since the Spartan occupation of Dekeleia. However, although the people rapturously welcomed Alkibiades' return, not all of Athens was jubilant and his political enemies bided their time.

XENOPHON

It is during his account of the oligarchic revolution of 411 BC that Thucydides' history comes to an abrupt end half-way through a sentence. Why he stopped at this point is unknown but there is enough internal evidence from his history to show that he outlived the conclusion of the war and that the fate of Athens influenced his analysis of events. Our main source for the last part of the war is the Athenian Xenophon, who starts his narrative by literally finishing Thucydides' last sentence.

Xenophon was a most interesting man: a pupil of Socrates, a pro-Spartan, he demonstrated remarkable qualities of leadership. After the Peloponnesian War he had taken part, as a Greek mercenary, in a civil war between the Persian king, Artaxerxes II, and his younger brother Cyrus. In 401 Cyrus had marched from Asia Minor to Cunaxa (in modern Iraq) but, although he had nearly defeated his brother, he was killed in the battle. The 10,000 Greek mercenaries had successfully overwhelmed the enemy but they now found themselves not only without a paymaster or a cause but isolated in a hostile territory. Artaxerxes invited the Greek leaders to a conference and then promptly seized them; the mercenaries then elected Xenophon to lead them back home to friendly territory. Despite harassment from the Persians and a journey through the unmapped and mountainous regions of what is now eastern Turkey, the Greeks reached the Greek colony of Trapezus (Trebizond, now Trabzon) on the south coast of the Black Sea in good order. As they came over the pass above the city they let out the famous cry '*Thalassa, thalassa*'; (The sea, the sea) – the element that had become part of the Greek soul. Xenophon recorded this remarkable exploit in an account known as the *Anabasis* (The Expedition). As a historian he lacked the meticulous care of Thucydides and so our understanding of the last phase of the Peloponnesian War does not have the clarity and definition of the earlier parts.

Cyrus and Lysander

The Persian king, Darius II, was anxious to halt the waxing of Athenian power and sent his younger son Cyrus (the same Cyrus who was to eventually rebel against his brother) to Asia Minor to act as viceroy and co-ordinate Persia's aid to Sparta. The Spartans had also appointed a new commander, Lysander, who as well as being a gifted commander had the ability, unusual in a Spartan, to establish good personal relations with non-Spartans. He soon became a friend of Cyrus and the financial aid Sparta required for her fleet was secured on a firmer footing. Then, during an absence of Alkibiades', Lysander was able to entice the Athenian fleet into a disadvantageous engagement at Notium. Although he was not present, the fickle Athenians blamed Alkibiades and he was not re-elected general for the following year. Fearing his enemies in Athens would seize the opportunity to prosecute, he withdrew and retired to a private castle he had built on the Kherronnesos.

At this time Spartan law only allowed commanders to be appointed for one year, so Lysander was replaced by a far less able man. The Athenians were able to take the initiative and in 406 defeated the Spartan fleet in a major naval battle near the small island of Arginoussai off the coast of Asia Minor. Their victory was marred by heavy casualties: although only thirteen ships were lost, over 5000 of their crews drowned. Considerable resentment was fanned among the people of Athens by claims that the generals in charge had failed to attempt to rescue the sailors, and it was decided to try them *en masse* in the Assembly. It happened that on that day Socrates was the chairman of the executive and he refused to conduct the trial as it contravened an Athenian citizen's right to an individual hearing. The sentiment and hysteria was such that the people ignored his objection and condemned all the generals; the six

The Parthenon

who happened to be in custody, including the son of Perikles, were summarily executed. Later, as we saw happen with the decision over Mytilene, the Athenians regretted their decision. The episode is a further example of the irrational and emotional behaviour of which the Athenian democracy was capable; as the philosopher Aristotle recognized, the weakness of ancient democracy was that it could easily degenerate into ill-considered ochlocracy (mob-rule).

The Defeat of Athens

The Spartans, shaken by the defeat at Arginoussai, were prepared to offer terms but the Athenians were in no mood for peace and rejected the overtures. The disaffected Aegean subjects of Athens now urged the Spartans to reappoint Lysander to the command and, since technically he could not be commander-in-chief, he was made second-in-command. He quickly obtained further subsidies from Cyrus and mustered a large fleet to confront the Athenians in the Hellespont. In 404 the Athenian generals, perhaps demoralized by the events after Arginoussai, allowed themselves to be manoeuvred into a vulnerable position at Aegospotami. Alkibiades, from his stronghold, observed their weak position and warned them of the impending danger. The Athenians ignored his advice and allowed Lysander, in a surprise attack, to catch their fleet beached. Only ten Athenian ships managed to escape and over 170 were captured; Lysander executed the Athenian prisoners and now sailed through the Aegean unchallenged. Athens' vital corn ships from the Black Sea were halted and wherever Lysander found Athenians he drove them back to Athens. The population of the city swelled but there was no food, and it was only a matter of time before Athens was forced to seek peace. The weapon of hunger had brought the Athenians to their knees and after protracted negotiations Athens was force to surrender unconditionally. Sparta's allies, in particular Corinth and Thebes, wanted to see her total destruction, but Sparta, mindful of her need to balance and limit the power of rival city-states, wished to keep Athens as a force to check Theban ambitions and refused to wipe her out. The empire was disbanded, Athens was forced to become an ally of Sparta, had to surrender her remaining ships, and the walls of the city were dismantled to the sound of flute music while the freedom of Greece was proclaimed.

Athens' defeat, whatever its causes, had revealed the limitations of her imperialism. Recognized for her enterprise and cultural poise, she above all other city-states should have been best equipped to foster some form of unity among the Greeks, but her misuse of power and her exclusion of her allies from a share, either in governing the empire or in its rewards, left her isolated and ultimately defeated. Sparta had shown great tenacity in winning the war but she was ill-suited to foster harmony among the Greeks since her policy was limited by the constant concern to suppress the subject people of Lakonia and Messenia. The Peloponnesian War, then, did not enhance the cohesiveness of Greece but weakened the city-states, leaving them more vulnerable in the long term to outside forces.

CHAPTER SIX

The Fourth Century

The fourth century BC in Greek history has a complex and often bewildering succession of wars and unstable alliances. The politicians of the major city-states chauvinistically struggled to promote the dominance of their city over the others, and the constant hostilities degenerated into pettiness and muddle which is both irritating and frustrating to follow. Amid the fog of chaos two important factors do emerge: the shattering of the myth of Spartan invincibility on the battlefield; and, more important for Greece, the dominance of Macedonia and the erosion of the political significance of the city-states in favour of monarchy.

Spartan Hegemony

After Athens had surrendered to Sparta in 404 Lysander abolished the democracy and supported the establishment of an oligarchy, which became known pejoratively as the Thirty Tyrants (one of whom was Kritias, a pupil of Socrates). Backed by a Spartan garrison in the Acropolis the Thirty's rule was arbitrary and vindictive and a democratic opposition in exile soon formed. Succoured by the Thebans, who were disgruntled at the Spartan peace settlement, the democrats seized a strongpoint in Attica and marched on the Piraeus, where the poorer people lived from whom the sailors came (and where the support for democracy was therefore strongest). In an attempt to dislodge the democrats, the Thirty Tyrants and their Spartan backers experienced a reverse and Kritias was killed. When Lysander sailed into the Piraeus with a Spartan fleet it looked as if the Athenians would suffer a fearful retribution but the Spartan government, with its customary fear of its own generals, attempted to curb Lysander's growing power and influence. Pausanias, one of the Spartan kings, was sent by land to take over. Lysander's policy of promoting extreme oligarchies was abandoned in favour of a more conciliatory solution and Pausanias was able to unite the moderates within the democratic and oligarchic camps so that finally the democracy was once more established in Athens.

SOCRATES

The initial years of the democracy were not a time of complete concord and some old scores were settled. One of the most compelling and tragic events, known to us through the writings of the philosopher Plato, was the prosecution of Socrates in 399. He was accused of impiety and corrupting the young, but in Plato's account, at least, it appears that his main crime was that he lived his life according to his principles. Socrates

Socrates

had never bowed to public opinion or political threats: in 406 he had resisted the demand to try the generals of Arginoussai, and under the Thirty he had refused to act illegally. His unswerving devotion to principle and law, rather than expediency, was in itself an affront to the sovereignty of the Athenian people. Goaded by Socrates himself (he dubbed himself the 'gadfly') into giving a severe sentence a jury convicted and condemned the sage to death. Even then Socrates refused to compromise and, rather than seeking voluntary exile, normally seen as a legitimate alternative, he demanded that the letter of the law be carried out and the poison, a cup of hemlock, be administered. Perhaps keen to exemplify his own philosophical position, which included a dispassionate preference for death over life, Socrates embraced his own end and became a martyr for philosophy, thereby exposing a fundmental flaw in democracy: the will of the people is not necessarily based on ethical principle.

Sparta soon assumed the mantle of Athenian imperialism and the former subjects of Athens found themselves under a harsher hand. While discontent against her was brewing in Greece, Sparta entered into hostilities with her previous paymaster, Persia, over the fate of the Ionian cities. The Spartan king, Agesilaos campaigned in Asia Minor but, although he gained some military success, no political advantage accrued to Sparta and he had to be recalled when resentment against Sparta spilled over into war on the mainland: in 394 Corinth and Thebes allied with Athens and declared war – a war which became known as the Corinthian War. The confederates were not strong enough to defeat her but Sparta, although she won two pitched battles, could not completely subdue the allies. Both sides became exhausted and it is perhaps ironic that it was the Persian king who settled the war in 387, proposing the terms of the treaty – known as 'The King's Peace'.

The continual fighting and wide geographical range of the conflicts which had characterized the Peloponnesian War led to the creation of a new type of soldier in Greece. Wars in the fifth century had been dominated by heavily-armed hoplites who, apart from the Spartans, were essentially amateurs recruited from the citizen body. After the Peloponnesian War there was a whole generation of Greeks whose only way of life had been fighting, and there now became available a large body of men who, like Xenophon's Ten Thousand, were prepared to sell their military skills as mercenaries. This in turn had an important effect upon the role and resources of the city-states as political entities: cash to pay mercenaries became more significant than the patriotism of local manpower. The superiority of the hoplite was challenged by new tactics developed by lighter-equipped mercenaries; the Athenian mercenary commander, Iphicrates, refined the tactics of the peltast (a light-armed soldier) by developing new weaponry – a long spear and more effective sword – so that on several occasions in the fourth century hoplites were worsted by lighter-armed mercenaries.

The King's Peace did not settle the issue of hegemony among the Greek city-states and Sparta's rivals prepared to renew the struggle. Athens revived her maritime ambitions and formed a new league, the Second Athenian Confederacy, composed of the cities and islands of the Aegean and Ionian Sea. The Confederacy, however, was only a pale shadow of the Delian League since Athens, conscious of her previous overbearing behaviour, imposed rigorous conditions of self-restraint upon her leadership. Lacking a determined and confident lead and suffering a severe shortage of funds, the Second Confederacy proved comparatively ineffective and soon overreached itself.

The Hegemony of Thebes

The Thebans had strengthened their position by constructing a Boiotian League around their leadership, making them the dominant city-state in central Greece and Sparta's most dangerous rival. Sparta's policy was to break up Theban control of the other Boiotian cities, and to intervene in their government; to that end in 382 a pro-Spartan oligarchy was installed in Thebes, supported by a Spartan garrison in the Kadmeia (the citadel of Thebes). But in 379, in a marvellously dramatic scene worthy of a novel, seven Theban exiles disguised as women were introduced to the post-prandial celebration of the pro-Spartan leaders. The celebrants were assassinated and the gates of Thebes were thrown open. The Spartan commander of the garrison found his position untenable and agreed to evacuate the Kadmeia.

At this time Thebes produced two remarkable leaders in Epameinondas and Pelopidas, who were to establish Thebes as the leading power in Greece. They constructed a new Theban army which would be able to challenge the Spartans both in tactics and resolution. The core of this army was an élite body of hoplites called the Sacred Band: professional soldiers paired in dyadic relationships and *in extremis* sworn to die for their partner.

After some years of exhausting and indeterminant warfare, in 371 Sparta, with the agreement of Athens and Persia, attempted to impose a general peace. Thebes agreed to the treaty but insisted on signing on behalf of all the Boiotian cities. Sparta refused to accept this threat to her hegemony in central Greece and the Spartan king, Kleombrotos, marched on Boiotia at the head of an army. On the plain of Leuktra Epameinondas led out the Theban army to face the Spartans. Pelopidas, leading the Sacred Band, was placed on the left of the Theban line in an extra-deep wedge formation opposite Kleombrotus and his Spartiatai. The Boiotian cavalry successfully drove the Peloponnesian cavalry from the field and then the Sacred Band charged, killing Kleombrotus and leaving 300 Spartiatai dead. Sparta's allies, who had not been engaged, retreated from the field. The myth of Spartan invincibility was destroyed.

Sparta's long-established dominance in the Peloponnese now came to an end in political turmoil, as many city-states which had been held in alliance by military coercion now rebelled. The Spartans appeared to have believed that the basis of their state demanded a clear and consistent policy (the restrictive control of the subject peoples of Lakonia and Messenia had determined her role in the Greek world); in order to safeguard her government she had aimed to keep other city-states weak through promoting dissension and strife and thereby maintaining the balance of power in her favour. Sparta's policy was now to prove an impossible straitjacket and, at a time when flexibility and change were required, she failed to adapt and consequently was humbled by her enemies.

The Thebans, aided by Sparta's erstwhile allies, now invaded the Peloponnese and hemmed in Lakonia by freeing the Messenians and helping the Arcadians build a new centre of resistance to the Spartans in the city of Megalopolis. Athens, fearful of the growing power of her neighbour Thebes, switched allegiance and formed a coalition with Sparta. In 362 Epameinondas once more demonstrated Theban superiority in battle over the Spartans near Mantineia but in the fighting he was mortally wounded. His death (Pelopidas had already been killed in battle) was an irreplaceable loss and Thebes was unable to sustain the necessary momentum to confirm her dominance.

The Arts

In the fourth century architects and artists moved on from the purity of fifth-century forms to pursue more refined and sensual representations. Although temple construction continued, some of the great buildings of the period had different functions: for example, the theatre at Epidavros, the Leonidaion at Olympia, and the monument of Lysikrates at Athens. Sculptures, like Praxiteles' Hermes and Dionysus at Olympia, are more sensuous than the hard athletic poses of the fifth century. The nude female statue now appears for the first time, confirming the sculptors' new interest in softer and more rounded forms.

The literary scene lacked the freshness of the fifth century. It was an age where oratory dominated and speeches were polished into elaborate creations, as is demonstrated in the works of Demosthenes. The intellectual giants of the age were Plato and Aristotle. The former, a pupil of Socrates, recorded his master's thoughts and dialectic technique in his Socratic dialogues but his literary activity also covered just about the whole spectrum of philosophical enquiry. Aristotle, after his tutorship of Alexander the Great, settled in Athens and founded the Lyceum which supplanted Plato's Academy. He was a remarkable polymath whose works on science, ethics, politics, aesthetics and metaphysics have made him one of the most influential thinkers of all time.

The Rise of Macedonia

Xenophon closed his account of Greek history with the battle of Mantineia. For the subsequent events we have to rely on the written speeches of orators and later writers. The next twenty-five years saw the decline of Theban power and the lack of any firm leadership in Greece by any of the city-states. This confused and weak situation was in marked contrast to the ascending star of the Macedonian state to the north. The Macedonians were not considered truly Greek by the city-states: they did not speak 'proper' Greek and had a political system and a culture which was more akin to a 'barbarian'; they were not civilized, in the literal sense, as they did not live in city-states (the mark of a true human being, Aristotle said, was that he lived in a *polis*) governed by an oligarchy or a democracy, but they were a tribal people ruled by monarchs. By Greek standards Macedonian habits and customs were bizarre and uncouth: a Macedonian youth's initiation to manhood, for example, was achieved by single-handedly slaying a lion (it is doubtful if there were many lions left in northern Greece by the end of the fourth century BC, and perhaps this is the reason why). To the Greek mind Macedonians seemed to be mainly interested in drunken wassailing, producing an irrationality and wildness more associated with beasts than men. Greek and, later, Macedonian, prejudice was to have important political implications in terms of their ability to co-operate.

Until the second half of the fourth century BC, Macedonia's role in Greek politics had been very limited. Despite its comparatively large geographical area and population, it had always been politically weak The development of its potential had been inhibited partly by its geographical position and partly by the constitutional nature of its monarchy. The country was basically split into two halves: the lowland area between the rivers Axios and Haliakmon, and the mountainous hinterland which was less settled and was hemmed in by predatory enemies to the north, east and west. The monarchy, although operating a centralized government, was weak: the succession of the king was not based upon an absolute rule of primogeniture but an elective system was preferred whereby the potential candidate, chosen from the royal family, had to receive the approbation of the Macedonian nobility. Legitimacy tended to rest with the success of the politically adept rather than an ordained biological pedigree. A consequence of this haphazard form of succession was that claimants could only secure the throne by the defeat of rivals, and even when established a king had to continually beware of usurpers promoted by palace factions. This, along with the hostility of her wilder neighbours, left Macedonia enfeebled.

Philip II

In 357 BC after acting as regent for two years for his nephew Amyntas, Philip II was elected king. During his reign Macedonia was to become the leading power on the Greek mainland. What brought this about? A theoretical view, which emphasizes the importance of the role of individual free will in history, might ascribe it to the character and policy of Philip II; a more historicist view – where the current of history is perceived to be subject to some immutable forces or laws which sweep individuals along in the tide of their own inevitable and natural direction – would argue that the political, economic and social circumstances of Greece were now ripe for the emergence of Macedonia as the dominant state. Whatever a contemporary historian may feel, ancient commentators believed that it was the personalities of individuals that influenced events. Our Greek sources saw Philip's role as crucial and painted a florid and remarkable picture of the man, although much of the evidence is inevitably hostile as this 'barbarous' monarch imposed his unwelcome dominance over the rest of Greece.

Under Philip Macedonia acquired a new cohesiveness which enabled him to overwhelm the disunited Greek city-states of the south, but when he was elected to the throne he was beset by the customary challenges that faced a Macedonian monarch, and it would have been difficult to predict the success he was to achieve. Faced with a divided court supporting rival claimants and hostile neighbours eager to attack his kingdom, Philip employed a combination of diplomacy and force to defeat his enemies. For Philip, who had perhaps learnt from an earlier experience as a hostage at Thebes, diplomacy meant the assassination of rivals and the liberal use of bribes, buying time from his enemies until he was in a position to defeat them. He recognized that the prosperity and security of Macedonia depended ultimately upon an effective army and he built up a new professional force. The infantry was recruited from Macedonia's hardy peasants, whose loyalty was focused on the king rather than any particular locality, and a highly-trained cavalry was built up around an aristocratic corps known as the Companions.

Once Philip had firmly established his right to the throne he was able to defeat his hostile neighbours piecemeal, not only securing

Macedonia's frontiers but enlarging his kingdom at their expense. It seems clear that from an early stage he had a broader view of Macedonia's destiny than merely solving its problems through military might: he recognized the cultural superiority of the city-states to the south and not only built himself a new capital at Pella, modelled on a Greek city, but introduced Greek intellectuals and artists to his court.

Athens, because of her interests in the north of the Aegean, especially the Khalkidike, had been content to see Macedonia weak. The statesman Demosthenes realized that Philip's expansionist policies represented a threat to Athenian interests and denounced the ambition of the Macedonian monarch in a series of speeches: in those known as the *Philippics* he has left us with an unsurpassed example of rhetorical invective. Although Demosthenes worked hard to ally the Greeks against Macedonia his warnings were unheeded until it was too late. Philip, however, outmanoeuvred Athens and gradually absorbed the cities of the northern Aegean seaboard, including the Khalkidike and Amphipolis. At the same time his conquests eastwards enabled him to set his kingdom on a sound financial footing by fully exploiting the gold and silver mines of Mount Pangaeus.

Philip now turned his attention to the south. He had already intimidated Thessaly into an alliance, and he soon became involved in the politics of the city-states of central Greece. Thebes, her power waning, had become engaged in a long-drawn-out war with her neighbour Phocis over the control of the sanctuary at Delphi. Phocis, despite its relative weakness, by using the treasure of the offerings to Apollo deposited at the sanctuary by grateful users of his oracle had been able to fund a large mercenary force, and the war, known as the Sacred War, had ground on for a decade. In 346 Philip, on the basis of his military power and his own desire to be seen as the leader of the Greek states, interfered and acting as arbiter brought the war to a close. With the threat to the independence of the Greek city-states thus becoming apparent, Demosthenes was able to create an alliance between Athens and her old enemy Thebes.

THE BATTLE OF KHAIRONEIA

The inevitable confrontation now came to a head and in 338 Philip marched down on central Greece to meet Athens, Thebes and their allies in battle. By this time the Macedonian army was the most experienced on the mainland. The infantry, heavily armoured and equipped with long pikes, fought in a solid line – a phalanx – about ten men deep; the front ranks, probably with different lengths of spear, were designed to present a solid line of spearheads to the enemy while the ranks behind raised their spears to various heights to protect the whole line from missiles falling from above. Intense training made the infantry phalanx flexible in action but as impenetrable as a hedgehog. The main body of the cavalry was also heavily armoured, carrying a powerful lance (the sarissa) and trained to make lightning charges.

The two sides met near Khaironeia in Boiotia. The Greeks probably numbered about 38,000 and the Macedonians about 32,000, but Philip's troops were well-seasoned veterans whereas the Greeks, apart from the Thebans, were inexperienced (the Athenians, for example, had not fought a land battle for a generation). Philip employed a tactic which was often to prove successful against Macedonia's enemies. On the left of the Macedonian line, opposite the Thebans and the Sacred Band, he placed the heavy cavalry led by his son Alexander with the Companions, and he himself took up position with the crack royal guard (the Hypaspists) on the right opposite the Athenians. He advanced the

Greek Black Figure vase

Macedonian line at an angle to the Greeks' battle-line so that the right wing came into contact first, but then executed a partial retreat drawing the Athenians after him. Mistaking the retreat and sensing victory, the callow Athenians pursued Philip's right wing in some disorder. The Greek line lost cohesion and began to pull over towards the Athenians, but the disciplined Thebans, fearing lest they be outflanked on their right, stood steadfastly to their positions. The Greek line cracked and a gap appeared; into this opening thundered Alexander and the calvary, quickly isolating the Thebans who without support were surrounded and annihilated. With the most effective corps of the Greek army destroyed, the cavalry, able to attack the Greek line from behind, rolled back the Greek centre. Meanwhile Philip had halted the retreat of the Macedonian right wing and his veteran infantry counterattacked, driving the disordered and inexperienced Athenians before them. With the battle won Philip called a halt to the pursuit of the defeated enemy.

The League of Corinth

As his subsequent actions demonstrated Philip had not been intent on massacring the Greeks at Khaironeia but forcing them to accept his leadership. Demosthenes had prophesied a dire fate for Athens if Philip was victorious but his expectations were proved wrong. Anxious to court Athenian public opinion, Philip sent Alexander with a military escort to return the ashes of the Athenian dead who had fallen in the battle, and he exacted no punishment but merely demanded Athens should ally herself with Macedonia. After his victory he marched through Greece receiving the submission of city-states, settling political and territorial disputes. Only Sparta refused to recognize his hegemony, but she was no longer a significant power to cause him trouble and he contented himself with marching his army through Lakonia as a demonstration of force. At the sanctuary to Zeus at Olympia, where the Olympic Games were held every four years, Philip began a circular monument (that shape often indicated a dedication to a hero) known as the Philippeion, in which were placed gold and ivory statues of Philip and his family (the foundations and the statue bases can still be seen today).

In the year after Khaironeia, Philip called a conference of the Greeks at the Isthmus of Corinth and bound them, by oaths of allegiance to the Macedonian royal house, into the League of Corinth. The rivalry of the city-states had kept Greece divided and weak and Macedonia had profited from this discord. Philip had fully exploited the advantages of monarchy, where disparate groups within the state could be united by loyalty to the crown so that Macedonia, with resources far greater than a city-state, could act with the consistency and determination allowed to a centralized authority.

Although Philip now considered himself the leader of the Greek people, the Greeks themselves were far from enthusiastic about the prospect. The whole political theory of the city-state was founded on its ability to exercise autonomy and this had now had to be surrendered to the 'tyranny' of the king of a 'non-Greek' neighbour. Philip himself was aware that it would need more than the sham of an alliance to unite the Greeks behind him. At the time when he was about to intervene in the Sacred War, the Athenian politician Isocrates had written a speech in which he had urged him to unify the Greeks by leading them on a crusade of revenge against the Persian Empire. After Khaironeia, Isocrates sent a letter to Philip appealing to him once more to campaign with the Greeks against the national enemy Persia.

Philip was not insensitive to the political advantages of diverting people from domestic dissatisfaction by uniting them in some cause against an external foe, but there were other reasons, apart from binding the Greeks and Macedonians together in a joint exercise against an ethnic enemy, which made the invasion of the Persian Empire an attractive proposition. Macedonia had been turned into an imperial power and the political and social mechanisms which had made Philip militarily successful needed to be satisfied with the rewards of conquest: both material – land and cash – and psychological – continued success and prestige. Booty and territory taken from the Persians could satisfy these demands. At the formation of the league of Corinth he announced his intention of invading the Persian Empire on behalf of the whole Greek nation, and a year later his general, Parmenion, crossed over into Asia Minor and established a bridgehead for the invasion. Philip, however, was not destined to lead that invasion himself.

The Assassination of Philip

Polygamy seems to have been traditional among the Macedonian kings, and the practice may well have been a consequence of the uncertainty of the method of succession. Philip had six wives but his senior queen was Olympias, the mother of Alexander; his only competent son. Perhaps lest he and Alexander were both to perish in the coming Persian expedition and Macedonia be left without an immediate successor, Philip decided in 336 BC to take another wife. This new marriage caused some estrangement between Philip and Olympias and Alexander (though, in reality, any child by Philip's new wife could not have been a rival to the mature Alexander). Philip eventually smoothed over the resentment and, possibly as a mark of conciliation, the marriage of his and Olympias' daughter Kleopatra was arranged. During the celebrations, however, Philip was assassinated by a young Macedonian noble, Pausanias. Philip had many political enemies who might have been involved in his death, but Pausanias' motives may simply have been personal.

In 1977 the Greek archaeologist, Manolis Andronikos, excavating a royal burial mound at Vergina in Macedonia, found an intact tomb. It consisted of two chambers, in each of which, among the many fine artefacts found, there was a stone vessel containing a gold box. In each box were found partially burnt human remains, a man in the larger one from the main chamber and a woman in the other. Although there was no direct evidence to identify the occupants of the tomb. Andronikos believed that the style of the artefacts pointed to a date at the end of the fourth century BC. Other evidence seemed to indicate that the Vergina tomb was that of Philip II: the discovery of a likely portrait of Philip among a series of very small ivory heads, which had probably been studs attached to a piece of wooden furniture placed in the tomb; and the fact that the greaves (leg armour) found in the tomb were designed for a man with one leg shorter than the other – Philip was known to have walked with a limp through a wound he had received.

The evidence was not conclusive but the identification has been confirmed by a remarkable reconstruction of the head of the dead king. The charred bones contained within the larger gold box were sent to

Manchester University, where the fragments of the skull were reassembled and the muscles and tissue of the face reconstructed. The portrait that emerged was astonishing: it was clear that the dead man had suffered a horrific wound to the right side of the face which had caused severe damage to the top part of the eye socket and cheekbone and would have most certainly resulted in the loss of the eye. It is known from an ancient source that during a siege in 354 BC Philip lost his right eye when he was shot by an archer from the city wall. So Andronikos' identification of Philip II's tomb has been confirmed by the dead man himself.

CHAPTER SEVEN

Alexander the Great

Philip's Legacy

When Alexander was proclaimed king on the death of Philip in 336 BC he was only twenty years old. The position in life of the son of an exceptional father must always be difficult: comparison of son with father is likely and if the son is to establish his own separate identity and not live in the shadow of his father he must surpass him or be condemned as unequal, and therefore a failure. Alexander was so to outshine his father that he has probably stolen some of the light that should be bestowed on Philip: any judgement of him must take account of the immense progress Macedonia made under his rule, from a weak and insignificant state to the most powerful nation in Greece.

Any assessment of Alexander and his achievement is beset by the difficulty of disentangling the historical facts from the many legends that not only arose after his death but were also promoted during his lifetime. Our main informant about Alexander and his campaigns is the writer Arrian, who lived in the second century AD but used more contemporary sources now lost to us. His sober narrative and careful analysis is a welcome contrast to much of the romantic writing about Alexander, although it is also true that Arrian's sources were Alexander's followers, notably Ptolemy I, who were likely to give a favourable picture of their leader.

Alexander had been well trained for kingship and Philip had shown every confidence in his military and diplomatic ability: giving him the command of the Companions at Khaironeia, for example, and sending him to accompany the ashes of the Athenian dead. He had also engaged

Aristotle

Aristotle as his son's tutor, so Alexander was not only accomplished in the traditional Macedonian pursuits of fighting and hunting but he had a developed interest in learning and culture. (The poet W.B. Yeats suggests that Aristotle 'played the taws upon the bottom of the king of kings', but the reality was probably rather different.) Despite the attention his military exploits and his political achievements demanded, Alexander retained his interest in culture and learning all his life and on his travels he was accompanied by a group of experts in their various fields. It was said that such was his love of Homer that he slept with a copy of the *Iliad* under his pillow. If this was indeed his habit it probably relates to the story that Alexander believed that he was not only descended from but actually was a new Achilles – beloved of the gods, destined to destroy his Asian enemies and, having chosen the life of fame, to die young.

Alexander's Accession

Immediately upon his accession Alexander acted with the decisiveness and ruthlessness for which he became well known. Potential rival claimants to the throne were executed, and his mother Olympias even put to death the infant daughter of Philip's last queen and forced the mother to commit suicide. (The child could not have been a threat to Alexander and this terrible killing must have been a vindictive act of revenge by Olympias.)

The news of Philip's death was welcomed by Macedonia's enemies and insurrections broke out. Demosthenes congratulated the assassin and urged the Athenians to abandon their treaty with Macedonia. While Alexander was subduing the peoples to the east and north of Macedonia, Demosthenes obtained cash from the Persian king, Darius III, to finance a rebellion at Thebes. Alexander acted quickly. Breaking off his engagement, he marched south to besiege the city; on the fourth day of the siege the Macedonians assaulted the Theban positions and by evening 6000 Thebans lay dead and 30,000 of the population were prisoners. Alexander ruled that the Thebans had acted treacherously in breaking the alliance and he decided to make them an example to the other Greek cities. The population was sold off into slavery and the city, so recently the dominant power in Greece, was razed to the ground, only the temples and the house of the poet Pindar being spared. Alexander was a passionate man, capable of acts of cruelty which he demonstrated on more than one occasion, but no doubt the Macedonian royal house was a hard school of life. Resistance in the remainder of Greece collapsed, Athens and many other cities hastening to send their apologies to Alexander. As an example to inspire fear the destruction of Thebes was certainly a success, but such methods destroyed the hope of creating concord and a union between the Macedonians and the Greeks, which Philip had tried to nurture.

Alexander's Invasion of Asia Minor

Alexander was now ready to turn his mind to the conquest of the Persian Empire. In a book about Greece this is not the place to go into a detailed history of Alexander's campaigns but the consequences of his conquests were so important that it is perhaps appropriate to give a brief account. When he began his campaign the Persian Empire was not strong and

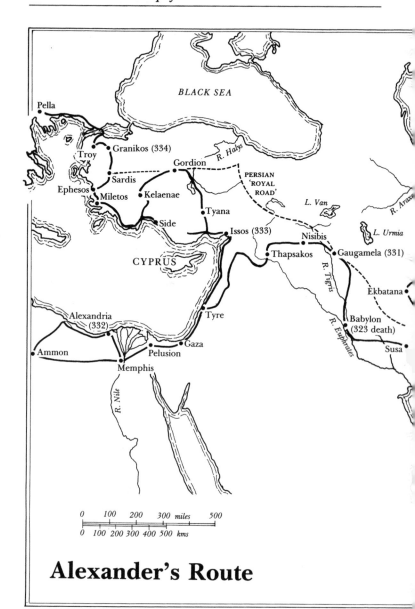

Alexander's Route

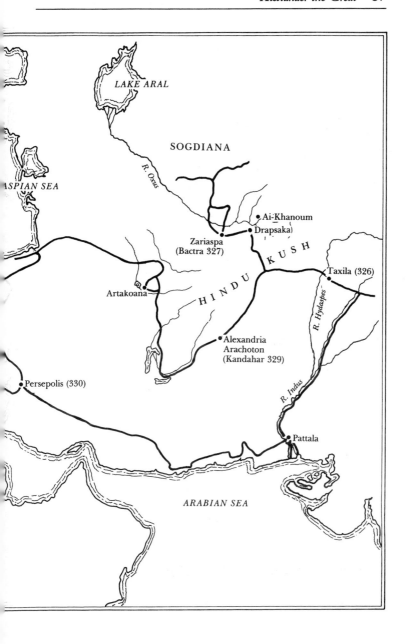

LAKE ARAL

SOGDIANA

R. Oxus

ASPIAN SEA

• Ai-Khanoum
Zariaspa   • Drapsaka
(Bactra 327)

H I N D U   K U S H

• Taxila (326)

Artakoana

R. Hydaspes

• Alexandria
Arachoton
(Kandahar 329)

• Persepolis (330)

R. Indus

• Pattala

ARABIAN SEA

although Darius III could call on greater resources to put in the field, the battle-hardened Macedonian army was superior both in equipment and tactics. Persia's main strength had always been in its cavalry and Persian infantry were generally poorly armed and trained, but since the beginning of the fourth century the native armies had been stiffened by the use of Greek mercenaries.

After Alexander had crossed over to Asia Minor in 337 with an expeditionary force of about 40,000 (less than half were Macedonians and probably less than a quarter were drawn from the Greek states of the League of Corinth), he was immediately opposed by Darius' generals at the River Granikos. Despite an awkward crossing of the river the Macedonians effected a landing and routed the Persian army; Alexander celebrated by sending 300 suits of captured armour to Athens, dedicated to Athena on behalf of himself and the Greeks (except for the Spartans who still resisted alliance). He then advanced through Asia Minor 'liberating' the Greek cities – they were not all welcoming to the Macedonian monarch. He also disbanded his navy; this might seem a strange decision but he knew that it was weak and he feared it might be defeated by the powerful Phoenician and Egyptian squadrons who made up the Persian fleet. Although disbanding the navy meant abandoning some of the islands in the Aegean to the Persians and risking the cutting of his own communications with Macedonia, he planned to make the enemy fleets inoperable by seizing their land bases.

The Battle of Issos

Having reduced Asia Minor Alexander crossed over into Syria. Darius now appeared at the head of the Persian imperial army and confronted the Macedonians at Issos (near Iskenderun in modern Turkey). The choice of ground suited the smaller number of Macedonians but the battle was fiercely contested with the Greek mercenaries and the Persian cavalry threatening disaster to the centre and left wing of the Macedonian line. Alexander, however, made a cavalry charge on the Macedonian right which overwhelmed the Persian left wing and, leading the Companions, then rode behind the enemy line to seek out Darius himself. (During the excavations of Pompeii, the Roman town destroyed by the eruption of Vesuvius in AD 79, a floor mosaic was found in a room in the House of the Faun. This superbly executed mosaic, which is now in the National Museum in Naples, depicts the moment at the Battle of Issos when Alexander, hazarding his life, confronts the Persian King of Kings. The Macedonian cavalry, with a forest of lances, are pressing back the Persians. Alexander, cuirassed but without a helmet, is shown in profile. Darius, wearing a so-called Phrygian cap [the mark of an oriental], is mounted on a chariot and his face is depicted frontally; in his eyes there is a look of fear and disbelief as his charioteer hastens to drive him to safety. The tessera [cubes of coloured stone or glass] of the mosaic are very fine, allowing for subtle gradations of colour and flexibility of line. The scene and the quality of the work suggest that the Pompeii mosaic is probably a copy of a Hellenistic painting [perhaps originally on a wooden panel] famous in the ancient world, but now lost.)

Darius managed to flee the battle but his mother and his queen were among members of the royal family who were captured with the Persian baggage. Alexander was careful to treat these prisoners with great respect, as he was probably already thinking of usurping Darius' position. Darius at this stage attempted to negotiate a peace by offering to cede formally the territory Alexander had already conquered and to give the hand of his own daughter to Alexander in marriage. Alexander, however, rejected the terms and, rather than pursuing Darius into Mesopotamia, proceeded to march south along the seaboard of Palestine, denying the Persian fleet access to its ports. Tyre (in Lebanon) proved the most resistant but eventually fell after a seven-month siege. Egypt, happy to throw off the Persian yoke, now capitulated. While in Egypt Alexander, enhancing the legends of his own divinity, visited the desert sanctuary of Ammon (in the Greek mind equated with Zeus, the father of the Greek gods), whom, it was later said, he claimed as his father; whether he really believed he was divine is a moot point but he certainly was to receive worship as a god from his non-Greek subjects. Alexander's attitude to the religions he encountered throughout his empire was tolerant and he allowed freedom of worship. Before leaving Egypt Alexander laid the foundations of Alexandria, which was to become Egypt's capital and one of the most famous cities of antiquity.

Gaugamela and Rebellion in Greece

Once Alexander had secured the Mediterranean seaboard the Persian navy surrendered and he now led his army into Mesopotamia. In 331 he met Darius once more in battle, this time at Gaugamela (Iraq) near the River Tigris. The Persians had prepared the battlefield so that their advantage in numbers could be decisive. Alexander initially used the same tactics Philip had used at Khaironeia, advancing his battle-line at an angle so that the right wing reached the enemy line first. But this time the heavy cavalry was also on the right. The Macedonian line, if the Persians' superior numbers threatened to outflank it, could be collapsed into a massive rectangle (like the famous squares of the British army at Waterloo). Alexander, as usual leading the Companions, charged with the cavalry and managed to punch a hole in the enemy's left wing. The battle was fiercely contested in several quarters but the success of Alexander's charge proved decisive and Darius fled the field, hotly pursued by Alexander.

This defeat broke the resistance of the Persian imperial army and Darius became a fugitive. Alexander's forces now marched virtually uncontested from one Persian regional capital to the next: from Babylon his advanced forces captured the Persian royal treasure at Susa and amongst the bullion were found the two statues of the tyrant-slayers Harmodios and Aristogeiton taken by Xerxes from Athens, which Alexander now returned. In Athens Demosthenes was urging the Athenians to rebel and give their support to Sparta, which had challenged Macedonian suzerainty in the Peloponnese. The Spartan king, Agis, with the aid of most of the Peloponnesian cities and a large body of mercenaries, had defeated a Macedonian army and was threatening to wrest southern Greece from its control. The Athenians, however, held back from breaking their treaty with Macedonia. Alexander had left his experienced and trusted commander Antipater to rule Macedonia as regent and control the Greeks. Antipater now marched south with a large force and in a fierce battle defeated the Spartans (Agis died in the fighting). Although the Athenians had hesitated to rebel this time, there was still a general feeling against Macedonia and Alexander, as is demonstrated by the easy acquittal of

Demosthenes when he was prosecuted by his enemy Aeschines, essentially on the grounds of taking an anti-Macedonian stance.

Alexander's response to the rebellion in Greece was lenient and, after the capture of the Persian capitals Persepolis and Ecbatana, he allowed the Greek troops which the League of Corinth had been required to contribute to return home, taking with them generous gratuities. At Persepolis Alexander had fired the royal palace; although there is some mystery as to the reason, it seems probable that he burnt it down to demonstrate that the Greeks had taken revenge for the burning of their cities, especially Athens, by Xerxes in 480.

Alexander's Empire

Though the destruction of the palace may have symbolized the end of a war of revenge, Alexander did not intend to end the campaign. He now moved swiftly through Persia in pursuit of Darius and at Hekatompylos, just south of the Caspian Sea, his advance guard found the king, who had been stabbed a few hours earlier by his own man Bessos, dying by the roadside. Darius was given a burial worthy of a king and eventually Bessos received the punishment reserved for a regicide of a Persian monarch. Alexander's treatment of both was appropriate for the successor of Darius and his policy was now quite manifest: he, Alexander, had succeeded to the throne of the Great King, the King of Kings.

As the legitimate Persian monarch Alexander began to adopt Persian customs and Persian nobles were received at his court and gave him due regal honours. There was, inevitably, opposition among the Macedonians to this cultivation of both Persian habits and the Persian nobility. In 330 there was a plot against Alexander that implicated Philotas, the commander of the Companions and the son of the general, Parmenion. Philotas was condemned to death and, because Macedonian law demanded the execution of all male relatives of traitors, Parmenion, who had served both Philip and Alexander so well and already lost two sons in the campaign, was also put to death. A couple of years later Alexander killed with his own hand a member of the court, Kleitos, who was taunting him about his Persian habits. When Alexander tried to introduce the Persian greeting of prostration before the king the Greeks and Macedonians resisted, on the grounds that such servility was only suitable for barbarians. The philosopher Kallisthenes openly refused to comply with the order and, although Alexander rescinded the command, he was later accused of conspiring against Alexander with the royal pages, to whom he was tutor, and he was executed.

The death of Darius did not bring a close to Alexander's conquests and he pushed on into Sogdiana (modern Uzbekistan in the USSR), where he married a Sogdian princess, Roxane, famed for her beauty. He continued on into Bactria (Afghanistan) and into the Indian subcontinent. When he had defeated an Indian king, Poros, at the River Hydaspes he wanted to push on into India but his army called a halt to his conquests: his men were exhausted by a decade of war and refused to go further. He could only concede to their wishes and began the long march back.

Alexander now devoted himself to organizing his vast empire; the extraordinary and progressive political vision he had was of concord and unity between the Macedonian and Greek peoples and the Persians. At

Alexander the Great

Susa in 324 eighty of the Companions were married to eighty noble Persian women and Alexander took as his second wife Barsine, the eldest daughter of Darius. Ten thousand Macedonian soldiers who had taken native women had their relationship solemnized as marriage and were released from military service. Thirty thousand Persian youths were trained as Macedonian soldiers, and Asiatics were drafted into the Companions. Persians were appointed as governors and administrators and new cities were built throughout the empire for Greeks and Macedonians to colonize (at least sixteen named Alexandria were founded).

This policy encountered considerable opposition among the traditionally conservative Macedonians, and at Opis in 324 Alexander had to nip a mutiny in the bud. If he had lived longer, perhaps with his immense prestige and capacity for action he could have seen his dream of a joint empire come to fruition. In 323 BC, however, while he was at Babylon Alexander caught a fever and suddenly died – thus bringing true his belief that, like his alleged counterpart Achilles, his life was to be brief as well as famous.

Alexander is perhaps the most heroic figure of antiquity; although only thirty-three when he died, the scale of his conquests was incredible and his political vision unequalled. Many of his achievements, however, were to fade with his death because there was no ruler, endowed with his authority, capability or likemindedness, to follow him. Alexander had changed the world. The Macedonian monarchy, influenced by its contacts with the oriental kingdoms, now infused the Greek mind not only with an alternative concept to the city as the only appropriate model for government, but also furnished the individual with a more universal perception of mankind: man was not merely a citizen of a small city-state while the rest of humanity was alien but he was part of a universal empire which embraced all mankind. The city-states which had dominated the politics of the Greeks were now superseded by a series of monarchies which created larger units of government throughout the lands of Alexander's conquests. These monarchies, often termed Hellenistic monarchies (because of their Greek basis), were in turn ultimately to furnish the model for the development of the Roman Empire.

CHAPTER EIGHT

The Hellenistic World

Alexander's Family

With Alexander's death the coherence his reign and conquests had brought to the Greek and Persian worlds disintegrated. He had made no plans for the succession and the vast territories he had conquered were soon carved up by his ambitious generals into independent and rival kingdoms. Among the royal family Alexander had a half-brother, Philip Arridaeus, but he suffered from some mental disability which made him unfit to rule and he became a mere pawn in the power struggles of the generals. Roxane was pregnant at the time of Alexander's death and when she gave birth she produced a son and possible heir to his father's throne, but his tender age and oriental blood left him vulnerable to the machinations of the Macedonian nobles. When her husband died Roxane had demonstrated the customary ruthlessness of the times by inveighling Alexander's Persian queen, Barsine, into a trap. Unaware of Alexander's demise, she rushed to Babylon upon a treacherous summons from Roxane and was promptly seized and murdered. A few years later, in 310 BC, Roxane herself and her son, known as Alexander IV, were to meet a similar fate. Kassandros, the son of Antipater, Alexander's faithful viceroy of Greece, first defeated and executed Alexander's mother Olympias and then captured Roxane and her son; after a few years' incarceration he had them both put to death. Such was the violent end of Alexander's royal house.

The death of Alexander had incited the Greeks to rebel once more, and Athens sounded a clarion call throughout Greece for a war of independence. After some initial successes for the Greek allies, Antipater received the aid of a Macedonian fleet and an army from Asia Minor. After defeating the Athenians at sea and overwhelming the allies on land, he enforced terms upon the Greeks. For Athens her surrender meant the end of her proud tradition of naval power and the abolition of her democracy. With its cessation died one of its most ardent exponents, Demosthenes: the great orator and politician, hounded in exile by his Macedonian enemies, took poison to avoid capture and certain execution.

The Hellenistic Kingdoms

For twenty years after Alexander's death war raged among his generals as they vied for the territories of his vast empire. Gradually several states arose upon the ruins of Alexander's conquests, and the most successful of the commanders proclaimed themselves kings and established dynasties. These kingdoms have become known as Hellenistic because, although their ruling dynasties were usually Macedonian, their culture was

Ptolemy I of Egypt

predominantly Greek and their courts and administration were serviced by Greeks. In Egypt Ptolemy and his descendants ruled as Hellenized pharaohs until the last Ptolemaic queen, Cleopatra, and her consort Mark Antony committed suicide in 30 BC after their defeat at the hands of Julius Caesar's great-nephew, Octavian.

Seleukos, the commander of Alexander's crack infantry, acquired the most extensive of the Hellenistic kingdoms. After he had gained control of much of the eastern part of the empire, including Persia and Syria, it looked as if Macedonia too would fall into his hands, but just as he was about to set out for the mainland he was murdered by one of Ptolemy's sons, whom he had unwisely befriended. Seleukos' successors, known as the Seleukids, continued to rule the Near East for some time, but Alexander's policy of fusing the Greek and Persian peoples into one commonwealth was let slip so that the Persians, resenting Macedonian superiority, effected a nationalist revival and the Iranian plateau was split off from the Seleukids' more westerly possessions to form a Persian kingdom under the native dynasty of the Parthians (traditionally founded in 247 BC).

Macedonia was fought over by many rival commanders but eventually was ruled with some stability by the descendants of Antigonos, another of Alexander's generals. It was Antigonos' son Demetrios, known as 'the Besieger' (a nickname he had acquired after a complex, although unsuccessful, siege of the island of Rhodes), who freed Athens and re-established democracy there in 307. A brilliant but headstrong soldier, he was an inveterate adventurer and his dramatic life and exaggerated personality reflect perfectly the chaotic but romantic era of the Hellenistic Kingdoms. It was said that he had caused the death of his father in a crucial battle against Seleukos in 301: after Demetrios had successfully charged with the cavalry he pursued the retreating enemy too far, allowing his father and his forces to be surrounded and cut down. After further adventures Demetrios was finally captured by Seleukos, who treated his captive kindly, but rather than bear the shackles of inactivity Demetrios drank himself to death in 283.

It is the personalities of the historical characters of the Hellenistic period which dominate the pages of our sources. One of our informants is Plutarch, a Greek who lived in the second century AD when Greece was part of the Roman Empire. He published a set of biographies, the '*Parallel Lives*', of Greeks and Romans whose lives he felt had run similar courses. Among other interests he was concerned with moral philosophy and his biographies emphasized moral examples and precepts, so that he focused more on anecdotal material which exemplified the private vices and virtues of his subjects than on historical facts. Plutarch's influence on the Renaissance was considerable; among his debtors were Montaigne and Shakespeare.

Antigonos Gonatas

Demetrios' son was another Antigonos, for some obscure reason nicknamed Gonatas (meaning 'kneecap'). After a difficult beginning to his reign he finally established firm control over Macedonia at the end of the 270s BC. Greece was then invaded by a group of migrating Celts; they were driven out and crossed over into Asia Minor where they were defeated by the Hellenistic king of Pergamon (Pergamum) and settled by him in an inland area which became known as Galatia. (Some stone sculptures found in Italy, one known as 'the Dying Gaul', are probably copies of a series of bronze statues set up at Pergamon to celebrate the Celts' defeat.) No sooner had Antigonos Gonatas helped in driving out the Celts than he was attacked by his neighbour, King Pyrrhos of Epiros. Pyrrhos was another of the bold adventurers of the age and he had recently returned from campaigning in Italy and Sicily. In Italy he had achieved two victories over the Romans but his casualties had been so high that he has given his name to 'a Pyrrhic victory' – one gained at too great a cost. Although Pyrrhos was a brilliant military tactician he had little political acumen and he failed to consolidate his military successes into lasting gains. In 272, after an unsuccessful attack upon Sparta, he was cornered by Antigonos; as he was retreating into the city of Argos he was killed, so it is said, by a tile thrown from a rooftop by an old crone.

The death of Pyrrhos gave Antigonos some respite, but five years later Athens allied herself with Sparta and, with the support of the Egyptian king, Ptolemy II, attempted once more to throw off the yoke of Macedonian domination. Antigonos laid siege to Athens and, after a Spartan attempt to relieve the city failed, she was forced to come to terms. She had already lost her seapower when Antipater had defeated her in 322, and this capitulation to Antigonos Gonatas signalled the end of any hopes Athens had for political leadership in Greece, although the city itself was to remain the Greek intellectual centre. Despite his victory over Sparta and Athens, Antigonos found himself constantly challenged by external enemies so that he was unable to stamp his authority on Greece.

The Leagues of Akhaia and Aitolia

Although it was not possible for any single city-state to stand up to Macedonia, two confederacies of smaller communities evolved into powerful political alliances, capable of matching Macedonia's resources. In the Peloponnese the Akhaian League united the city-states of southern Greece, and to the north of the Corinthian Gulf, the Aitolian League brought together the communities of central Greece. Both leagues were federal states which enrolled members beyond their borders, shared common citizenship, were self-governing, and carried out corporate action – a rare achievement among the Greeks. In 251 the Akhaian League, under the leadership of Aratos of Sikyon, almost united the whole of the Peloponnese and, after the death of Antigonos Gonatas in 239, his son Demetrios II was hard-pressed to contain the Aitolian League, who, sallying forth from their mountain haunts, pursued a policy of rapacious plundering against their enemies.

In 229 the Spartan king, Kleomenes III, instigated a social revolution in Sparta and challenged the Akhaian League. Reviving the ideas of the ill-fated Spartan king, Agis IV, who had attempted to abolish debt and redistribute land in Lakonia, Kleomenes reintroduced this policy but also determined to extend the Spartan franchise to the subordinate peoples in Lakonia. Betrayed by his uncle to the conservatives, Agis IV had submitted to execution rather than start a civil war, but Kleomenes outmanoeuvred his opponents in Sparta and introduced his revolutionary programme. The Akhaian League, which was dominated by conservative oligarchies, feared revolution breaking out in their own cities and attempted to check him. After a series of setbacks, they appealed to Macedonia to intervene. Demetrios II had been killed in 229 and

Macedonia was now ruled by his cousin Antigonos Doson. In 222 he invaded Lakonia and forced a pitched battle at Sellasia, just ten kilometres north of Sparta. In a hard-fought engagement Antigonos Doson's superior numbers (28,000 Macedonians to Kleomenes' army of 20,000) told and the Spartans were crushed. Kleomenes fled to Egypt where he and his followers eventually killed themselves after a failed coup against the Ptolemies.

Macedonia now formed a 'Hellenic League', recalling the days when Philip II had established such a confederacy to unite the Macedonians and Greeks. Under Philip V, the grandson of Antigonos Gonatas, who came to the throne on the death of Antigonos Doson, the League attempted to establish peace throughout Greece and in 217 a conference was held at Naupaktos. According to the historian Polybios, it was at this meeting that the diplomat Agelaos warned the Greeks of 'a cloud in the West'. The cloud was Rome, which was at that very moment engaged in a desperate struggle against the Carthaginian general Hannibal, in what is known as the Second Punic War. After subduing its neighbouring peoples, the Latins, Etruscans and Samnites, Rome had come to dominate all of southern Italy. Her interest in the island of Sicily had led to a clash with Carthage and a series of wars which ended in the latter's total destruction. (Polybios had good reason to recall Agelaos' warning about Rome's imperial ambitions as he was to spend an important period of his life in Rome as a Greek hostage.)

The Arts

The Greeks of the Hellenistic age lived in a world which seemed far larger than the one their ancestors had understood. The constant sense of the citizen closely knit to his own community, the city-state, which had characterized the Classical period, gave way to a perception of the individual as being part of a universal commonwealth. Greeks and Macedonians in their thousands had followed in the wake of Alexander's conquests and settled within old or newly-founded cities across the various, and often unstable, kingdoms established by Alexander's successors. Old Greece, too, had its horizons expanded and its stability undermined: the city-states, their autonomy lost, were now subject to the Hellenistic monarchy and its continual power struggles. The feelings and attitudes generated by the opportunities and anxieties of these upheavals, combined with the new sense of the individual, emerge as potent characteristics within Hellenistic art.

The tenor of Hellenistic individualism is embodied in the various schools of philosophic thought that appeared during the period. The followers of Diogenes (*c.* 400–325 BC), the Cynics in particular, but also the Epicureans (Epicurus 341–270) and the Stoics (the followers of Zeno 335–263), pursued the goal of 'self-sufficiency' as a means of insulating the individual from the fickleness of Fortune and the vagaries of the outside world.

Concentration upon the individual is reflected by a new focus within the visual arts: Hellenistic sculptors, painters and even architects were intent upon representing the inner experience and feelings of the individual. Portraiture, for example, which was in great demand, sought not only to express the public roles of individuals but also to reveal their inner character and temperament. The sculptor Lysippos (*c.* 370/360–305) was one of the first artists to develop a style of dramatic representation, as in his famous portraits of Alexander, by capturing the feelings of his subjects in the moment of heroic crisis. This sense of theatre became such a significant ingredient in Hellenistic art that it often led to an overdramatized, baroque style – as, for example, in the famous Laodoön now in the Vatican Museum. Even in the traditionally conservative medium of architecture there was an appeal to personal emotions through such devices as dramatic settings and mysterious inner spaces. Greek architects, however, spent much of the period building cities and royal palaces in the new areas of Hellenism: Egypt, Syria, Asia Minor and Mesopotamia. On the mainland some impressive secular buildings were erected, as, for example, the 'Tower of the Winds' and the Stoa of Attalos (reconstructed by the American School) at Athens.

The chief schools of sculpture were no longer in Greece but were those of Pergamon, where the Dying Gaul was sculpted, Ephesos and Rhodes. The mainland of Greece produced little, but what has survived demonstrates a conservative trend; and the emergence of a neoclassical style, particularly practised in Athens, recalls the achievements of the past. Perhaps the most famous Greek sculptures of the period, the

Aphrodite of Melos (Venus de Milo) and the Nike (Victory) of Samothrace (both in the Louvre), both exhibit in a curious blend these neoclassical and baroque traits. However, for all its vigour and technical competence Hellenistic art often smacks of contrivance and seems to be but a shadow of the achievements of the Classical period.

CHAPTER NINE

Roman Greece

The Macedonian Wars

Philip V, probably as a result of Hannibal's early victories in Italy and in his fear of Rome's growing interest in the Adriatic Sea, made a crucial mistake by allying himself with Carthage. After Carthage was defeated for the second time in 201 Rome was persuaded by Macedonia's enemies in the Aegean, Rhodes and Pergamon, to mount a major campaign against Macedonia. Although Philip prosecuted the war with great energy he was not supported by the Greeks and, with no options left, he was forced to engage the Roman legions in battle at Kynoskephalai (meaning 'Dog-Heads') in Thessaly. The Macedonian phalanx again demonstrated it was unstoppable in a forward charge but the Roman commander, Quinctius Flamininus, after driving off the Macedonian cavalry, attacked the flanks of the phalanx and scored a notable victory. It was Rome's first decisive success over the Macedonians but it was enough to establish Roman ascendancy in the whole of Greece. Philip was compelled to seek terms and Flamininus, in what must have been an unexpected move, proclaimed the freedom of all the Greek cities.

Roman attitudes to Greece at this time seem remarkably naïve: did Flamininus or the Roman Senate really believe that restored autonomy would bring harmony and peace to Greece? The Greeks immediately celebrated their liberty by not only falling out with each other but also antagonizing their liberator. Hardly had Flamininus made his declaration of freedom before he was marching on Sparta where a new revolutionary leader, Nabis, was proposing yet another social revolution involving the redistribution of land, but this time with plans to extend it over the whole of the Peloponnese. The Roman Senate consisted of aristocratic landowners, who could be described as innately conservative and were, therefore, suspicious of any political programme which aimed at upsetting the existing social hierarchy. The weight of Roman arms soon crushed Sparta. But no sooner had peace been established in the Peloponnese than the Aitolians, who had previously supported Rome against Macedonia, invited the Seleukid king, Antiochus III, to free Greece from Rome's overlordship. Although Antiochus had been successful in restoring Seleukid dominance in the East, his expedition to Greece failed miserably: the quixotic Aitolians failed to provide support and he was easily driven out by the legions. While the Romans were thus engaged, Philip V had managed to restore Macedonia's power, but his successor Perseus was embroiled by Pergamon, Macedonia's dangerous rival, in a war against Rome. After some stern resistance Macedonia's fate was decided in a pitched battle at Pydna in 167. Once again the Macedonian phalanx proved susceptible to attack from the flanks and Rome gained a decisive victory.

Perseus of Macedon

Until this third war against Macedonia Rome had sought to promote its image in Greece as that of the benevolent protector, but the Senate now took harsh measures against Macedonia and its sympathizers. Perseus was captured and deported to Rome as a prisoner and Macedonia was broken up into four federal states. In Aitolia 500 were executed, in Epiros 150,000 were sold into slavery, and from Akhaia 1000 hostages, including the historian Polybios, were taken to Rome. Throughout Greece resentment against Roman interference grew, and it was only a matter of time before the Romans, impatient of Greek politics, revoked their promise of freedom. As the result of a squabble between the Akhaians and the Spartans, in 146 the Roman general Lucius Mummius sacked Corinth as an example to all Greeks who might resist Rome. Apart from the temples the whole of the city was destroyed: so complete was the destruction that the archaeological remains a visitor to Corinth sees today are nearly all Roman except for the delightful temple of Apollo, its monolithic Doric columns testifying to its early date.

The Roman Annexation of Greece

Rome had attempted to police Greece without annexation but, the policy having failed, northern Greece was now converted into the province of Macedonia with direct rule from Rome. A short while later central and southern Greece became the province of Achaea (Akhaia). In the wake of Roman government followed Italian traders eager to exploit the prosperity of the Hellenistic world. The island of Delos now became an important entrepreneurial centre and its slave market was reputed to be able to sell 10,000 people a day. The island still has the remains of the large houses, with their expensive mosaic floors, built by wealthy Roman businessmen.

Rome was now the dominant power in the eastern Mediterranean and in 133 BC Attalos III, the king of Pergamon, bequeathed his kingdom to the Roman people. He had probably, by this gesture, hoped to spare his people from the trauma of conquest; in fact his action proved no salvation since the rapacity of the Roman tax collectors soon stripped Pergamon, now the province of Asia, of its prosperity and assets. Roman commercial exploitation, usury and taxation reduced the Greek people to such a penurious and desperate state that when Mithridates, the Hellenistic king of Pontos (on the south coast of the Black Sea), went to war with Rome in 88 he was welcomed by the Greeks as a liberator. In Asia Minor the people rose up and were said to have massacred 80,000 Romans and Italians on the same day, and much of Greece immediately allied itself with Mithridates. However, in 86 the Roman commander, Lucius Cornelius Sulla, easily defeated Mithridates at Khaironeia and in the same year captured Athens, which had unwisely joined in the rebellion, and shipped most of her celebrated works of art back to Rome.

Greece now entered an era which debilitated her morale and exhausted her reserves. The Roman masters of the Mediterranean fought out a series of disastrous civil wars, often on Greek soil, as they struggled among each other to gain power: in 49, during the last days of the Roman Republic, Julius Caesar defeated his rival Pompey on the plains of Thessaly at Pharsalos; in 42 Caesar's assassins, Brutus and Cassius, committed suicide after their defeat at Philippi in Macedonia at the hands of Mark Antony and Octavian; and in 31 Mark Antony and his consort Cleopatra, the last Ptolemaic queen of Egypt, were defeated by Octavian in a naval engagement at Actium off the west coast of Greece. Octavian took the name Augustus and established an autocracy at Rome to become the first emperor. (Plutarch recalled that his great-grandfather was one of the Greek porters who carried supplies to Antony's camp at Actium.)

Greece under the Roman Empire

Augustus' rule brought peace to the empire, the *pax Romana*. Although Greece itself was now to enjoy a period of peace and stability previously unknown in its history, it was not a time of great prosperity and many of its once magnificent cities suffered from decay and desertion. It did, however, find favour among the Roman emperors as a centre of culture and learning, Athens in particular benefiting from Roman patronage as the intellectual capital of the Graeco-Roman world. In AD 66–67 the Emperor Nero, who was besotted with Greek culture, toured Greece competing as an athlete and performer in a variety of contests, and naturally, because who could defeat an emperor, won all events in chariot racing, recitation and lyre-playing. A more balanced philhellene was the emperor Hadrian (AD 117–138) who spent much of his reign touring all the provinces of the empire; he had an admiration for all things Greek and organized an extensive building programme throughout the country. Several of the fine buildings he erected in Athens can still be seen today: his library and the beautiful arch which was an entrance to the city, as well as the massive temple to Zeus which owed its completion to Hadrian.

Hadrian's successor was the Emperor Antoninus, known as Pius (AD 138–161), who invited the wealthy and talented Athenian Herodes Atticus to be tutor to the future emperor, Marcus Aurelius (AD 161–180). Herodes spent much of his wealth on adorning his native city and the Odeum (Odeion), one of the impressive theatres that are sited at the foot of the Acropolis, was built by him; at Corinth he rebuilt and enlarged the Peirene fountain and the Odeum. His pupil Marcus Aurelius was so imbued with Greek culture that he was more comfortable writing in Greek than Latin, and was an ardent follower of Stoicism (the philosophical system founded by Zeno, a Cypriot, at Athens at the end of the fourth century BC – Zeno and his followers used to meet in a *stoa*, a roofed colonnade, hence they were labelled stoics). While Marcus was campaigning on the Danube frontier (in modern Yugoslavia) against the empire's Germanic enemies he recorded his thoughts in a daily journal, now known as his *Meditations*. His perception of morality and perspective of life, as they emerge in the *Meditations*, demonstrate how closely Stoic ethics at this time paralleled Christian thought.

CHAPTER TEN

Byzantium

Late Antiquity

After a period of peace, broken only by an incursion into central Greece in AD 175 by a northern tribe, the Costoboci, the Goths appeared on the northern frontier in about AD 250. The Emperor Valerian had the walls

Diocletian

of Athens rebuilt and the Isthmus of Corinth fortified, but this did not save Athens from being captured and pillaged by the Goths in 267.

Throughout the third century the Roman Empire was dogged by problems. In particular, it seemed less able to deal with its external enemies than in the past. One reason lay in the unstable system of imperial succession, with the political supremacy of the army leading to a series of usurpations of the emperorship. When Diocletian seized the throne in 284 he attempted to resolve the problems by dividing the Empire into two, with two emperors (*Augusti*), each with a nominated successor (*Caesar*) – the 'tetrarchy'. Four rulers could spread themselves across the Empire and have a better chance of defending all the frontiers than one.

Diocletian's Caesar and subsequent successor as Augustus in the East was Galerius, who chose Thessaloniki in Greece as his base. He built a large palace and a magnificent arch to celebrate his military victories (the remains of both can still be seen), but the most spectacular surviving monument is his own mausoleum. It is ironic that, as one of the worst persecutors of Christians, (according to one of our sources, Lactantius), his mausoleum should have been converted into the Church of St George. The building is a rotunda, and beautiful early Christian mosaics, mainly in gold, cover the interior of the soaring dome.

In 306 Constantius, the Augustus in the West, died at York while campaigning in Britain, and his troops declared his son Constantine Augustus. Diocletian's mechanistic system of succession had not taken account of the inherent loyalty of the Roman soldiers to the kin of their commanders, and the tetrarchy soon collapsed amidst civil war which was finally concluded in 324 when Constantine emerged as sole emperor. Apparently converted to Christianity, he now established a new Christian capital for the Empire on the site of the Greek city of Byzantium on the Bosporos, and it soon became known as Constantinople (Constantinopolis, 'the city of Constantine', now Istanbul). Constantine's promotion of the Christian religion was to change the world; its adoption by the Roman Empire converted the state into a theocracy and the emperor became God's vicar on earth (Constantine even received the title of the Thirteenth Apostle). Christian theologians, from having contemplated the apocalyptic destruction of the Empire as the worthy fate of the pagan persecutor, now equated eternal Rome with the world triumph of Christianity.

Byzantine Greece

The Roman Empire had already shown signs of splitting in half and Constantine's decision to found a capital in the east helped foster a division between the Latin-speaking western and the Greek-speaking eastern Mediterranean which determined much of the political complexion of the Middle Ages and has left vestiges in European culture and thinking today. By the end of the fourth century there were two empires and the fate of the western was to be very different from that in the east. The western provinces of the empire were to succumb to invasions of Germanic tribes and Roman government collapsed, whereas the Greek-speaking part of the empire, although it was to be threatened with extinction on several occasions, survived into the mediaeval world and became known to modern historians as the Byzantine Empire.

Western Europeans have characterized the Byzantine Empire as Greek but its subjects, notwithstanding that they spoke Greek, thought of themselves as Romans and their empire as the direct inheritor of classical Rome. In reality, the Hellenistic east imposed its cultural influence on the Byzantines and their capital. (A parallel may be made with modern Turkey where the government has seen the country's future as bound in with Europe but the people, and indeed Istanbul, retain a strong oriental and Islamic cultural influence.) Constantinople, as the political and intellectual centre, became the largest city in mediaeval Christendom and its bishop, known as a patriarch, established his authority over the patriarchs of Alexandria, Antioch and Jerusalem, despite their claims to greater antiquity.

The supremacy of the Patriarch of Constantinople was unlike the primacy of the Bishop of Rome, the Pope, over the western churches, and the early Christian tradition in the eastern churches of decision-making in ecumenical councils rejected the growing autocracy of the Pope. The different perception of Church hierarchy and the split between Greek and Latin theology created difficult relations; over the centuries, resentment and disagreements led to a schism (into what are

Hagia Eirene, Constantinople

now called the Orthodox Churches and the Roman Catholic Church), culminating in 1054 in the Pope and the Patriarch of Constantinople excommunicating each other.

The history of Byzantium was often a struggle for survival. In the east, from the seventh century, the empire had to contend with the expansion of Islam, with the Arabs overrunning Syria, Egypt and North Africa; in the west the Slavs, the Bulgars and, from the eleventh century, the Normans, the Franks and Venetians attacked the empire. Finally, the Turks absorbed Anatolia and the empire's remaining European territory until Byzantium was extinguished in the fifteenth century.

When the Roman Empire divided into eastern and western halves, Greece's interests, for geographical and cultural reasons, were identified with Byzantium rather than the West, but Greece, and in particular Athens as the heart of classical pagan culture, had to surrender her position as the forum of Hellenic civilization to Christian Constantinople. For much of Byzantine history, Greece remained a relative backwater and Athens' status sank to little more than that of a small provincial town. In the fifth century the German tribe of the Visigoths, who had been driven across the Danube by the savage Huns, defeated a Roman army and marched through Greece, devastating the cities and carrying off booty as they moved on to Italy in search of richer pickings.

Slavic Settlement

The sixth century, however, saw a series of new invaders who penetrated the frontiers of the empire, seeking land on which to settle. The most prominent were the Slavs, Bulgars, Avars and Patzinaks. Despite extensive defensive measures undertaken by the Emperor Justinian (527–65), the Slavs, who emanated from the Pripet marshes in the hinterland of eastern Europe, poured down into Greece and began to settle. The scale of settlement is uncertain and has aroused considerable controversy: how far the Greek population was displaced by Slavs and to what degree Greece was slavified has been a matter of bitter dissension among scholars; especially strong rebuttals of any dilution of the Greek race have come from those anxious to trace a continuity from the Classical Greeks to the present day. What is certain is that during the eighth century a plague swept through the empire leaving large areas of Greece depopulated and available for the new immigrants. The Emperor Constantine VII Porphyrogenitos (literally 'born in the purple' – the imperial colour – indicating the legitimate descendant of an emperor) recorded how Greece was left open to the 'barbarous' Slavs and became known as Sclavinia. During the ninth and tenth centuries, Byzantine emperors strove to pacify and subjugate these immigrants and the Church helped achieve a cultural victory through conversion to Christianity, so that the Slavs in Greece became assimilated into Byzantium.

During the immigration of the Slavs from the sixth century onwards, northern parts of Greece were also being settled by another group of people, whose language stemmed from Latin. The Vlachs were largely shepherds who drove their flocks from winter grazing in the plains to summer pastures in the mountains. This pattern of transhumance was mentioned by Anna Komnena, the Byzantine princess and historian of the eleventh century, and not only has this way of life continued into the modern era but the Vlachs have survived today as an identifiable group.

Although the Slavs and the Vlachs were the main immigrants into Greece, the Byzantines also had to contend with the fierce Bulgars who had settled in the lands south of the Danube. By the ninth century, under their khan, Simeon the Great (893–927), they had established a rival empire and had overrun much of northern Greece. It was not until the eleventh century that the Byzantines regained the initiative and the Emperor Basil II destroyed the Bulgar empire. Basil was a formidable and totally ruthless commander and for his exploits against the Bulgars he became known as the Bulgaroktonos (the Bulgar slayer). After capturing a Bulgar army in 1014 he had 14,000 prisoners blinded and returned to their leader Samuel, who was said to have suffered a fatal stroke as a result. (It was during Basil's reign that the state of Kiev was converted to Christianity and a new era of development began for Russia; Byzantine civilization still has, it may be argued, a significant influence on the political culture of the Soviet Union today – for example, in the centralized, bureaucratic and secret government of the Kremlin which has a precedent in Byzantine practice.)

During the centuries of pressure Byzantium also lost control of both the Aegean and the Adriatic Seas. The main Mediterranean islands, like Crete and Sicily, fell into Arab hands, but by the end of the eleventh century the western powers were beginning to take the initiative. At the time of the conquest of Britain by William I the Normans were also seizing southern Italy and Sicily, and it was not long before they found a pretext to attack Byzantium, occupying the island of Corfu and even penetrated as far as Thessaly on the mainland.

Islam and the Latins

The end of the eleventh century proved disastrous for Byzantium. The Turks had emerged as the new power in the east, and after destroying a Byzantine army Turkish settlers began to overrun Anatolia. At the same time the Turks captured the Holy Land and western Christendom launched the Crusades to free the Holy Places from Islam. To reach their objective the crusaders had to pass through Byzantine territory and an uneasy co-operation arose between the Byzantines and the westerners. (Anna Komnena recorded the Byzantine distrust of the 'brutish and unmannered' knights who descended upon Constantinople; and the cultural gap between the Latin west and the Greek east created an atmosphere of hostility which many western adventurers were only too happy to exploit.) In 1146 Roger, the Norman king of Sicily, attacked

Greece and sacked the mediaeval city of Thebes which had grown rich on the silk trade. Fifty years later the Normans once more invaded Greece and the Byzantine emperor, in a state of weakness, turned to the growing naval power of Venice. The Venetians, who controlled the Aegean, gave their help at the price of access to the trade markets of the empire. They ruthlessly exploited their privileges and, although subsequent emperors attempted to curtail Venetian dominance, Byzantium found their former ally the most deadly of foes.

In 1199 the Fourth Crusade was prepared in France and the crusaders hired a Venetian fleet to reach the Holy Land. However, when payment was not forthcoming for the Venetians, the crusade turned into an expedition bent on raising cash through plunder. In a disgraceful attack the Adriatic city of Iadera (Zadar) was sacked and crusaders slew fellow Christians. The Venetians, buoyed up by 'this success', exploited western prejudice against Byzantium and persuaded the crusade to attack Constantinople rather than go to the Holy Land. In 1204 the Fourth Crusade besieged the first city of eastern Christendom, thereby staining for ever the good name of the West in eastern Christian eyes. Constantinople had eluded capture by any enemy since its consecration by Constantine in AD 330 and it was the one city of antiquity that had not been sacked, thus bridging the divide between the ancient and mediaeval worlds. It was full of treasures from the ancient world (from precious works of art to the countless manuscripts of ancient authors); the rapacious crusaders breached Constantinople's previously impregnable walls and proceeded to burn down much of the city. What treasures remained were carried off and became dispersed around Europe. A visit to the Treasury of San Marco in Venice gives a glimpse of some of the Christian treasures Constantinople contained.

THE LATIN KINGDOMS

The crusaders broke up the Byzantine empire into a series of Latin kingdoms. Venice was allotted the Greek islands but their subjugation was left entirely to individuals. Marco Sanudo, a nephew of the doge, sailed to the Cyclades and established what was to become the most stable and successful of the Latin states, the Duchy of the Archipelago (1207–1566). In the last half of the sixteenth century the Turks drove the

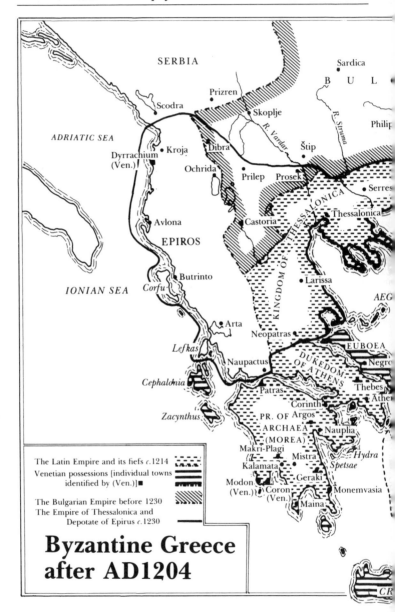

SERBIA

Sardica

B   U   L

Prizren

Scodra

Skoplje

R. Vardar

R. Struma

Philip

ADRIATIC SEA

Dyrrachium
(Ven.)

Kroja

Dibra

Štip

Ochrida

Prilep   Prosek

Serres

THESSALONICA

Castoria

Thessalonica

Avlona

EPIROS

KINGDOM OF

Larissa

IONIAN SEA

Corfu

Butrinto

AEG

Arta

Neopatras

EUBOEA

Lefkas

Naupactus

DUKEDOM
OF ATHENS

Negro

Cephalonia

Patras

Thebes

Athe

Corinth

Zacynthus

PR. OF   Argos

ARCHAEA
(MOREA)

Nauplia

Makri-Plagi

Mistra

Hydra

Kalamata

Spetsae

Modon
(Ven.)

Geraki

Coron
(Ven.)

Monemvasia

Maina

The Latin Empire and its fiefs *c.*1214
Venetian possessions [individual towns
    identified by (Ven.)]■
The Bulgarian Empire before 1230
The Empire of Thessalonica and
    Depotate of Epirus *c.*1230

Byzantine Greece
after AD1204

CR

Trnovo

Mesembria
Anchialos

BLACK SEA

R I A

Marica

Heraclea

Adrianople

LATIN
EMPIRE   Constantinople

Heraclea (Ven.)

Nicomedia

Sea of Marmara

Gallipoli
(Ven.)   Lampsacus

Nicaea

ros

Abydus   Brusa

Tenedos

Poimanenon

nnos   Adramyttium

SEA

EMPIRE OF
NICAEA

Lesbos

Pergamum

ara
Chios   Smyrna

R. Meander

dros

Icaria   Miletos   Antioch

Samos

SULTANATE OF RUM
(SELJUK TURKS)

Naxos

OM OF THE   Attalia

HIPELAGO   *Cos*

Rhodes

0   50   100   *miles* 150

0   50   100   150   *kms*

Scarpanto

andia

Latins out of the islands but western influence upon the Cyclades has left many traces which can still be observed in the buildings, memorials, language and religion – the Roman Catholic Church is even today an important force among the islanders.

In the north of Greece the Lombard Boniface of Montferrat established an ephemeral Latin kingdom at Salonika (1204–23). In central Greece the Burgundian Othon de la Roche founded the Frankish Duchy of Athens (1205–1460), which at the beginning of the fourteenth century was taken over by the Catalans and then fell into Florentine hands until the Turkish conquest. In the south Geoffrey de Villehardouin, the nephew and namesake of the historian, helped subdue the Peloponnese and emerged as 'the prince' of Akhaia. The peninsula was divided up among his followers into twelve baronies and the ruins of their castles still dominate the strongpoints of the Peloponnese. Through Geoffrey's daughter the principality passed to the Angevins of Naples, but by the end of the fourteenth century some mercenaries, known as the Navarrese Company, had taken control. By the beginning of the next century the Byzantines had managed to recapture the Peloponnese, garrisoning the formidable fortresses of Mistra (which became an important centre of Byzantine culture), near the old city of Sparta, and Monemvasia, on the east coast. The west coast islands of Greece, Cephalonia, Zante (Zakinthos) and Ithaca, were already in Italian hands before the Fourth Crusade but throughout the fourteenth century they changed hands between the Italians, Venetians and Byzantines until, near the end of the fifteenth century, they were conquered by the Turks.

After the sack of Constantinople some members of the Byzantine court had managed to hold on to parts of the empire. In north-west Greece, in the mountainous country of Epiros, Michael Angelos Komnenos established his rule under the Greek title of despot, and the territory remained independent until 1336 when it was reunited with the revived Byzantine empire. However, as Byzantine power once more faded, Epiros was fought over by Latins, Serbs and Albanians. The Albanians, whose origins are obscure but perhaps represent the pre-Hellenic Indo-European people of north-western Greece (known in antiquity as Illyrians and Epirotes), became the dominant population in that area when the Turks took control in the middle of the fifteenth century. After 1204 Theodore Lascaris, the son-in-law of a former Byzantine emperor, established his rule at the city of Nicaea in Asia Minor. The Empire of Nicaea, as it became known, grew in power and, after a new dynasty had been established by Michael Palaeologos, Constantinople was recovered from the Latins in 1261. With the establishment of the new dynasty Byzantium entered its last phase but the events of 1204 had so thoroughly weakened the empire that it was only a matter of time before it succumbed to the Ottoman Turks.

The Ottoman Turks and the end of Byzantium

The Ottomans, those Turks who claimed to have been originally ruled by Osman, emerged during the fourteenth century as the most powerful of the Turkish peoples in Asia Minor. The Byzantines had hoped to use the Ottomans to contain the growing power of the Serbs, who were threatening the Empire's European territory, but the Ottomans soon proved a far more dangerous enemy. By the fifteenth century they had conquered the empire's European territory, controlled Asia Minor, and had overrun the remaining Latin Kingdoms of Greece; Constantinople was all that was left to the Byzantines. Despite a brief respite in 1402 when the Ottoman sultan was defeated by Timur (Tamerlane), the Mongol conqueror, it was only a matter of time before Byzantium was to be snuffed out. When Mehmet II became the Ottoman sultan he determined finally to capture Constantinople. The city was now just a pale shadow of its former self and the last Byzantine emperor, Constantine XI Palaeologos, could call on only 8000 defenders, most of them Latin mercenaries, to oppose the 200,000 Turkish besiegers. Despite pleas for help Western Christendom failed to send aid and, after fifty-three days of battering by canon, on 29 May 1453 the defences were breached. Constantine fell fighting to the last and the city was captured. Although it was some years before all Byzantine territories were conquered, the fall of Constantinople marked the end of Byzantium.

The Arts

Byzantine art and architecture, from its development in Late Antiquity

Church of the Dormition, Daphni

until the fifteenth century, was firmly focused on the celebration and interpretation of Christianity. Artists and architects responded to a tradition which established conventions and forms of representation – iconography. The tradition based its legitimacy on theophany (the revelation of God to man) but stylistically evolved as the time-worn norms of ancient classical art and architecture were disintegrating; compositions and images no longer sought to depict a naturalistic ideal but to reveal the divine essence. There appear to have been many influences at work in shaping the stylistic trends of Byzantine art and although the result is often an abstraction of realism the previous Graeco-Roman concern with form is never entirely forgotten.

The main building and artistic programmes were geared to devotional exercises such as churches, martyria (mausolea for saints and martyrs) and baptisteries. The early churches had been based upon the basilical plan (a secular building of the Roman Empire, probably Greek in origin) – for example, Ayios Dhimitrios (St Demetrius) and Panayia Akheiro-poietos ('Made without hands') at Salonika. Whereas in the West church construction based upon the basilica has remained the dominant form, in Byzantium a centrally-planned domed building became preferred. The technical key to such buildings was the mastery of constructing a circular dome upon a square. In the sixth century Justinian's architects used this technique to create the unique Hagia Sophia (Holy Wisdom) in Constantinople. This vast cathedral was the largest Byzantine building and despite several earthquakes it has survived until the present day (now converted into a museum). The scale of the dome was unsurpassed until Michelangelo designed St Peter's in Rome in the sixteenth century.

Most Byzantine churches are more modest in size than the Hagia Sophia and the majority of those surviving in Greece are by western standards relatively small. Byzantine church walls were decorated with devotional programmes of mosaics or frescoes, and portable pictures of the Holy Family – known, in the singular, as an icon ('likeness') – were on prominent display (later, often on a screen – iconstasis – which separated the congregation from the altar in the eastern apse). In Byzantium icons held such a vital role in the reverencing of the divine (as they still do in the Orthodox Church today) that in the eighth century accusations of idolatry against the devotions paid to icons culminated in a movement, known as Iconoclasm ('the breaking of images'), which condemned the role of icons and caused a great rift in Byzantine society. The Iconoclasts were eventually to be defeated but during their period of dominance, apart from the destruction of portable icons, figural decoration was removed from many churches.

With the confirmation of the role of icons fresh programmes of decoration were developed in Constantinople – the capital seems to have taken the lead in artistic style and set the tone throughout the empire. By the eleventh century decorative programmes had reached remarkable levels of sophistication: for example, the monastery churches of Hosios Lukas (near Delphi), the Nea Moni (on Chios) and Daphni (just outside Athens) demonstrate the potency of Byzantine representation and the integral nature of a Byzantine church's design and its interior decoration. It has been suggested that the interior of churches constituted microcosms of the Heavenly Order on earth: Christ as Pantocrator ('The ruler of all things') dominates the dome, the highest point in the church, and the Heavenly hierarchy is spread out below; all these images, as icons, demand the devotion of the worshipper.

Many other minor arts flourished in Byzantium, mainly reflecting theological concerns: for example, decorative sculpture, enamels, gold

The interior of the dome, 'Christ Pantocrator', Daphni

and silver work, ivories, liturgical tapestries and illuminated manuscripts. In Greece the greatest repository of the Byzantine artistic and cultural inheritance has been the Orthodox Church, especially the monasteries: for example, on the peninsula of Mt Athos, in northern Greece, where there are still several active monasteries which pursue a strict mediaeval order, forbidding the presence of women, or indeed anything female apart from chickens.

Byzantine literature has tended to be criticized for its lack of originality and narrow theological focus: Byzantine scholars were, perhaps, on the one hand too wedded to their passion for theology, and on the other too conscious of their role in preserving the classical Greek past. It was, however, the Byzantines' awareness, which in the circumstances might be thought rather paradoxical, of their pagan inheritance which encouraged them to reproduce copies of the classical texts which provided an invaluable contribution to the preservation and transmission of the works of classical authors. One positive element of the destruction of Byzantium was that it brought to western Europe Greek scholars and their libraries of manuscripts, which were to play a significant part in the genesis of the Renaissance.

PART II

Greece from 1453 to the Twentieth Century

COLIN NICOLSON

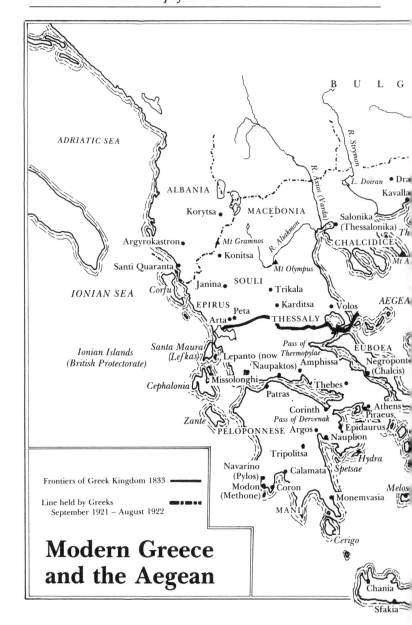

B   U   L   G

ADRIATIC SEA

R. Strymon

• Dra

L. Doiran

Kavalla

ALBANIA

R. Axios (Vardar)

Korytsa •

MACEDONIA

Salonika
(Thessalonika)

Th

Argyrokastron •

Mt Gramnos

R. Aliakmon

CHALCIDICE

Mt A

• Konitsa

Santi Quaranta •

Mt Olympus

IONIAN SEA

Corfu

Janina

SOULI

• Trikala

AEGEA

EPIRUS

Peta

• Karditsa

• Volos

Arta • •

THESSALY

*Santa Maura
(Lefkas)*

Pass of
Thermopylae

EUBOEA

Lepanto (now
Naupaktos)

Amphissa

Negropont
(Chalcis)

*Ionian Islands
(British Protectorate)*

Cephalonia

Missolonghi

• Thebes

Patras

Corinth

• Athens

Piraeus

Zante

Pass of Dervenak

Epidaurus

PELOPONNESE

Argos •

Nauplion

Tripolitsa

Hydra

Navarino
(Pylos)

• Calamata

Spetsae

Modon
(Methone) •

Coron

Melos

Monemvasia

MANI

Cerigo

**Modern Greece
and the Aegean**

Chania

Sfakia

Frontiers of Greek Kingdom 1833 ▬▬▬

Line held by Greeks
   September 1921 – August 1922 ▰▰▰▰

I A

BLACK SEA

Marica

Constantinople
(Istanbul)

Sea of Marmara

● Alexandropoulis

Gallipoli ●

ros

Tenedos

os

EA

Dardanelles

● Kydones
(Aivalik)

ASIA MINOR

Lesbos

● Smyrna (Izmir)

ra

Chios

● Chesme

ros

Samos

Naxos

Cos

Rhodes

| 0 | | 50 | | 100 | *miles* | 150 |

| 0 | | 50 | 100 | | 150 | *kms* |

Scarpanto

kleion (Candia)

TE

andia

CHAPTER ELEVEN

The Eclipse of the Greek World
1453–1715

During the two and a half centuries after the fall of Constantinople the Greek world passed entirely under the sway of rulers who were alien in language, culture and religion. Already, by 1453, the tremendous surge of conquest had swept away most of the bastions of Balkan Cristianity and penetrated deep into central Europe. By 1459 all of Serbia apart from the city of Belgrade had fallen to the Turkish onslaught. By 1461 they had swept through the fortifications protecting the Isthmus of Corinth, poured into the Peloponnese, and captured Mistra, dispersing the sparks of Byzantine civilization to light temporary fires in the islands, in remote monasteries and, more permanently, in the universities of Northern Italy.

For the next few centuries, the Greeks were merely spectators and victims in a struggle for dominance of the eastern Mediterranean between the two greatest powers of the age: the Ottoman Empire and the Republic of Venice. Both were expansionist: the Ottoman Empire was driven by the dictates of Holy War and the need to satisfy its warrior class, and the Venetians by a potent combination of commercial energy and Christian zeal. The apparently unequal struggle was sustained by the Venetians by a combination of wealth, diplomacy and sea-power which made the tiny republic a constant thorn in the side of successive sultans. For the next two centuries a battle for control over the eastern Mediterranean was fought out on Greek soil, and the fate of many Greeks was determined by the fortunes of these aggressive rivals. Control of strategic bases on the Greek coast and in the islands of the Aegean and Adriatic was fiercely contested, and was regarded by both sides as essential to their interests and survival.

For the Venetians, the Ionian islands Kerkira (Corfu), Kefalonia (Cephalonia) and Zakinthos (Zante) were vital staging posts for their galleys as they carried the produce of the Levant northwards to swell the ever-growing wealth of their city. Corfu in particular was essential to their interests, and although they managed to retain it until the end of the nineteenth century, the Turks never ceased in their attempts to take it from them. The fortresses of Rio and Antirio, facing each other across the narrow entrance to the Gulf of Corinth often called 'Little Dardanelles', were regarded by both as rich prizes. On the northern shore, Naupaktos (Lepanto) was fortified by the Venetians in the fourteenth century and later developed by the Turks as an important naval base. Further south, the wide bay of Navarino (Pylos) was a harbour of great attraction, while the castles of Modon (Methone) and Coron (Korone), often called 'the eyes of Venice', controlled the entrance to the Adriatic, and provided a beach-head to the Peloponnese. Massive fortifications serve as a testament to their great strategic importance.

The huge island of Euboia and the town of Khalkis (Negroponte), regarded by the Ancients as the key to the Greek mainland, was another constant source of rivalry. In the Aegean the Venetians strove to maintain a hold over Crete, Cyprus and the smaller islands, which were essential links in their trade with the Orient. All these territories served as a battlefield for control of the eastern Mediterranean in the centuries when no Greek state existed. The Greek people were intimately involved in the struggle; their lives were directly affected by the fortunes of the contestants and many of them played a crucial role on both sides.

The Struggle Begins

In 1499 war broke out over Venetian alarm at the increasing growth of Turkish sea-power. They had good reason to fear a challenge to what had previously been their monopoly. In 1500, in a battle near the island of Sapienza, they were severely defeated by the Turkish fleet, losing Modon and Coron, Navarino, and the port of Lepanto which became a linchpin of Turkish naval power in the eastern Mediterranean. The Venetians gained some recompense in the capture of Cephalonia by the great Spanish captain Gonzalo de Cordoba, and in 1502 of Santa Maura (Lefkas), but the treaty that ended the war in 1503 was a bitter pill for them to swallow. Apart from the two vulnerable footholds of Monemvasia and Napoli di Romania (Nauplion), the whole of the Peloponnese had fallen to the Turks, and remained in their possesion with short interludes for the next 330 years.

This disaster for the Venetians was ominous for the whole of Christian Europe, demonstrating that the Turks were rapidly developing the naval capacity to mount a battle at sea. Largely through the expertise of his Greek subjects, the Sultan was building shipyards along the Golden Horn and employing foreigners and North African corsairs to design and captain Ottoman ships. The Empire was becoming one of the great naval powers of the Mediterranean, and if the Turks were able to generate the same momentum of conquest at sea as they had displayed on land, no crowned head of Europe could rest easily in his bed.

The Reign of Suleiman the Magnificent

In 1520 Suleiman I, the greatest of all the Ottoman rulers, began a period of extraordinary Turkish expansion and creative energy which rivalled the greatest days of Byzantium. Scarcely a year after his accession he launched a campaign deep into central Europe. In 1521 Belgrade fell, and in 1526 the flower of Magyar nobility was slaughtered at Mohacs. By 1529 the Ottoman armies were pressing at the gates of Vienna. Had not unusual weather come to the aid of the defenders, the whole of European history would have been radically altered.

In 1522 Suleiman turned his attention towards the easternmost bastion of Christianity, Rhodes, which since 1306 had become the centre for the activities of the Knights of St John after their expulsion from the Holy Land. By the beginning of the sixteenth century they had transformed the town of Rhodes into a great complex of fortifications, hostels, storehouses and churches. The religious function of the Order had largely become a cloak for piracy, and the great red cross that emblazoned the sails of their ships was feared throughout the Mediterranean by Muslims and Christians alike. This combination of Christian zeal and lawlessness infuriated the Turks, who found the existence of a

Suleiman I

nest of Christian pirates so close to their coastline an unbearable provocation. In 1522 Suleiman sent an army of 100,000 men and a huge fleet against them; after a six-month siege the Knights were forced to transfer their activities to Malta, and the Greek population of Rhodes swelled the ranks of the Sultan's Christian subjects.

In 1534 the fragile peace between the Sultan and the Venetian Republic broke down again. After the Venetians had managed briefly to recapture Coron through the efforts of the great Genoese admiral, Andrea Doria, the Sultan ordered his admiral, Barbarossa, to settle accounts with the impudent Italian republic. A Turkish fleet landed on Corfu, but although the island was laid waste, the town of Kerkira, its defences refined by Italian military engineers, was able to resist the limited artillery that Barbarossa had with him. Later in the same year, at Preveza, near the spot (Actium) where Octavius Caesar and Mark Antony had fought centuries before, the Venetian fleet was destroyed.

The impact of these events upon the Greek people was considerable. The battle of Preveza forced Venice to accept the limitations of her ability to challenge the Ottomans by force of arms. In 1540 the Republic gave up its last footholds in the Peloponnese: Napoli di Romania, which had for centuries been the focal point of Venetian administration; the Gibraltar-like fortress of Monemvasia; and the islands of Paros and Syra (Syros). For the next quarter of a century relative peace reigned; the Venetians, chastened by the battle of Preveza and maintaining the delicate balance between profit and confrontation that so bemused and infuriated the Christian world, settled for a policy of co-operation with the Ottoman Empire.

The Loss of Cyprus

In the last half of the sixteenth century a great naval confrontation between Christianity and Islam took place in Greek waters. It began in 1570, when Suleiman's successor, known to history as Selim the Sot, decided to outdo his great predecessor by carrying Ottoman power deeper into Europe than ever before, and establishing Turkish naval hegemony in the Mediterranean. His first target was Cyprus, ruled by the Venetians since 1489 but a centre of Greek population and culture since ancient times. In July 1570 the Turks landed a huge army near Limassol and began a campaign that was to be marked by particular barbarity even by the standards of the age. The Venetians desperately sought the support of Christian Europe against a mortal threat to their position in the Levant, but also to the survival of Christian Europe. Attempts to save Cyprus by a joint Papal and Spanish fleet assembled in Suda Bay, Crete, ended in fiasco when rival admirals sailed home without engaging the enemy. In Spetember 1570 Nicosia fell, resulting in a massacre of 30,000 people, and the Turks laid siege to the last Venetian outpost on the island, the fortress of Famagusta.

The great walls of Famagusta proved to be a much more difficult barrier than Selim had envisaged. Eager to proceed with his assault upon Italy and central Europe, he assembled at Gallipoli in the spring of 1571 an enormous fleet of some 200 vessels, many of them drawn from as far away as Egypt. By April 250,000 men were camped before the walls.

Huge cannon specially constructed for the task made great breaches in the Venetian fortifications, firing 150,000 balls in the course of the siege. For months the city held out, defying assault after assault and costing the attackers over 50,000 casualties, but by the end of July the situation of the garrison and the Greek inhabitants had become intolerable. On 1 August the Venetian commander, Marcantonio Bragadino, accepted Ottoman terms of surrender.

The Turks, infuriated by Famagusta's resistance, decided to make an example of Bragadino by visiting on him a horrible catalogue of cruelty and humiliation: after a mock execution, his nose and ears were cut off and he was forced to crawl around the city kissing the ground; he was then tied in a bosun's chair, hauled to the top of a galley spar, and finally flayed alive; his skin, stuffed with straw, was paraded through the streets and symbolically consigned to a slave prison. Nothing could have been more calculated to blow apart the cosy relationship that had developed between the Venetians and the Ottomans since the battle of Preveza. There was now no possibility of agreement between Venice and the Sultan, and the horrific events of the fall of Famagusta alerted the whole Christian world to the dangers of Turkish expansionism, and strengthened the growing movement towards a new Holy War with the Ottoman Empire.

The Battle of Lepanto

In May 1571 Pope Pius V stitched together a Christian League with Venice and Spain to meet the threat of Turkish expansion. A combined fleet assembled at Messina under the command of the 24-year-old bastard son of the Emperor Charles V, Don John of Austria. Once again geography dictated that Greece would be the battlefield upon which the forces of Islam and Christianity came together. On 7 October 1571, in the narrow straits leading from the Gulf of Corinth, one of the greatest naval battles in history was fought out.

In the summer the Ottoman admiral, Ali, had gathered his ships for a campaign that would leave the whole of Europe open to his armies. The first task of any naval commander in the age of the galley was to secure a plentiful supply of galley-slaves: during that summer Ali raided the coasts of Crete and the islands, combing the villages for fit young men whose fate was to be chained for the rest of their lives to the oar of a Turkish warship. Next the Venetian naval base of Corfu became his target; pillage and destruction, and even the reduction of the fortress, were secondary to the desperate search for slaves. By the time Ali's fleet anchored off Lepanto, 14,000 Greeks had been captured. Two hundred galleys and 30,000 men, strengthened by 10,000 Janissaries from Negroponte, awaited the signal to leave Little Dardanelles and sail northwards.

The Christian fleet of some 200 ill-assorted Papal, Venetian and Spanish ships arrived at Viscando, near Preveza, on 8 August. Jealousies and rivalries threatened to make the Christian campaign as disastrous as that of the previous year, but news of the horrible fate of Bragadino strengthened the resolve of the fleet, particularly of the sixty Venetian vessels withdrawn from the defence of Crete. Henceforth the campaign took on the character of a crusade. Don John decided to stake all on a massive naval battle that could well decide the fate of Europe. If the Christian fleet was lost, he believed there would be nothing to prevent the Turks from mounting an unimpeded advance upon Rome and Venice.

The last great battle fought by oar-powered ships began on the morning of 7 October 1571, off Oxia Island in the Gulf of Patras. For an observer in the hills overlooking the narrow stretch of water the sight must have been awe-inspiring. The huge Turkish fleet, driven by a following wind, bore down upon the Christians in a great crescent that stretched from shore to shore. The Christian fleet, divided into three parts and outflanked on both wings by the enormous arc of Turkish galleys, bore up against the wind from the entrance to the Gulf. In the Christian fleet were adventurers and idealists who had come from all over Europe to be part of the great confrontation: aboard the galley *Marquesa* was the young Spaniard Miguel de Cervantes, who would lose his left hand in the ensuing conflict; commanding three English galleys was Sir Thomas Stukely, an English pirate and soldier of fortune who was reputedly the son of Henry VIII; Giacomo IV, last Genoese duke of Naxos, commanded 500 men in the service of the mercenary Andrea Doria; also in Doria's fleet were many French volunteers, including the famous Crillon, who had defied the disapproval of their king to take part in this great undertaking.

After an opening shot fired from Don John's flagship *Real* (now magnificently restored in the Maritime Museum of Barcelona), 400 ships began a furious close-quarters bombardment with cannon and arquebuses, longbows and crossbows. Ottoman success at sea, as on land, had been based upon the discipline, skill and fanaticism of the Janissaries, the Sultan's élite corps of Christian converts; galleys had been used simply as mobile platforms to enable foot-soldiers to swarm on to the decks of the enemy. The Christian fleet depended upon cannon power rather than upon boarding tactics, and many galleys had been ordered to remove their rams and replace them with extra cannon, making them highly mobile gun platforms. Spearheading the fleet were six galleases, huge, cumbersome vessels that had to be towed into action by smaller galleys; each of these monsters was furnished with forty heavy cannon, and their decks were packed with sharpshooters armed with arquebuses firing balls that could pass straight through a man at 200 paces. The destruction wrought by this unprecedented firepower upon the massed foot-soldiers cramming the decks of the Turkish vessels, and upon the naked bodies of the galley-slaves straining at their oars beneath, was appalling. The great crescent of the Turkish fleet buckled as galleys caught in the withering fire shuddered to a halt and staggered out of line.

Suddenly, as the fleets joined battle, the wind changed direction, bringing further confirmation to the faithful that God was on their side. As Don John's flagship bore down upon Ali's galley, *Sultana*, the Turkish admiral fell, pierced through the head. Spanish soldiers swarmed over the side of the stricken vessel, their triumph made sweeter by the discovery of the Admiral's personal fortune below its decks. Many Greek galley-slaves on the Turkish vessels mutinied, flinging aside their chains and swimming desperately towards dry land to begin the weary journey back to the villages and islands from which they had been kidnapped only a few months before. By four o'clock the battle was over, and the Gulf of Patras was littered with the debris of battle. The Turks had lost 25,000 men, 117 large cannon and 180 ships. The Christian fleet that put into Corfu, to a welcome of three days of fireworks and feasting, carried a huge treasure in gold captured from the holds of

Turkish captains; the green banner of the Prophet from Ali's vessel went to the King of Spain, while the Pope was rewarded by the captured banner of the Sultan. The Christian losses were comparatively light: 7000 men, 4800 of them Venetians, and only twelve galleys. (Of the English volunteers, ten lost their lives.)

The victory at Lepanto inspired enormous euphoria throughout Christian Europe. The military effects of the battle were not as great as contemporaries believed, but the psychological impact of the victory after centuries of Christian retreat in the face of militant Islam were incalculable. Lepanto quickly passed into the mythology of western civilization, inspiring Titian, Tintoretto and Veronese, and poets as diverse as James I and G.K. Chesterton. Once again the position of Greece had placed her in the cockpit of the struggle for dominance between Europe and Asia. Thousands of Greek people – as captains, galley-slaves and shipbuilders – had been participants in the last battle of the age of man-powered vessels. It was a mark of the supreme historical importance of Greece as the fulcrum between East and West that the last battle of the age of sail would also be fought in Greek waters.

The Fall of Crete

After Lepanto Greece lay once again forgotten by the world, trapped beneath the rival empires that dominated the eastern Mediterranean. Venice, the immediate threat to its existence removed, managed yet again to re-establish its profitable relationship with the Ottoman Empire, which fell into a period of spectacular decadence as the eunuchs and women of the harem vied with corrupt officials to control a succession of incompetent sultans. However, in 1639 Sultan Murad IV, reviving for a while the great Ottoman military tradition, turned his attentions towards the Venetian colony of Crete.

The origin of the renewed conflict lay in the chronic piracy that afflicted the Mediterranean from slavers and corsairs based in North Africa, Malta and a variety of harbours and hiding-places throughout the sea. The Turks depended heavily on the corsairs of Tunis and Algiers, and employed the services of men like the Greek renegade Dragut or the Calabrian Ochialli when it suited their purposes, while the Venetians turned a blind eye to the activities of the Knights of St John. In 1644 a squadron of Christian pirates from Malta captured several richly-laden Turkish vessels and carried them off to Crete, where the Venetian authorities were unable or unwilling to deliver them up. The Sultan decided that the time had come to sweep the Venetians out of their last important stronghold in the region. Orders were given for an assault upon the island.

In the spring of 1645, a vast Ottoman fleet set out from the Golden Horn and the Dardanelles and moved slowly southwards collecting supplies from Chios and transporting Janissaries from their barracks at Navarino. On 24 June the armada established a beachhead west of Chania and began the long task of disembarking the huge quantities of men and materials that were the hallmark of Turkish military strategy. Throughout the summer Venetian resistance was steadily reduced. In August Chania fell; three months later the great bastion of Rethymnon proved little obstacle to the weight and science of Turkish siege warfare. It seemed that the whole island would succumb before the end of the campaigning season, and that Selim's successor, Ibrahim the Mad, perhaps the most debauched and degenerate of all the sultans, would secure a triumph of arms to equal those of the great Ottoman conquerors.

In fact, the great Venetian fortress of Candia (Herakleion), under commanders like Francesco Morosini, defied the Turkish siege for no less than twenty years. Its walls, designed a century before by the military architect Michele Sammicheli, were over three miles long and rein-forced by seven great bastions. The Turks were never able to gain command of the sea and Venice continued to supply the garrison despite all efforts to seal it off. The waters of the Aegean were littered with the wrecks of lumbering Turkish supply ships which had failed to run the blockade. Venetian ships based in Zante attacked the Turkish garrison at Patras, burning and plundering the town, and Venetian agents stirred up a revolt against Turkish rule in the Mani, In 1654 the Ottoman fleet was destroyed in a great naval battle.

The Venetians were unfortunate that their attempts to hold on to Crete coincided with the ascendancy in Constantinople of the great Koprulu family. Successive members of this family of Albanian converts introduced into Ottoman administration a reforming zeal that had not been seen since the time of Suleiman the Magnificent. By 1667 Koprulu was determined to put an end to the festering and ruinously expensive siege of Candia. By using the narrow Canal of Chios and introducing a convoy system for Turkish galleys, he assembled an army of 80,000 men equipped with siege cannon of unprecedented size. In 1669, in what one historian has called 'the greatest feat of arms of the age', involving two and a half years of systematic bombardment, mining and frontal assault, Candia finally fell. For the Venetians the loss of their last commercial and military outpost in the region was a crippling blow. For the Greek population of Crete it meant the end of the flourishing post-Byzantine culture that had survived on the island under Venetian protection since the fall of Constantinople. Hundreds of Greek writers, icon painters and intellectuals were dispersed to Italian cities like Padua, to the Ionian Islands and to Mount Athos. Those who remained passed under a Turkish domination that would last until the twentieth century.

Venice's Indian Summer in the Peloponnese

Even before the fall of Candia, the Turks began their last attempt to expand their rule into central Europe. In 1683 a force of well over 200,000 men began what has been called 'the most important campaign in Turkish history' – operation Kyzyl Elma (Red Apple), aimed at Vienna. Like the campaign of Suleiman the Magnificent 154 years before, it ended in disaster. The Poles sent the Turkish army fleeing in disorder; the Austrians pushed deep into Hungary; the Grand Vizier was strangled in his tent; the Janissaries revolted; and the Sultan himself was deposed.

This disaster presented the Venetians with the opportunity to regain lost ground in Greece. Led by Morosini, the veteran of the siege of Candia, and the German mercenary Koenigsmarck, Venetian armies marched inland from their bases in the Peloponnese, pushing the Turks northwards beyond the Gulf of Corinth. In 1686, after an absence of 146 years, they entered Naupleon and reoccupied the fortifications built by their ancestors in the fourteenth century. The following year they took the colossal mediaeval fortress of Acrocorinth and repossessed

Monemvasia, last occupied by them in 1540. Venetian soldiers occupied Porto Leone (Piraeus), carried off the ancient lions that marked the entrance to the harbour, and laid siege to the Turkish garrison on the Acropolis.

It was during this campaign that a Venetian cannonball exploded the gunpowder stored in the ruins of the Acropolis by the Turkish garrison, seriously damaging the Parthenon. This hardly caused a stir at the time: for the Turks, the Acropolis represented simply the remains of a long-forgotten infidel tribe, no more worthy of preservation than any of the other piles of stones littering the landscape of their empire; nor did the Venetians feel that these roofless pagan columns, so unimpressive and insignificant compared with the great churches of Venice and Rome, should be allowed to delay the serious business of reducing a Turkish stronghold.

Having taken the insignificant village of Athens and its fortress, the Venetians laid siege to a place that had far more historical and strategic importance for them, Negroponte, the centre of their mediaeval empire in the Aegean. This was a prize almost as significant as Crete for Venetian arms, but hope of regaining former glories by crossing the 'Black Bridge' came to an unheroic end: Koenigsmarck was forced to retreat after 15,000 of his men were struck down by malaria. Within a year Athens was lost again and Venetian rule was restricted to the Peloponnese.

Venice escaped further humiliations through the efforts of her allies. In 1697, 30,000 Turks were slaughtered at the battle of Zenta in Hungary and the Sultan was forced to sign the Peace of Karlowitz, losing vast territories in Hungary and Transylvania. The Venetians, fortunate beneficiaries of this triumph, found themselves confirmed in possession of the Peloponnese, Santa Maura and the island of Aegina. For the next thirty years, Venice tried to rebuild its historic position in Greece. Nauplion once more became Napoli di Romania, capital of the Venetian colony in the Peloponnese: French engineers repaired and strengthened Palamedes fort, the great citadel that rivals Candia as a masterpiece of military architecture; new churches, public buildings and warehouses were built, and Nauplion returned to something of its former glory.

While the Sultan's armies were fighting for survival on the Danube, the Venetians were briefly able to establish a garrison of 8000 men on the island of Chios, posing a serious threat to Turkish control of the vital entrance to the Straits. In underestimating the resilience of the Turks, the Venetians were making a mistake that would be repeated many times in the next two centuries. The revived Venetian empire in Greece was built on sand. As early as 1695 a large Turkish fleet, supported by sixteen Corsair vessels, swept them off the island of Chios. A great shipbuilding programme provided the Turks with a modern sailing fleet to replace its outmoded galleys. By 1713 they were ready to move against the Venetians in the Peloponnese, which posed an immediate threat to Constantinople that could not be ignored.

On 1 January 1715, a Turkish army of 70,000 lay encamped on the plain of Thebes. The new Turkish fleet, built largely by Greek shipwrights in the slipways along the Golden Horn, and crewed and captained mainly by Greeks, had destroyed Venetian naval superiority. In June the islands of Tinos and Aegina, which had been in the hands of Venice for five centuries, were captured by the Ottoman fleet. On the mainland the Turks crossed the Isthmus of Corinth, captured Acrocorinth on 7 July, and rapidly reduced Argos. Benefiting from their command of the sea, they recaptured Navarino, Modon and Coron with ease, landed reinforcements in the southern Peloponnese, and laid siege to Nauplion. Despite the great efforts the Venetians had made over the previous thirty years to strengthen its defences, there was to be no repeat of the epic siege of Candia: within a few weeks the city fell to the overwhelming numbers and modern artillery of the Turks.

The existence of Venice itself was now seriously threatened. In the summer of 1716 the Turks landed a force of 30,000 men on Corfu, the most Venetian of all the Greek islands and one that was absolutely essential to the Republic's position in the Adriatic. Within weeks the whole island apart from the town of Kerkira was in Turkish hands; thousands of terrified inhabitants crowded into the town hoping that they would be saved by the massive walls of the citadel, the twin peaks of which, protecting the harbour and the town, had survived numerous sieges. In fact the Corfiots were saved by events taking place hundreds of miles away in the Balkans where, on 5 August, Venice's ally Prince Eugène of Savoy defeated 120,000 Turks at Peterwardein, forcing the

Sultan to lift the siege of Kerkira and confirm Venetian occupation of the island until the end of the century. The rest of Greece lay firmly in Turkish hands, and would remain so until history provided the opportunity for freedom. But both the powers that had dominated the lives of Greek people for centuries had shown unmistakable signs of collapse. The opportunity for Greeks to take control of their own destinies could not be long delayed.

CHAPTER TWELVE

Survival and Resurgence
1716–1820

Life under Foreign Rule

For nearly four centuries after the fall of Constantinople Greeks were no longer in control of their own destinies, but dependent on the changing fortunes of the two great powers that dominated their ancient homelands, the Ottoman Empire and the Republic of Venice. They were reduced to the status of pawns, suffering or prospering as the two giants sank from imperial and commercial dominance in the sixteenth century to senility and decline in the eighteenth.

Although the power struggle between Venice and Turkey went on sporadically in the Peloponnese and amongst the islands, no war was fought in the area where most Greeks lived – Asia Minor, northern and central Greece – until the nineteenth century. The Greek heartland lay behind the lines in the great struggle between Islam and Christianity, far from the depredations of the Sultan's Tartar irregulars or the Hapsburg and Russian armies that invariably left a trail of pillage and destruction in their wake. Compared with the populations who suffered in the wars that devastated Germany, Italy and central Europe during this period, the Greeks could be counted fortunate.

However, although ordinary Greek people may have escaped the ravages of war, their lives were none the less structured by the dictates of the Ottoman war machine. The Empire required constant military activity to oil its wheels; generals, officers, ordinary soldiers. janissaries, and even the Sultan himself, depended upon a regular provision of plunder that could only be provided by continuous expansion of the frontier. The Greeks, as the most important of the Empire's subject

The Sultan surrounded by Janissaries

peoples, were profoundly affected by this: their taxes paid for the sultan's wars; their agricultural system was structured by the dictates of the Turkish feudal system; their children formed the élite corps of the Sultan's army; they built, captained and crewed the Sultan's battle fleets, and provided the highest officials and diplomats of the Ottoman state.

The non-Muslim inhabitants of the Sultan's territories were not regarded as his subjects but as cattle (*rayah*), a resource to be tapped for manpower and cash in pursuit of the endless Holy War. As Christians, Greeks could play no direct part in the armies or administration of the Islamic state. If they fulfilled Ottoman requirements they were respected as 'people of the Book' and left alone. Their customs, laws of inheritance, social hierarchies, organizations and religious activities were of no interest whatever to the Sultan, so long as they paid their taxes and did not disturb the tranquillity of the state.

Greeks benefited and suffered as a result of this contemptuous tolerance. No attempt was made to convert them to Islam, to recruit them for military service, or interfere with their daily lives. Indeed, far from persecuting the Church, sultans made it the cornerstone of administration for their Christian subjects. From the moment that Mehmed the Conqueror confirmed the appointment of the Patriarch

Gennadios in 1454, until his successor was hanged outside his church in 1821, the Greek Patriarch was regarded as an official of the Ottoman state, responsible for the administration of all Christians in the Empire. Just as the basis of law for Muslims was the Sharia, or religious law, Christians were subject to their own religious rule. For most Greeks, therefore, the important matters of everyday life were governed, not by a corrupt Turkish governor or *hodjibashi*, but by the priests and primates of the Orthodox Church. For centuries the Church was the guardian of Greek identity, keeping alive language and tradition, running schools, training priests and supporting monasteries.

It was not surprising, therefore, that many Greeks preferred Turkish rule to that of Venice, which was never forgiven for the treachery of 1204 and was also suspected of undermining the Orthodox Church by seeking converts to Latin Christianity. Their regime was marked by heavy taxes and high-handed bureaucracy. Few Greeks fought for the Venetians, but many played an important role in the Turkish war effort.

The early period of Turkish rule imposed upon the Greeks a series of regulations that constantly reminded them of their inferior status. In theory, they were forbidden to bear arms or to ride horses, although in practice this usually meant dismounting at the approach of an Ottoman potentate. Their houses could not overlook their Muslim neighbours; they could not wear Muslim dress, and were sometimes made to wear distinctive black clothing. Christian churches were not allowed to be built near mosques and bell-ringing was strictly controlled to avoid disturbing the Faithful with ostentatious religious buildings or loud displays. The enforcement of these regulations was at the whim of local officials, and most of them had fallen into disuse by the beginning of the eighteenth century.

Greek Influence in the Empire

Apart from certain discriminatory taxes, the imposition that most shocked contemporary opinion and provided rich propaganda for the Greek cause was the *devshirme*, or 'tax of children', which was enforced in the early years of Turkish rule. Every four years Ottoman officials toured the Empire selecting promising Christian children to be trained in the skills of administration or war. They were converted to Islam and brought up to form an élite group dedicated to the service of the state; the strongest were assigned to the Corps of Janissaries, a force that inspired terror from the Euphrates to the gates of Vienna. Ironically, thousands of Greeks must have spent their lives fighting Christians as part of an army renowned for its religious fanaticism and willingness to make any sacrifice to further the cause of Islam.

The brightest recruits from the *devshirme* were trained to become the Sultan's most trusted officials, administrators and advisers. Because no Turkish aristocrat could demean himself by taking on the function of a clerk or merchant, the administration of the state lay entirely in the hands of the products of the Christian levy. No office was beyond their reach, and virtually all the Grand Viziers until modern times were Christian converts. On the many occasions when Sultans were half-witted or given over to debauchery, these officials became the *de facto* rulers of the Empire. The history of the Ottoman Empire is studded with men and women of Greek extraction who had a powerful influence on its destiny. Many of the Empire's most powerful and creative people were converts.

Sinan, a Greek boy carried off in the *devshirme* of 1491 and trained in the Palace schools, became the greatest architect of the Ottoman Empire. At the time of his death in 1588 at the age of ninety-one, dozens of his buildings adorned the cities of the Empire. Among his eighty-one mosques, the great Selimiye complex at Edirne and the huge Suleima-niye dominating the skyline of Istanbul are regarded as the crowning achievements of Ottoman architecture. Eighty-four of Sinan's buildings can still be seen in Istanbul alone.

Many rich and powerful Greeks suffered a violent fate. 'Ibrahim', carried off by pirates from his home in Parga and sold to a rich woman in Constantinople, became Grand Vizier to Suleiman the Magnificent. Eventually he fell victim to the intrigues of Suleiman's wife and died in the traditional manner, strangled with a bowstring by deaf mutes. The Greek Michael Cantacuzenos became one of the richest merchants of Constantinople, with a huge library of ancient manuscripts now held by the monks of Athos. He was executed in 1578 as an 'overmighty subject'. Kosem, a Greek girl sent to the Harem after abduction from her home

Sultan Ibrahim

in Corfu, became one of the most powerful and fascinating women in the history of the Ottoman Empire; for decades, as the favourite of Sultan Ahmed and the mother of Sultans Murad IV and Ibrahim (the Mad), she dominated the Seraglio and virtually ruled the Empire. In 1652 she too fell victim to the bowstring, bringing to an end the period known as the 'Rule of Women'.

The Effects of Turkish Rule

The propaganda generated by the long rivalry between Greece and Turkey has emphasized the cruelty and oppression of Ottoman rule. Certainly the Turks reacted violently to any attempt by subject people to challenge their authority; nations like the Armenians, who constantly rebelled, suffered reprisals that amounted to genocide. But on the whole the Greeks did not challenge Turkish domination (until the nineteenth century), and remained the most favoured and co-operative of the Sultan's non-Muslim subjects. On the whole, cruelty and oppression by Muslim overlords was not a part of the everyday lives of most of them. In Asia Minor and Thrace they lived reasonably settled and prosperous lives, subject to discriminatory treatment, but living under the laws of their own religion and community. In cities like Constantinople, Smyrna (Izmir) and Salonika, they prospered because of the limitations of the Ottoman system. In large parts of the more mountainous areas of the Greek mainland and the Peloponnese the Turks were never fully able to establish their dominion and the population was ruled by Greek officials appointed by the Sultan, gaining a control over their own destinies that was rare in most of Europe at this time.

Revulsion against the nature of Turkish rule should be measured against the standards prevailing in Christian Europe during these centuries. Chroniclers of Turkish brutality would be hard-pressed to equal the horrors of the Thirty Years War, the Inquisition, or the massacre of Moors, Aztecs and Incas at the hands of Christian fanatics. Long after the *devshirme* became defunct in the middle of the seventeenth century, the inhabitants of Christian Europe were liable to be press-ganged, condemned to the galleys, or conscripted to a lifetime of military service. Judicial torture and cruel methods of execution were part of the legal process in most of western Europe until at least the nineteenth century. Despite the hardship and uncertainty of Turkish rule, it is doubtful whether the many Greeks would have preferred the life of the millions of Christians who lived as serfs or feudal tenants in central Europe, Russia or France, where families were liable to deportation, torture and even execution at the whim of feudal landlords.

It was the neglect and indifference of the Ottoman state and the corruption and unpredictability of its officials, rather than any systematic oppression, that characterized Ottoman rule. The greatest danger came, not from local officials, but from the lawlessness and anarchy that stemmed from lax government. Christian and Muslim pirates terrorized anyone living near the sea. The mountains were dominated by local bandit chieftains known as *klephts*. Invested by the passage of time with an aura of romantic adventure, klephts were often rapacious warlords who preyed as much upon the Christian population as upon the Turks.

In the mountains of the Peloponnese and the Pindus a constant struggle took place between klephts and gangs of Greek and Albanian *armatoli* who were employed by the Turks to control them. Fighters shamelessly changed sides according to the current opportunities for plunder. It is not surprising that during the centuries of Ottoman rule there was considerable movement of population out of the lawless mountainous regions as people sought a more settled and prosperous life in Thrace, Constantinople and the cities of western Asia Minor. The region that is now modern Greece became a primitive and underpopulated backwater of the greater Greek world.

Eighteenth-Century Changes

As early as the end of the seventeenth century, successive military defeats marked the beginning of the decline of the Ottoman Empire. For the Greeks living under the rule of the Sultan, this had profound consequences. A major reason for this decline was the collapse of the remarkable line of rulers that had created one of the world's great Empires. Absence of any settled form of succession had resulted in the wholesale murder of prospective heirs, culminating in the slaughter of nineteen brothers and seven pregnant widows by Sultan Murad III (1574–95). Fratricide was replaced by the institution of the Cage, by which heirs to the Sultanate were confined in the Harem and denied any access to the outside world. Ibrahim (the Mad) spent no less than twenty-two years in the Cage, which virtually guaranteed that he would be naïve, ignorant of the world, and probably half-witted. This grotesque emasculation of the line that had established an empire from the Euphrates to the Atlantic meant that power was often a prize to be squabbled over by the chief wife, the chief black eunuch, the Grand Vizier and the palace Janissaries.

The decay of the sultanate was only the most spectacular symptom of the collapse of the system that dominated the lives of the Greeks. Once Turkish military expansion stopped, the whole system, depending as it did upon plunder and conquest to reward its élites, began to fall apart. Janissaries, deprived of the rewards of successful campaigns, became a corrupt hereditary clique that preyed upon the people and threatened the security of the sultans. The Turkish warriors, or *spahis*, who had originally been given land only for their lifetime, evolved into a settled and hereditary landowning class. This affected the Greek population by introducing a permanent Turkish landowning class that took over large areas of the most fertile land. Deprived of the rewards of conquest, the demands of Turkish officials on the Christian population became more insistent.

As the power of the Sultan declined, his ability to control his vast territories faded away; all over the Empire virtually independent states appeared, owing only nominal allegiance to Constantinople. In northern Greece officials transformed themselves into local potentates, while in the Peloponnese Greek chieftains and landowners took over the administration. Amongst the Christian population at local level a remarkably democratic system of self-government began to emerge.

The eighteenth century saw an upsurge of Greek power and influence

Etchi Bashi, the chief cook of the Janissaries

in the Empire. In Constantinople Greeks formed what was virtually a self-governing community under the Patriarch, comprising over one-third of the total population. In the Phanar district along the Golden Horn one can still find examples of the great palaces of wealthy Greek merchants, who became known as 'Phanariots'. The contempt of the Turkish aristocracy for commerce and administration propelled members of the eleven leading Greek families of Constantinople into positions of unprecedented power and influence. As early as 1669 Pangiotaki of Chios was in control of Ottoman foreign policy. Another Phanariot, Alexander Mavrokordatos, was the chief Ottoman negotiator at the Treaty of Karlowitz. After 1709 Phanariot families became hospodars (governors) of the provinces of Moldavia and Wallachia (modern Rumania), posts that rewarded the incumbent with huge powers of patronage and immense revenues. By the end of the eighteenth century Phanariot Greeks had secured a hereditary right to many of the highest positions in the Ottoman state, including *hospodars* of the Danubian provinces, interpreter to the Chief Admiral, and governors of the Peloponnese and islands.

By the end of the century the Greeks had become indispensable to a system that was stifled by conservatism and inertia. The three 'nautical islands' of Spetsae, Psara and Hydra controlled one of the greatest merchant fleets of the Mediterranean; in Constantinople, Salonika and Smyrna a wealthy Greek merchant bourgeoisie was becoming the most dynamic economic force in the Empire. Some historians have suggested that Greeks were gradually taking over the Ottoman Empire from within; certainly many of them – churchmen, rich merchants, state officials and landowners – had a strong vested interest in maintaining their privileged position within the existing order.

But such was the pace of change at the end of the eighteenth century that the time was fast approaching when Greeks would have to choose between continuing to prosper under an alien system, or risking all in an attempt to create an independent Greek state.

The Origins of the War of Independence

The very forces that were propelling Greeks within the Empire into a position of unprecedented power and influence were also pushing them towards a confrontation that challenged the very basis of their relationship with the Turks. Two major influences can be detected in the events leading up to the war of independence in 1821: a belief that Russia was prepared to champion the Greek cause; and the growth, largely within the expatriate intelligentsia, of the ideas of modern nationalism.

Ever since Tsar Ivan III had married the Byzantine princess Sophia Paleologos in 1472, the Russian emperors had nurtured ambitions of ruling over a restored Byzantine Empire. This goal was encapsulated in the prophecy of a mediaeval monk that the Tsars would one day found a 'Third Rome' beside the Bosporus. In the second half of the eighteenth century these dreams seemed on the point of fulfilment in the schemes the Empress Catherine the Great. At their height her ambitions encompassed a grandiose scheme to have her grandson, Constantine, crowned Emperor in Constantinople. Clearly this carried massive implications for the Greeks, and Catherine's ambitions raised the hope that at last the dream of liberation from Turkish rule would be brought about through Russian intervention.

Early in 1770 Catherine sent the Orlov brothers to incite a rebellion in the Peloponnese. Throughout the peninsula klephtic chieftains, believing the long-awaited liberation was at hand, encouraged the people to rise up and throw off the Turkish yoke. In fact, the Orlov expedition proved to be an ill-planned and costly fiasco. Having taken Navarino, the Russian force, hopelessly ill-equipped and ineptly commanded, was defeated at Tripolitsa and forced to beat a humiliating retreat to the coast. Orlov's fleet scored an important victory at Chesme (on the Turkish coast opposite Chios) and occupied Paros, where the Russian fleet spent the winter of 1770. From Catherine's point of view the expedition had succeeded in its aim of distracting the Turks, but for the Greeks of the Peloponnese this premature rebellion was a disaster, bringing down upon them thousands of Albanian irregulars whom the Sultan ordered to ravage the Peloponnese in retribution.

In 1774 the Russians forced Turkey to sign the Treaty of Kutchuk Kainardji, which gave them the right to appoint consuls in the Ottoman Empire and allowed them ill-defined rights to interfere on behalf of Orthodox Christians. In the same year a commercial convention gave

Greek merchants the right to trade under the Russian flag, a concession that proved to be a great stimulant to the growth of the Greek merchant fleet. Catherine's schemes soon dissolved in the realities of international politics, but the activities of Russian consuls who manipulated the 'right' to intervene on behalf of the Orthodox Christians implanted the dangerous delusion that it was only a matter of time before Russian armies would liberate them from Turkish rule.

The Roots of Greek Nationalism

The outbreak of the French Revolution in 1789 provoked a ferment of expectation amongst educated Greeks, but the rise of Napoleon Bonaparte had a more concrete impact, epitomized by the changing fortunes of the Ionian Islands. In 1797, after dissolving the Venetian Republic, Bonaparte occupied Corfu, Zante and Cephalonia, proclaiming them 'more important to me than the whole of Italy'. Then in 1799 they became the Septinsular Republic, under Russian control, before they reverted to France in 1807 and became a base for French intrigue with the Sultan's rebellious vassal, Ali of Janina (Ioannina). After 1814 they passed under the protection of Britain, where they remained until 1864. These experiences brought together all the forces that were propelling Greece towards change: the example of the French Revolution, the hope of Russian or British patronage, and experience of self-government and representative institutions. The islands acted as a beacon for hopes that soon all Greeks would control their own destinies.

The Congress of Vienna, which met to settle the affairs of Europe after the defeat of Napoleon in 1814, did nothing to satisfy Greek aspirations. The Ottoman Empire had not taken part in the conflict, and its affairs played no part in the deliberations of the peacemakers. The conservative statesmen who now dominated European affairs, epitomized by the Austrian Chancellor, Count Metternich, were determined to stamp out any movement that threatened to rekindle the fires of revolution, and the reactionary Tsar of Russia, Alexander I, seemed a most unlikely candidate to be the patron for a Greek rebellion. But the shocks and excitements of the previous thirty years had unleashed forces that were propelling Greeks towards revolutionary action.

In the eighteenth century there had been a powerful revival of Greek consciousness all over the Greek world. Hundreds of books were published in Greek; wealthy merchants established libraries; the Church sponsored schools to teach the young about their heritage; political and cultural societies, many of them secret, met throughout the Ottoman Empire and in the Greek expatriate communities to discuss the prospects of freedom.

Large expatriate communities had come into being in many European cities, particularly in Venice, Marseilles, Geneva and Moscow; there was even a flourishing Greek merchant colony in Calcutta. Like the Jews, the literate, educated and wealthy expatriate Greeks of the late eighteenth century were valued and influential members of their adopted communities, who had hung on to their cultural identity during centuries of foreign rule. Like the Jews also, the Greeks were excluded from their historical homeland, and increasingly obsessed with the glories of their past.

Discussing Greek emancipation ran up against a fundamental problem. The majority of the people who spoke Greek and professed the Orthodox religion lived cheek by jowl with the Turks, many of them in Constantinople itself; many of the most highly educated and articulate Greeks were scattered throughout Europe. It was only in certain small and relatively poverty-stricken areas, like the Peloponnese, that the Greek population could be defined as a nation in the modern sense, and full emancipation could be brought about only by destroying the Ottoman Empire. Eighteenth-century Greek nationalists struggled to define what was meant by 'Greece' at this time. Some writers, like Adamantios Korais, emphasized the continuity between Ancient Greece and contemporary orthodox Greek speakers, contrasting the glories of the past with their present degradation. This 'Hellenism' made modern Greeks aware of their heritage, but encouraged an obsession with the past which had little practical relevance, and raised grandiose expectations which would prove impossible to achieve.

Nothing could have been more alien either to the Ancient or to the Byzantine Greek than the idea of the nation state. This was the solution of those who had been influenced by the ideas of the French Revolution, such as the thinker and publicist Rhigas Pheraios. He advocated the establishment of a Greek Republic which would include Constantinople, large tracts of Asia Minor where Greeks formed a significant part of the population, and most of the Balkans on the coast of the Black Sea. Greek would be the dominant language and culture of the new state, and representative institutions based on those of revolutionary France would create a sort of liberal Byzantine Republic. In 1798 Rhigas was betrayed and handed over to the Turkish authorities in Belgrade, who took his ideas seriously enough to have him strangled and thrown into the Danube.

The Etairia Philike

The spark that would transform intellectual ferment into action was a revolutionary society known as the *Etairia Philike*. Founded in the fast-growing Russian port of Odessa in 1814, it rapidly developed a following throughout the expatriate Greek community. Much of its prestige came from its fostering of the belief that it was backed by influential people in St Petersburg, perhaps even by the Tsar himself. Great store was laid on the appointment of the Corfiot Greek, John Capodistrias, as Russian foreign minister. The Etairia held a vision of a liberated Greece that was very similar to that of Rhigas, but its members went much further than propaganda and philosophy, believing that the time had come to throw off the Turkish yoke by armed force.

Their plans envisaged simultaneous uprisings in the Balkans and the Peloponnese, which would have the effect of pushing Russia into an Orthodox Crusade to sweep the Turks out of Constantinople. Essential to the success of these schemes was the need to mobilize other Balkan peoples, and above all Imperial Russia. Capodistrias's persistent rejections of the leadership should have warned them of the Tsar's hostility, while the belief that other Balkan peoples would wish to substitute a 'neo-Byzantine' for an Ottoman rule showed how much the Etairia had succumbed to its own propaganda. It underestimated the reluctance of many Greeks within the Empire to disturb the status quo from which they were benefiting. The Patriarch and most leading churchmen condemned any challenge to the existing order, fearing the loss of their privileges and the Islamic backlash that would follow an uprising;

wealthy Greek merchants shunned it, fearing the destruction it would bring to their favoured trading position; and rich Greek landowners, or 'primates', were content with the powerful positions they held within the existing order and were very reluctant to risk all in an uprising.

None the less, the propaganda of the Etairia's agents, with its hints of Russian support, persuaded many influential Greeks in the Peloponnese – the most ethnically heterogeneous Greek province – to join the cause. The powerful klepht Theodore Kolokotronis, Petrobey Mavromichalis, governor of the Mani, and Germanos, Bishop of Patras, all pledged their support. Because most of the inhabitants were simple peasants to whom the idea of 'nation' and a constitution meant little, the Etairia realized that the support of the tiny educated élite would be decisive. Many klephtic chieftains, churchmen, landowners and merchants in the Peloponnese were persuaded by its claims that the opportunity to throw off foreign rule was at hand.

After being rejected by Capodistrias, the leadership of the Etairia passed to a Phanariot officer in the Russian army, Alexander Ypsilantis. Plans for a simultaneous rising in the Balkans and the Peloponnese went ahead, but the difficulties of securing a co-ordinated Balkan strategy foundered when the Serbs, who had just won their independence after a long unaided struggle against the Turks, showed no inclination to shed more blood for the Greeks. Despite the fact that preparations in the Peloponnese were in their infancy and many Greeks remained very reluctant to act, Ypsilantis pushed ahead with foolhardy plans to raise a rebellion in the Principalities alone, in the hope that this would act as a catalyst for Slav and Russian support.

Ali of Janina Lights the Fuse

We shall never know whether these rash plans would have yielded to the warnings of Capodistrias, for in 1820 matters began to move rapidly towards a climax through the activities of Ali Pasha, 'the Lion of Janina'.

Since his appointment over thirty years before as Turkish governor, this formidable Albanian warlord had carved out a virtually independent state for himself in Epirus and southern Albania. In 1803 he subdued the fierce Suliot clansmen at the battle of Nikopolis, provoking the deaths of

Ali Pasha

scores of women and children who threw themselves over a precipice near the monastery of Salonga rather than surrender to him. In 1817 he persuaded the British, to the lasting disgust of Greek nationalists, to sell him the port of Parga. By 1820 he ruled a mini-state which stretched from Durazzo to the Gulf of Arta. He controlled the klephtic chieftains of the Western Pindos, and his sons, Veli and Mukhtar, dominated most of the Peloponnese. His power was such that it could be ignored neither by the Greek national movement nor by the Sultan.

Ali's capital, Janina (Ioannina) remains one of the few cities of Greece where a visitor can still find substantial evidence of the Muslim past. Impressive mosques, religious schools, libraries and public buildings remain as an evocative legacy of the brief flowering of a power that justified the presence of representatives of several European states. Foreign visitors, including Byron in 1809, testified to the mixture of opulence, decadence and cruelty that characterized his court. Befuddled by the effects of the 36-course meals set before them, they naïvely recorded Ali's promises to build a free and liberal Greece under his benign rule.

By 1820 Ali's pretensions had so enraged the Sultan that he sent an army of 50,000 men to lay siege to Janina and bring him to heel. This provoked a crisis for the Etairia, which believed that it must act while these two oppressors were locked in combat; the victory of either of them was likely to be a disaster for the Greek cause, but while they fought each other there was an opportunity to light the spark that would ignite the various explosive forces waiting to be detonated in the Balkans.

In February 1821 Alexander Ypsilantis crossed the River Prut dividing the Russian and Ottoman Empires, on a mission to begin the Greek Revolution. In June he was confronted by an overwhelming Turkish force at Dragatsani and within hours his inexperienced force, including 800 members of a student brigade, were slaughtered by the triumphant Janissaries.

In retrospect, we can see that this suicidal assault upon the might of the Ottoman Empire was based upon heroic delusions. The calculation that Rumanians would rise in support of a Greek Phanariot whose clique had for decades oppressed them as agents of the Sultan, or that the Serbs and Bulgars would rush to arms to become subjects of a revived Byzantine Empire, were soon exposed as Hellenist fantasies. Amongst the non-Greek subjects of the Empire there was no response to Ypsilantis's gesture. The Tsar, far from seeing it as a rallying call for action, responded with embarrassment and hostility, dismissing Ypsilantis and allowing Turkish troops to cross Russian territory.

In one sense, however, the sacrifice of Ypsilantis achieved its goal in full measure. The idea that the Greek cause would be carried forward on a tide of Balkan revolution may have perished at Dragatsani, but far to the south, in the mountains and islands of Greece, news of his brave and foolhardy gesture had indeed unleashed ferocious and long-suppressed forces. Across the mountains and peninsulas of mainland Greece, leaping like flames from island to island in the Aegean, religious war, class conflict and atavistic strife between competing warlords broke out in an orgy of destruction that was to last for nearly ten years. The Greek revolution had begun.

CHAPTER THIRTEEN

The War of Independence
1821–32

The Illusion of Victory, 1821–24

On 25 March 1821 Germanos, bishop of Patras, one of the Peloponnesian members of the Etairia, raised the flag of revolt in the monastery of Ayia Lavra near Kalavrita. Visitors are still shown the small church and the flag raised to proclaim the start of the struggle for independence. In reality this symbolic event was insignificant at a time when the Etairist conspiracy and the popular uprising were already sweeping through the Sultan's Greek lands. In the far north, the treasurer of the Etairia had landed weeks earlier on Mount Athos and had been welcomed by the head of the Esfigmenou monastery; hundreds of monks declared themselves ready to fight for the cause. As early as 2 April the war-loving clans of the Mani had risen under their leader Petrobey Mavromichalis and laid siege to the Turkish strongholds of Monemvasia, Kalamata and Navarino.

The agents of the Etairia would have preferred to wait until the Russians had committed themselves to the cause, but two things seem to have precipitated the rising in the Peloponnese. Firstly, the Turks summoned the Greek leaders to Tripolitsa, and to many of them it must have seemed safer to take the dangerous leap into open revolt rather than place themselves in the power of the Turkish governor. Secondly, the leadership was outflanked by an enormous upsurge of popular enthusiasm fuelled by the widespread belief that Russia would support the cause, by conviction that the moment had arrived to seize the lands of their Turkish neighbours, and above all by long-standing feelings of religious antagonism. From the end of March onwards, the 40,000

Turkish inhabitants of the Peloponnese were driven from the lands where many of them had lived for generations. Over half of them were killed in the first few weeks of the uprising, and the rest fled in terror to the crumbling fortresses that the Turks had inherited from their Venetian predecessors.

Amongst the Greeks, caution was soon swept away by the relentless speed of events. In April the shipowners and captains of the three nautical islands, Hydra, Spetsae and Psara, joined the revolution, giving the Greeks control of the seas and making the position of many of the Turkish fortresses impossible to sustain. In August Navarino and Monemvasia fell, and in the autumn of 1821 the Greeks concentrated on the large towns of Tripolitsa and Nauplion. On 5 October Tripolitsa surrendered amidst scenes of carnage and cruelty that made a lasting impression on those who had come to Greece filled with idealistic notions about the nobility of Ancient Greece. 'The prisoners were taken

Prince Demitrios Ypsilantis

out of the town,' reported the British Consul, 'and above 12,000 men, women and children were put to death by their inhuman conquerors. Some were hanged, others impaled, many roasted alive by large fires ...; upwards of 200 Jews, who were inhabitants of the city, were put to death, some of them by crucifixion.'

'European' Greeks like Demetrios Ypsilantis were disgusted by the behaviour of the chieftains. They realized that, although some success had been achieved, long-term prospects of survival were less promising. Although the reduction of Tripolitsa was followed a few months later by the capture of Acrocorinth, Nauplion remained stubbornly in Turkish hands, as did the two strategically important towns of Coron and Modon. Little progress had been made outside the Peloponnese, and the European powers had welcomed the uprising with hostility to the Greek cause. Serious divisions were beginning to appear amongst the revolutionaries, and above all Sultan Mahmud II, distracted by other pressures throughout 1821, had made no real effort to crush the rebellion.

The Sultan's Response

The traditional Ottoman response to rebellion was to crush it by intimidation and terror. The Greek revolt was not seen as an expression of national self-determination, a concept that was meaningless to the Sultan, but as an attempt by greedy individuals to usurp power for their own ends. Above all, it was seen as a religious phenomenon: all Christians within the Empire were judged responsible for the excesses of the Peloponnesian chieftains and were liable to communal punishment. In particular, the Patriarch of Constantinople, as a high Ottoman official responsible for the conduct of the Christians in the Empire, now paid the price of centuries of privilege. Despite his solemn excommunication of the Greek rebels, he was taken to a gate outside the Patriarchate, and there hanged on Easter Sunday 1821. After three days his body was cut down and given to the traditional enemies of the Greeks in the Empire, the Jews, who dragged it in triumph to the Golden Horn.

The execution of the Patriarch marked the beginning of a campaign of terror designed to deter any Greek within the Empire from joining the revolt. Throughout the spring hundreds of prominent Greeks –

churchmen, merchants, shopkeepers and artisans – were publicly executed in Constantinople, Smyrna (Izmir) and Adrianople (Edirne). Muslims were encouraged by the religious authorities to punish the Greek community for its sins, and as news of Greek atrocities in the Peloponnese became known, thousands were massacred in Rhodes, Kos and Cyprus. The Anatolian town of Kydonies (Aivalik) was reduced to rubble and its community of 30,000 massacred. In March 1822 the arrival on the island of Chios, whose Greek population was one of the most prosperous and contented of the Empire, of hundreds of nationalists from Samos provoked an onslaught by the Turks in which thousands of Chiots were killed and enslaved. Sacks of human remains were taken to Constantinople and strewn around the streets of the capital. The Chios massacres, depicted in the huge painting by Delacroix in the Louvre, brought great publicity to the Greek cause.

In northern Greece, the Turks had little difficulty in crushing all resistance. The Etairist Papas, who had succeeded in rousing the monks of Athos and had won a victory at Ierissos, advanced upon Salonika only to be checked by the Turks at Sedes and forced to abandon his followers. Salonika was deterred from any future rebelliousness by a massacre that crippled the city for decades. The chieftains of north-west Greece, separated by hundreds of miles from the centre of the rebellion, stood no chance of making headway against an overwhelming Turkish force; after a disaster at Nausa, where some of them emulated the Suliots by throwing themselves into the falls of the Arapitsa, their best fighters were forced to trek southwards to join the revolt in the Peloponnese.

The Sultan and his Grand Vizier regarded Ali Pasha's rebellion as far more threatening than the temporary independence of the Peloponnese, and Turkish energies were chiefly directed at reducing Ali's stronghold in Janina. By the beginning of 1822, Ali was forced to sign an armistice and retreat to a final refuge on the island of Itch-Kale. There, on 5 February 1822, surrounded by 50,000 hostile troops, he was struck down by assassins. His head was sent to Constantinople to be displayed on a dish in the Seraglio as an example to other over-mighty subjects.

The fall of Ali Pasha allowed the Sultan at last to concentrate his forces upon the revolt in the Peloponnese. Turkish strategy was conditioned by the geography of Greece: even today few roads run from west to east across central Greece, and at that time it was unthinkable to send an army through the mountains that provided a perfect habitat for Greek guerrillas. Any advance had to be made along the plains and river valleys of the east and west coasts, and even then could not avoid passing through the narrow defiles of Makrinoros and Thermopylai. In the spring of 1822 Turkish armies mounted a two-pronged advance southwards. Their objectives were to subdue the area north of the Gulf of Corinth, relieving Athens where a starving Turkish garrison was still holding out, and capturing Missolonghi which controlled the entrance to the Gulf of Corinth. They would then cross the Isthmus, take Acrocorinth and advance to the relief of Nauplion. It seemed unlikely that the Greek insurgents in the Peloponnese, weakened by factionalism and without a regular army or financial resources, stood any prospect of surviving such an assault.

In fact 1822 proved to be a triumph for the Greeks. The Turkish army in the north-east, consisting of some 20,000 men under Dramali Pasha, set off from Larissa in July and for a while swept all before it. The Greek chieftain Odysseus allowed the Turks to pass freely through his territory, and although the garrison holding the Acropolis fell before the Turks could relieve it, they captured Thebes and crossed the Isthmus of Corinth virtually unopposed after the Greeks surrendered the apparently impregnable fortress of Acrocorinth without a fight. There seemed to be nothing to stop them from advancing to the relief of Nauplion and reconquering the Peloponnese. The government left in panic for the coast, thousands of refugees fled the advancing Turkish army, and many of the more fickle klephts took to the mountains and considered the possibilities of changing sides. It appeared that the Greek revolution was doomed.

With nothing seeming capable of stopping the fall of Nauplion, Demitrios Ypsilantis rallied a few hundred followers in the crumbling citadel of Argos and stood in the path of the Turkish army. With victory in his grasp, Dramali Pasha decided to abandon his campaign and retreat to Corinth northwards through the narrow defiles called the Dervena-kia, which in his overconfidence he had failed to secure. It was here that the Turkish army was ambushed and massacred by the guerrillas of Kolokotronis and Dikaios. Dramali Pasha and 17,000 of his men perished in the débâcle and the subsequent fall of Corinth. Within a matter of weeks the starving Turkish garrison of Nauplion capitulated.

The western Turkish army, fresh from its triumphs over Ali, was equally unsuccessful. In July, advancing from its bases at Arta and Vonitsa, it encountered an ill-assorted combination of irregulars and European volunteers blocking its path at Peta. After a disastrous sequence of misunderstandings and incompetence, the Turks won a significant victory and advanced on their main objective, the strategically important town of Missolonghi (Mesolongion). Here their campaign, like that of Dramali in the east, ended in humiliation and defeat. The Turkish commander, his army ravaged by disease and harried by Greek irregulars, committed suicide on Christmas Day 1822, and his men retreated northwards in disarray. Henceforth Missolonghi became a symbol of the Greek cause out of all proportion to its military worth.

The events of 1822 had demonstrated the limitations of the Sultan's power and in the spring of 1823 the Turks repeated their previous strategy with even less success. Logistical problems had proved insurmountable: Greek command of the sea made it impossible to land a force of any size in the Peloponnese. The only alternative was the laborious build-up of forces in northern Greece and a long advance through dangerous terrain controlled by klephtic chieftains. The summer campaigning season was simply not long enough for the Turks to marshal their resources and bring them to bear on the Greek strongholds in the south. The power and corruption of the Janissaries also proved as big a problem to the Sultan as to the Greeks.

Conflict within Free Greece

It was fortunate for the Greeks that the bravery of their sea-captains had achieved a temporary stalemate by 1824, because there seemed to be a real likelihood that Free Greece would tear itself to pieces in factional struggles before the world had even recognized its existence. The problem lay in the irreconcilable interests of the various groups that had taken the stage in 1821. The Greeks who had organized the revolution, Phanariots like Alexander Mavrokordatos and Ypsilantis, had a sophis-

Ships from the Greek naval force

ticated political philosophy based on Western European ideas. Their vision of Greece comprised far more than the rocky peninsula of the Peloponnese upon which they found themselves marooned, and they were determined to create a modern state. As they became more familiar with the violent customs and politics of this primitive backwater it must have seemed unlikely that much could be built on such unpromising foundations.

The Greek landowners, or 'primates', who formed the ruling class under the Turks found these new-fangled revolutionary ideologies disturbing and presumptuous. They had enjoyed considerable material and political power and many of them had been reluctant to begin the revolution in the first place; their chief concern was to retain their wealth and influence. The rich shipowners and merchants of the islands, many of whom, like George Koundouriotis, were Albanian rather than

Greek, had also done well under the lax Ottoman regime; although they saw advantages in self-government, they too were determined to safeguard their interests in the power vacuum that followed the expulsion of the Turks.

Despite the political sophistication of the Phanariots and the local influence of primates, churchmen and wealthy islanders, real power lay in the hands of the klephtic chieftains. It was Kolokotronis who had defeated Dramali Pasha and led the assault on Nauplion in 1822, and the Suliot Botsaris who had checked the Turkish advance in 1823; the Rumeliot, Odysseus, controlled the Turkish invasion route to the Isthmus of Corinth. Kolokotronis in particular had amassed huge quantities of plunder in the sack of Nauplion and was able to use it to maintain a private army. The new state was forced to depend on these men to defend it from the Turks, but they were determined to block the formation of state institutions that might curtail their power.

Given the complete lack of political experience of the illiterate masses, whose driving impulse in 1821 was religious and racial hatred of the Turks, and given the violent differences within the leadership, it is not surprising that Free Greece quickly descended into political fragmentation and civil war. During the course of the year numerous bodies with grandiose titles sprang up in the area conquered from the Turks, as the leading figures of the uprising scrambled to secure their positions. There was, however, a growing acknowledgement that anarchy could not continue. If the Greek revolution was to become more than a temporary uprising in a corner of the Ottoman Empire, some more concrete evidence of nationhood was required. The Greeks had no army, no means of raising revenue, no law-making institutions, no constitution and no accepted government. If they expected recognition and support from the world, there would have to be some central institutions with which the world could deal. The Phanariots were well aware of the need to establish them, but the indigenous leaders of the uprising had no intention of giving up their hard-won spoils to these 'foreigners'. When, in December 1821, a 'National Assembly' met at Argos, it soon became clear that it would only be allowed to exist so long as it had no power. On New Year's Day 1822, near Epidauros, an elaborate Constitution was proclaimed. It was full of subtle checks and balances designed to prevent the government from doing anything at all.

Unless Free Greece could establish the trappings of statehood and obtain a source of revenue, it seemed destined to be for ever at the mercy of the warlords. During the next two years, as the threat of invasion by the Turks receded, the contradictions between the various power groups developed into a virtual civil war. Regional rivalries between the Peloponnese and northern Greece complicated the existing differences between Phanariots, Primates, Islanders and Kapitani. By 1824 the factional fighting had become so serious that the government was forced to call on John Kolettis, the ex-physician of Ali Pasha, to bring in Rumeliot troops to put down and imprison Kolokotronis.

The Greek state at the end of 1824 was a travesty of the enlightened Byzantine revival envisaged by the Etairia. Torn to pieces by the self-interest and intrigues of its leaders, it had been met with indifference and hostility by the governments of Europe. The Sultan's policy of terror and intimidation had confined it to a small southern promontory of the Greek world, and the promise of Balkan revolution and Russian assistance had been exposed as Utopian dreams. 'The nation', wrote one of Metternich's advisers in 1825, 'is too young and at the same time too old for revolution. The great mass cannot yet be enticed by revolutionary ideas. The few powerful and somewhat developed men are altogether devoted to anarchy, in order to use, in the basest fashion possible, the misfortune of the majority for their own enrichment.'

The Coming of Ibrahim Pasha

The continuing uprising posed a threat to the Ottoman Empire that could not be ignored. By 1824 successive military disasters had forced the Sultan to accept that there was no prospect of crushing the Greeks by his own efforts and he therefore requested the services of his most powerful vassal, Mehemet Ali, Pasha of Egypt. Son of a tobacco dealer from Kavala, Mehemet Ali was, like Ali of Janina, another Albanian parvenu who rose to prominence within the Ottoman Empire. By the 1820s he had transformed the Ottoman province of Egypt into a significant military power in the eastern Mediterranean. He possessed an army trained by European officers, and a largely French-built navy that was capable of holding its own with the Greek fleet. Early in 1824 the Sultan offered to cede Crete to him and to allow his son Ibrahim to take the Peloponnese, in return for assistance in putting down the Greek revolt.

In the spring of 1824, while the Greek factions were struggling to reconcile their differences at a conference in Amphisa, Mehemet Ali's brother-in-law Hussein landed at Suda Bay in Crete and began to establish a base for the reconquest of the Peloponnese. In January 1825 a large Egyptian army under Ibrahim Pasha began disembarking at Modon. The Greeks were so preoccupied with factional strife that this strategically vital fortress had not been secured. A Greek fleet of seventy ships failed to prevent the troops landing, showing that the Greeks had lost their greatest military asset, command of the sea. In May the Egyptian army, trained and officered by men like Colonel Joseph Anthelme Sève ('Suleiman Bey'), who had seen service in the Napoleonic wars, captured Navarino, thus providing a splendid harbour for Ibrahim's fleet. Supplied and reinforced from Crete, Ibrahim threatened to 'burn and destroy the whole Morea'; a trail of burned crops, slaughtered livestock and empty villages marked the progress of his advance, and in Modon a slave market was opened where Greeks were sold as galley-slaves or forced to work in labour gangs.

Moving northwards along the coast, Ibrahim destroyed the medieval town of Kiparissia; in the south Mistra, which still had a population of 40,000 in the eighteenth century, was finally extinguished. Some strongholds, such as the massive Frankish castle of Karitena, were able to hold out for a while, but guerrilla methods that had succeeded against cumbersome Turkish armies in 1822 and 1823 did not work against Ibrahim's well-trained troops. Even the release of Kolokotronis and his appointment as commander-in-chief made little difference to Greek fortunes. By June Ibrahim's forces threatened Nauplion, but at the fortified mills of Lerna (Mili), where Hercules performed one of his labours, Demetrios Ypsilantis in a feat of scarcely less heroic proportions held up the Egyptian army with a force of not more than 250 men.

By the beginning of 1826 the position of Free Greece was desperate. Ibrahim's Egyptians controlled almost the whole of the Peloponnese, restricting the Greeks to a small pocket of territory from Nauplion to the Isthmus of Corinth; a Greek force was besieged in the Acropolis; and the

Turks had renewed their siege of Missolonghi, assisted by Ibrahim's forces. Some of the klephtic chieftains were planning to desert the cause and settle with the Turks, and in October 1825 the body of one of the most unreliable of these warlords was found suspended from the walls of the Acropolis, a symbol of the depths into which the cause had now sunk. When Missolonghi fell in April 1826, it was obvious that unless the foreign support could be mobilised Free Greece would soon revert to being a small province of the Ottoman Empire under Egyptian rule.

The attitude of the Great Powers had proved to be a great disappointment to the hopes of Greek nationalists. Statesmen at the Congress of Laibach, which was meeting as the revolt broke out, reacted with hostility: the Austrian Chancellor, Prince Metternich, superciliously asked what was meant by the word 'Greek', and the British foreign minister, Lord Castlereagh, offered no encouragement. Most disappointing of all to Greek hopes, the Tsar allowed Turkish troops to crush the rebellion in the Principalities. The French had a friendly relationship with Greece's most dangerous enemy, Mehemet Ali, and neither Russians, Austrians nor British welcomed the weakening of the Ottoman Empire, which would leave a dangerous vacuum in south-eastern Europe that might well be filled by a rival.

The Greeks were unfortunate that their quest for national independence came when it did. Europe was still dominated by the coalition that had defeated Napoleon. The spirit of the times was profoundly conservative, and any movement that sought change was seen as a rebirth of the dangerous spirit of revolution that had been put down at Waterloo. The Ottoman Empire represented the status quo, and the Greek rebellion seemed merely part of the revolutionary wave that had broken out all over southern Europe at the beginning of the 1820s. Most European leaders hoped that the Sultan would end these disruptive disturbances as soon as possible.

The Philhellenes

If it had been left to the hard-headed judgement of statesmen there is little doubt that the Great Powers would have stood by and watched with some relief while the Greek revolution was crushed. But the

Greeks had one enormous advantage over Balkan peoples like the Serbs, whose successful struggle for independence had been ignored by the world. The educated classes of Europe and America were steeped in the culture and philosophy of Ancient Greece, which had deeply permeated western European attitudes to art, philosophy, literature and politics. No European gentleman's education was complete without a knowledge of ancient Greek and a thorough grounding in Greek classics and literature. Many believed that the heritage of Ancient Greece lay not merely in books but that the actual descendants of the Ancient Greeks awaited deliverance from alien bondage. Greece had joined Italy as part of the itinerary of the Grand Tour, and many an adventurous wealthy young man 'dreamed that Greece might still be free'. In short, a Romantic attachment to Greece was deeply embedded in the consciousness of the educated classes of western Europe and America; it is not surprising that the Greek revolt evoked a response in the minds of the public that was very different to the calculating *realpolitik* of their rulers.

Like the volunteers in the Spanish Civil War, many philhellenes went to Greece to offer their services to the cause, and in the early months of 1821 large numbers of idealists, unemployed ex-soldiers and professional revolutionaries began to arrive. Many returned home immediately, their illusions about the nobility of the Ancient Greeks punctured by the horrors perpetrated by the modern ones; others found themselves stranded and destitute, unloved by Greeks who resented this influx of patronizing foreigners who know nothing of their traditional ways of warfare. Duels were so frequent amongst the touchy volunteers from Germany that they were called 'etiquette soldiers'. The introduction of European fighting methods led to a series of military disasters which contrasted with the success of traditional Greek tactics, which bore a remarkable resemblance to those of the Afghan mujaheddin.

The greatest success of the Phillhellene Societies in Europe and America was to raise money for the cause. The fortune collected by private subscription, and two Greek Loans floated on the London market, had an important impact on the situation. The government was strengthened against men like Kolokotronis who were defying it, and the civil war stopped abruptly when British gold arrived in Zante and rebellious klephts came to heel to share the spoils. Conspicuous

Frank Abney Hastings

consumption, rather than preparations against the imminent Egyptian onslaught, became the main activity on the streets of Nauplion.

Under the influence of two British soldiers of fortune, much of the money went into an attempt to create a modern Greek navy. Frank Abney Hastings, who had ended a distinguished career in the Royal Navy after challenging his flag captain to a duel, joined the crew of the Hydriot vessel *Themistokles* when the Greek revolt broke out; having distinguished himself in various naval engagements, he recruited a private force to serve the Greek government. Thomas Cochrane, Earl of Dundonald, had lived a life of such adventure – court-martialled, convicted of fraud, elopement, expulsion from the House of Commons, stripped of the KCB, independence fighter in several Latin American countries, hijacker of half the Brazilian navy – that in comparison the advantures of Hastings appear sadly suburban. Both men were convinced that the key to Greek victory lay in the weapon that had changed the whole nature of naval warfare – the steamship. In 1823 Hastings told Lord Byron that one steamship, with its manoeuvrability and ability to fire red-hot shot, could wipe out the Turkish fleet and win the war. In the spring of 1825, the Greek government ordered a 400-ton vessel, *Perseverance*, from a Deptford yard, to be paid for by the London Greek Committee, and two of the latest sailing frigates from American shipyards. With the arrival of Cochrane, the projected Greek navy assumed grandiose proportions. As a condition of accepting command of the fleet, he demanded six more steam vessels, two 74-gun ships of the line modified to carry exceptionally heavy guns, and a salary of £57,000, which was more than half the annual revenue of the Greek government. Mehemet Ali joined the naval race by buying a Margate steam-packet and converting it to carry three heavy cannon.

Like most of the military efforts of the Philhellenes, the schemes of Hastings and Cochrane ended in expensive fiasco. *Perseverance* burst its boilers on its way to Greece because it could not raise sufficient steam without exploding; when it eventually reached Nauplion in September 1826 it could not be used because its guns had not arrived. Of the American frigates only one, *Hope* ('Hellas'), was built; escalating costs and corruption had put the project beyond hard-pressed Greek resources. Of Cochrane's fleet, only *Enterprise* ('Epicheiresis') and *Irresistible* ('Hermes') were ever built; the others were either cancelled or left to rot half-built in the Thames.

The most useful, and best-remembered, contributor to the Greek cause was Lord Byron. He arrived in Greece in January 1824 with nine servants, a personal physician, and many handsome uniforms. After striving in vain to reconcile the Greek factions, he caught a chill and died in April at Missolonghi, before he could make any real contribution to the war effort. But the circumstances of his death, containing as it did all the components of fashionable European Romanticism, made certain that the Greek cause, like the Spanish Civil War a century later, became a stage upon which the dreams of liberals and idealists were played out. The fall of Missolonghi two years after Byron's death became a symbolic event out of all proportion to its military significance, galvanizing support for a cause that seemed to be on the point of extinction.

Lord Byron

The Great Powers to the Rescue

Byron's contribution epitomized the impact of philhellenism on the independence struggle. In practical terms it was limited or counterproductive, but its role in popularizing the cause and putting pressure upon European governments was of great importance. It partly explains why European statesmen, at the moment when Greece stood on the brink of defeat, decided to come to her aid. The huge groundswell of public emotion generated by Byron's death coincided with a belated realization that an end to the Greek crisis would best serve the national interests of the great powers.

The Tsar of Russia, Alexander I, believed that the Greek Revolution threatened the security of Europe, but he also saw himself as the protector of Orthodox Christians and events like the execution of the Patriarch and the massacre at Chios gradually pushed him into supporting some sort of Greek autonomy. By 1825 the Russians were prepared to accept the establishment of three small Greek principalities with limited autonomy under the Sultan, and as the war dragged on the new Tsar, Nicholas I, moved towards co-operation with Britain, to seek a way out of the crisis.

In Britain, the appointment of George Canning as foreign secretary in 1822 marked a move away from the initial hostility to the Greek cause. The pressure of public opinion combined with a pragmatic appraisal of Britain's interests gradually led him towards cautious support. His decision in 1823 to accept the right of the Greeks to impose a blockade was a significant shift away from neutrality and the beginning of a slow drift towards intervention on the Greek side.

In July 1825 the Greek government, fighting for its life against Ibrahim Pasha, asked the British to make Greece a British protectorate. Although the request was rejected out of hand by Canning, who realized that the other Great Powers would never accept it, he was already seeking an end to the war through international co-operation. In July 1827 Charles X of France, an ardent Philhellene, joined the British and Russians in signing the Treaty of London: a Greek principality was to be set up under the overall sovereignty of the Sultan, with its exact frontiers to be settled by later negotiations. Such was Greek desperation that they accepted this proposal, although it was a travesty of their national hopes. The Sultan and his vassal Ibrahim, believing rightly that they had all but won the war, refused to co-operate.

The Treaty of London stipulated that if its terms were rejected the Powers would 'impose' its provisions 'without the use of force'. How the rampant Ibrahim was to be persuaded to lay down his arms on the brink of victory was never explained to the Allied admirals instructed to enforce the treaty. The outcome was the great naval battle of Navarino, the most decisive event of the War of Independence (and the last naval battle fought between wooden sailing ships). On 20 October 1827 a British, French and Russian fleet under Sir Edward Codrington, with orders to prevent supplies reaching Ibrahim Pasha's army, confronted a Turkish and Egyptian fleet in Navarino Bay. Through panic or incompetence one of the Muslim ships opened fire. As usual before the age of instant communications, decisions that changed the course of history were left to commanders on the spot. Admiral Codrington, an ardent philhellene hungering for an opportunity to fight for the cause, gave the order for the Allied fleet to open fire. Within a few hours Ibrahim's fleet, outgunned and trapped against the shore, had been annihilated. The birth of an independent Greek state, however truncated compared with the inflated dreams of the Etairia, waited only upon deliberations and rival interests of the Powers.

The Establishment of the Kingdom of Greece

Foreign intervention came at the lowest point in Greek military fortunes, with the various rival Greek 'governments' confined to the north-east corner of the Peloponnese. No European statesmen had wanted a military confrontation with the Sultan, but the effect of cutting Ibrahim's supply routes meant that his effort to conquer the Peloponnese was now doomed, and the establishment of a Greek state inevitable. Its frontiers and the extent of its independence from the Turks remained in the balance, but the obduracy of Turkey was steadily pushing the Powers, however reluctantly, towards the establishment of an independent Greek kingdom, free from all association with the Ottoman Empire. The long-awaited Russo-Turkish war of 1828 finally destroyed any chance of limited Turkish sovereignty over Greece.

Greece's dependence upon the goodwill of foreign powers forced an end to the factional squabbling that had characterized the war. Even after the fall of Missolonghi rival national assemblies based at Aegina and Kastri had continued to expend their energies in a violent power struggle, but to retain the support of foreign governments and public opinion it was essential to establish an ordered government and administration. In May 1827 the rival assemblies met at Troizen and agreed on a series of constructive measures. The appointment of Sir Richard Church and Lord Cochrane as military and naval commanders gave direction to the war effort, and a new constitution brought an opportunity to escape from political anarchy. Most important of all, the assembly offered the presidency to John Capodistrias.

When, in January 1828, Capodistrias arrived to take up the role he had been so reluctant to assume in 1820, he made no attempt to hide his contempt for his new subjects. He believed that the 'Christian Turks' (landowners), 'Children of Satan' (Phanariots), 'robbers' (klephtic chieftains), and 'fools' (intellectuals), had nearly brought the revolution to disaster. Capodistrias himself was an authoritarian who had built his career in the Tsarist bureaucracy; he had no intention of respecting the new constitution, and was determined to impose efficient, authoritarian government. He had two goals: to seize as much territory as possible so as to influence the frontier negotiations, and to establish a modern state with a national army, a civil service and an efficient educational system. In both these endeavours he had little success: klephtic bands sent to capture territory still held by the Turks made little impression; Cochrane's naval efforts failed to match his triumphs in South America, and Hastings was tragically killed in a minor naval engagement.

In reality the future shape of the new state depended entirely upon the decisions of the Powers who, having briefly colluded at Navarino, were now bent upon preventing each other's predominance in the region. The British prime minister, the Duke of Wellington, was chiefly concerned with preventing Russia making the new Greek state into a satellite; his proposals for the degree of Greek independence and its frontiers varied according to his perception of how Russian designs could best be thwarted; and he was determined not to give Greece the Ionian Islands or the mainland opposite them, which he believed were essential to British strategic interests. The French landed an expeditionary force to oversee the evacuation of Ibrahim's army, hoping that this would give them lasting influence; while the Russians believed their victory over the Turks in 1829 gave them powerful leverage. The driving force of the protracted negotiations was not the interest of the Greek people but the suspicions and rivalries of the Great Powers.

Eventually the Powers decided that it would suit them best if Greece became a fully independent kingdom, and the search for a monarch began. No European royal family would have accepted the travesty of a kingdom suggested by Wellington. The first candidate, Prince Leopold of Saxe-Coburg (subsequently the first King of the Belgians), withdrew when he was offered a state which excluded Samos and Crete and

Greek Freedom fighter

stretched only as far north as the River Aspropotamos. Capodistrias was determined to push the frontier as far north as possible and refused to withdraw his irregular forces from north of the Gulf; he was rewarded when the British accepted Greece's right to this area. Prospective candidates for the Greek throne were now offered a northern frontier from Arta in the west to Volos in the east.

Capodistrias was now living on borrowed time. His attempts to build the foundations of a modern state were frustrated by a crippled economy, the absence of an educated class, and above all by the hostility of the leaders of the War of Independence, who resented his high-handed curtailment of the spoils of victory. On 9 October 1831 he was assassinated on the steps of the Church of St Spiridon in Nauplion by the Maniot chieftains, Constantine and George Mavromichaelis. His brief career foreshadowed a struggle between authoritarianism and anarchy that would be a recurrent theme in Greek history.

In May 1832 the Powers established a protectorate over Greece and accepted Otto, the seventeen-year-old son of King Ludwig I of Bavaria, as Otho I, first ruler of a small but independent Greek Kingdom.

CHAPTER FOURTEEN

Nationhood Unfulfilled
1832–1914

The Reign of King Otho

The huge Romantic paintings in Munich galleries showing the arrival of King Otho in Nauplion bear little relation to reality. Otho's new kingdom had been reduced to penury by nearly ten years of war and civil strife. Towns and crops had been destroyed; refugees from Asia Minor and the Islands roamed the streets or lived in makeshift shanties; thousands of armed men hung on to their weapons and used them to prey upon the civilian population. The American philhellene Samuel Gridley Howe came across 'six hundred persons, mostly widows and orphans, driven from their homes, hunted into the mountains like wild beasts, and living upon herbs, grass and what they could pick up from the rocks'. Another American described the blinded and mutilated victims who came in desperation to claim food donated by the American philhellene organizations.

Count Armensperg, the Bavarian official who headed the Regency during Otho's minority, was not popular. Bavarian soldiers attempting to impose order in the countryside were defeated and repulsed by the Maniots. Division of the country into ten provinces, or nomarchies, destroyed the traditional system of local self-government and weakened the authority of local chieftains. Active government by officials appointed from Athens (which became the capital of Greece in 1834) was hated by a population which valued its individualism above all else. There was constant friction over new taxes and the appointment of Otho, a Catholic, as head of a national Greek Church caused a schism with the Patriarch and offended conservatives.

The war and its unsatisfactory conclusion left a legacy that made Greece a difficult country to govern throughout the nineteenth century. Klephtic chieftains resisted attempts to disarm their followers, and Kolokotronis narrowly escaped death for his defiance of the new order. Local politicians resented the influx of Bavarians and Phanariot Greeks who excluded them from power. Soon Otho's refusal to grant a constitution became the focus of discontent, and in 1843 demonstrations backed by the army forced him to grant a new constitution with a two-chamber parliament consisting of a senate (*Gerousia*) appointed by the king, and a lower chamber (*Vouli*) elected on a wide franchise. The king still retained the power to veto legislation, appoint and dismiss ministers, dissolve parliament, and call elections when it suited him.

Otho remained at heart an autocrat, and the 'revolution' of 1843 merely substituted a clique of old independence fighters in place of the Bavarian and expatriate élite upon whom he had previously relied. Kolettis, who had learned his political skills in the court of Ali of Janina, was used by Otho to subvert the spirit of the constitution by means of bribery, patronage and intimidation.

At election time, klephts and brigands were employed to intimidate voters and candidates, and the distribution of official positions to supporters introduced a corruption into public life that persisted well into the present century. The army's morale was undermined by making promotion a reward for supporting the government. Political corruption became deeply entrenched.

The people might have accepted this political chicanery if the regime had been able to achieve material advances, but progress in raising living standards was minimal. In the 1850s the population of Athens was still only 20,000. There were no railways and hardly any metalled roads, making pack animals the only means of transporting produce. The balance of trade was constantly in deficit, and the export of currants provided virtually the only source of national income. Industry, apart from small-scale artisan production, did not exist. The prosperous wartime merchant fleet declined under the competition of steam, and huge foreign debts were a constant drain on resources. Ironically, many people left Greece at this time to settle in the more prosperous Greek-speaking parts of the Ottoman Empire.

The Great Idea

Few Greeks were satisfied after the war of independence. The kingdom was only the smallest and poorest part of the potential Greek state, and far more Greeks still lived outside than within it. Most people believed that progress could only come about if all their countrymen still living under Ottoman rule were liberated and incorporated in a much larger and more viable Greek state. It was out of this feeling of frustrated national destiny that the 'Great Idea' (*Megali Idea*) was forged, a dream of a Greece 'spanning two continents and five seas' that was the national obsession until it ended in disaster in 1922.

John Kolettis, in a speech that might have been made by virtually any Greek politician, summed up the essence of the Great Idea:

> A Greek is not only a man who lives within this kingdom, but also one who lives in Janina, in Salonika, in Serres, in Adrianople, in Constantinople, in Smyrna, in Trebizond, in Crete, in Samos, and in any land associated with Greek history or the Greek race. ... There are two main centres of Hellenism: Athens, the capital of the Greek Kingdom ... and 'the City' [Constantinople], the dream and hope of all Greeks.

This ambitious definition of 'the Greek nation' translated into practical politics the belief that the modern Greeks were the direct descendants of the Ancients. Suggestions that Romans, Huns, Slavs, Franks and Turks might have diluted the stock of Perikles were greeted with violent abuse. Even today a Greek analysis of the national character will begin with a discourse of the characteristics of ancient Athens and Sparta, rather like seeking an explanation for 'British disease' in the social habits of the Ancient Britons. This identification with the distant past spawned an aggressive modern nationalism which, according to Kolettis (himself a Vlach), gave the modern Greeks a right to claim lands held hundreds or even thousands of years before. The danger of the Great Idea was that it could only succeed at the expense of the Turks and other national groups that had settled in the Greek world over many centuries.

Attempts to revive Greece's classical heritage permeated every aspect of life under Otho. After 1834 Nauplion and Athens were reconstructed

Old Parliament Building in Athens

along neoclassical lines by German and French architects, in an attempt to reproduce the clean elegance of ancient Greek cities. Wide streets in geometric patterns, incorporating squares and open spaces, were lined with splendid public buildings like the University, the Academy and the Observatory. The Bavarian architect Gärtner was commissioned to build a Royal Palace on the north side of Sindagma Square, an a Frenchman designed a suitable neoclassical building to house the Parliament. Visitors to Athens in the nineteenth century describe a small, calm city of elegant tree-lined boulevards fronted by the houses of merchants and politicians, most of which have now, alas, disappeared beneath the still-rising tide of concrete. Nineteenth-century Athens was deliberately designed as the reincarnation of ancient glories.

Attempts were made to make the Greek inhabitants of Asia Minor aware of their heritage by setting up Greek schools staffed by teachers trained in the kingdom. These efforts were not helped by the imposition of a pseudo-classical language, known as *katherevousa*, which was an artificial tongue that had never been spoken by anyone. The attempt to impose it as an 'official' language cut ordinary people off from government, public life, and even from literature, and its alienating effects have been felt until recent times. But the Great Idea was far more than a cultural or educational movement. Greeks looked to the king and to politicians for concrete action to liberate the Ottoman Greeks and extend the boundaries of the kingdom. There was no surer way to secure popular adulation in nineteenth-century Greece than by pursuing aggressive foreign policies: as seemingly insoluble domestic problems crowded in upon Otho, he encouraged nationalist ambitions, believing that Greece must expand to survive and that foreign adventures might distract attention from the inglorious and corrupt realities of domestic politics.

In 1839, when Greece's old foe, Mehemet Ali, attacked the Sultan with French support, the Cretans rose up and demanded union (*enosis*) with Greece. Groups of nationalists crossed into Turkish territory and tried to stir up the local population. In 1854, during the Crimean War, Otho launched an ill-prepared attack across the border, hoping to take advantage of Turkish preoccupation. This adventure resulted in a double humiliation for Greece and established a pattern that would be repeated several times in the future: the Turks repulsed the disorganized and badly equipped Greek forces with ease; and the British and French, infuriated by this attack on their Turkish ally, landed troops at Piraeus and forced the king to accept a pro-British administration, occupation by British and French troops, and supervision of Greek affairs that continued for several years.

The Fall of Otho

These adventures showed the danger for Greece that pursuit of the Great Idea entailed, and the disparity between her grandiose ambitions and her ability to carry them out. In reality Greece was at the mercy of the Protecting Powers, who could choose to interpret their role as an excuse to intervene in Greek affairs whenever it suited their interests. Her vulnerability to coercion by the British navy was demonstrated in 1850 when, in an absurd caricature of 'gunboat diplomacy', Lord Palmerston imposed a blockade in support of the dubious claims of the Gibraltarian Jew, Don Pacifico. As long as the Powers remained determined to maintain the Ottoman Empire, it was difficult to see how the aims of the Great Idea could be achieved.

Lack of realism continued to warp the judgement of Greek politicians. As memories of the war faded, it too became part of nationalist mythology. That the rebellion was snatched from the brink of disaster by the intervention of the Powers was forgotten. The brutal and often treacherous klephtic chieftains, who so very nearly brought disaster to the Greek cause, were installed as epic heroes to rank with the giants of antiquity; their statues, striking herioc poses and clad in unlikely classical garb, proclaimed to generations of Greeks that victory could be achieved by heroism alone. The mythologizing of the events of 1821, which can be observed in any Greek museum, bred an unrealistic belief in the prowess of Greek irregulars and a contempt for the Turkish army, resulting in constant ill-organized and over-optimistic military adventures and frequent humiliating defeats.

Championing the Great Idea did much to redeem Otho in the eyes of many Greeks, but emphasis on securing liberty for the Ottoman Greeks focused attention upon the lack of political freedom at home. When the Italian struggle for independence began in 1859 younger Greeks were intoxicated with the triumphs of Garibaldi, but Otho tried to damp down popular demands to follow the lead of the Italian revolutionaries and strike boldly against the Turks. He seemed to be exposed as a cautious reactionary whose prestige was undermined by his Catholicism, his failure to produce an heir, and his association with corrupt and cynical politicians. In 1862 a series of rebellions broke out across the country, led by soldiers of the Athens garrison. A provisional government, led by Demetrios Voulgaris, a member of one of the leading Hydriot political families, called for the abdication of the king and a new constitution. The protecting powers advised Otho to leave, and at the end of 1862, almost thirty years after his triumphant arrival in Nauplion, he left Greece, as he had arrived, aboard a British warship.

Greece under George I

A plebiscite on Otho's successor in December 1862 resulted in an overwhelming vote for Prince Alfred, second son of Queen Victoria. International politics made it impossible for a member of the British royal family to take the throne, but the Greek people clearly continued to believe in close association with Great Britain, whose navy still controlled the destinies of the eastern Mediterranean. In fact, Britain was committed to the continuance of the Ottoman Empire and quite prepared, as she had already shown at the time of the Crimean War, to use force to control any Greek threat to its security. The monarch eventually chosen by the Powers was Prince William of Holstein-Sonderburg-Glücksburg, whose father in 1863 became King Christian IX of Denmark. William took the title George I, King of the Hellenes, which showed his commitment to *all* Greeks, not just those of the existing kingdom.

The revolution of 1862 had been fuelled by impatience to fulfil the Great Idea but also by hunger for political reform. Within a few months of the new king's arrival, substantial strides had been made towards the achievement of both these goals. Britain marked the beginning of the reign by ceding the Ionian Islands: at a stroke 250,000 people, who had always enjoyed a higher level of education and culture than on the mainland, were added to the existing kingdom, marking the greatest increase of territory since independence and swelling the population by one-fifth. This was followed in 1864 by a new constitution, which established what the Greeks called 'Crowned Democracy'. The Senate was abolished, and a single Chamber, elected on an extremely wide franchise, was established, making Greece in theory one of the most democratic countries in Europe. There was still considerable scope for arbitrary action by the monarch: George retained the right to appoint ministers without a majority, to dismiss parliament, to declare war and sign treaties, leaving an ominous vagueness over the monarch's right to intervene in foreign policy. The prospects of orderly political development were still dependent upon the good will of the king, and the growth of a maturity and moderation amongst politicians that had hitherto been in very short supply.

For the first few years of the new reign it seemed as if little had changed. When, in 1870, a group of wealthy British tourists were kidnapped and murdered by brigands on an excursion to Marathon (in what became known as the Dilessi Murders), it emerged that there had been over a hundred cases of brigandage in the previous eighteen months. In parliament corruption, fraud and vote-rigging provided a staple diet for the dozens of newspapers that fed upon the insatiable appetite of Athenians for political scandal and gossip. In the first seventeen years of George's reign there were nine elections and thirty-one governments. Governments continued to employ klephts and use the army to intimidate voters at election time, and government offices were openly traded for political favours.

The last decades of the nineteenth century saw the beginnings of economic growth. By its end nearly a thousand miles of railway and a rudimentary network of metalled roads had been built. In the sixties and seventies production of currants, still the only crop exported in any quantity, more than doubled. The draining by Scottish engineers of Lake Kopais, a huge marshy area in central Greece, brought much new and fertile land under cultivation. But industry was very slow to develop: only 7000 people worked in factories in 1877, and only 36,000 as late as 1917. This was offset by the impressive growth of the merchant fleet, which developed under Greek entrepreneurs, many of them living abroad, into one of the largest in the world. The opening of the Corinth Canal in 1893 made Piraeus one of the great ports of the Mediterranean. Syros, which had grown from nothing after independence to mount a serious challenge to the 'Greek' ports of Constantinople, Salonika, Alexandria and Smyrna, went into decline.

The Greek economy remained small and unbalanced, dependent on a single crop and burdened with debt repayments that amounted to 40% of the national budget, but its growth, however modest, led for the first time to the development of a small middle class which began to change the patterns of Greek political life. In 1875 the king appointed as prime minister one of the outstanding politicians of the century, Charilaos Trikoupis, a representative of the London Greeks. For the next twenty years he strove to reform the system, introducing measures designed to reform the administration and to boost the economy. Tariffs were introduced to protect infant Greek industry; taxes were raised to pay off the crippling national debts; government money was put into projects to improve the infrastructure of the economy; attempts were made to improve the quality of civil servants and to establish an independent judiciary. After fourteen years in England Trikoupis admired English institutions, and strove to substitute the stability of a two-party system for the atomized chaos of Greek politics. The king's acceptance of the principle that the government must come from the majority party was a large step in this direction.

In the end Trikoupis was defeated by the way in which the two-party system relentlessly adapted itself to traditional Greek politics. His bitter rival, Theodore Deligiannis, alternating in power with him for fifteen years, based his policy almost entirely upon a mindless opposition to everything Trikoupis attempted to achieve. Change of government meant the repeal of all measures passed by the previous administration, and the wholesale replacement of officials associated with it. Trikoupis tried to soften popular enthusiasm for the Great Idea and to concentrate on pressing domestic problems, but Deligiannis embraced an irresponsible and risky foreign policy with all the enthusiasm of a demagogue.

The problems, like those in any developing country, would probably have been overcome by the development of the economy and the growth of an educated electorate. But in Greece the economy and the fragile political consensus were constantly threatened by the demands of the Great Idea. Towards the end of the century two explosive developments strained the country's resources to breaking point: the drive towards enosis by the people of Crete, and the growth of Slav nationalism which challenged the supremacy of the Greeks amongst the Christians of the Ottoman Empire.

Crete and the Eastern Question

Crete, the 'Great Island, had strongly resisted Ottoman rule ever since 1669. Peasants were exploited by a landowning class largely made up of Greek converts to Islam, and a fierce tradition of mountain independence constantly challenged Muslim rule. Persistent uprisings put Athens under relentless public pressure to help the Cretan cause. In 1866 the leaders of a massive revolt demanded enosis and called upon Greeks everywhere to come to their aid. Volunteers, many of them serving officers, flocked to the island with the connivance of the Greek government, and Greek communities all over the world, like the one in Manchester which paid for a ship, raised money for arms and supplies. Athens tried to form a Balkan front, signing an agreement with the Serbs for a combined attack on the Turks.

Once again an attempt by Greece to carry forward her national goal by force was frustrated by the Powers. Diplomatic pressure and the threat of a naval blockade forced the king to abandon the Cretans to their fate. At a conference in Paris the Greeks were warned about the use of armed force and threatened with dire consequences if they continued to aid the Cretan insurgents. All the Greeks had to show for several years of high expectations was the Organic Statute, a promise of reform squeezed from the reluctant Turks by the Powers.

Some historians have wondered whether Greeks under Turkish rule should have developed their favoured position in the Empire and 'taken it over from within' instead of constantly challenging it. The Ottoman Greeks had regained the position they had held in the eighteenth century, and the Greek population of western Asia Minor was growing at a far greater rate than that of the Turks, giving them a majority in cities like Smyrna and a growing proportion of the population of Constantinople. Greeks like Alexander Katheordory Pasha, a deputy foreign minister, held important positions in the Ottoman administration, and Ottoman reforms led to the growth of a wealthy Greek middle class of shopkeepers, doctors and professionals. Greeks were active in banking, railway construction and shipping, dominating the commerce of the Empire to a greater extent than before 1821.

All this progress, and the survival of the Ottoman Greeks, was threatened by this disorganized activities of Greek nationalists. In 1870 the Sultan established an independent Church (Exarchate) for the Bulgarians. This was a shattering blow to Hellenism, striking at the root of the assumption that the Sultan still regarded the Greek Patriarch as the head of Orthodox Christians in the Empire and the Greeks as its dominant Christian minority. It marked the start of a Turkish strategy of 'divide and rule', but above all it heralded the challenge of Slav nationalism.

Further shocks occurred during the great 'Eastern Crisis' in 1875, when the Serbs and Montenegrins attacked Turkey. When Russia joined in there seemed to be a real prospect of the dissolution of the Ottoman Empire. With the Russian army only a few miles from Constantinople revolts broke out in Crete, Thessaly and Epirus. An excited Greek government prepared to gather up the spoils, but before the Greek army had a chance to fight, the news arrived that in the peace treaty of San Stefano Greek claims had been completely ignored. Russia wanted a 'Big Bulgaria' occupying the whole of the Aegean seaboard between

Salonika and Adrianople, which would effectively usurp Greek claims to Thrace; this exploded a central assumption of the Great Idea: Russia was now committed to Pan-Slavism as a vehicle for her expansion into the region, and Greeks could no longer dream of riding into Constantinople on the shoulder of the Russian bear.

The Treaty of San Stefano was greeted with outrage by the other Powers, and a Congress was held in Berlin under Bismarck's chairmanship to impose an international settlement. This was more palatable to the Greeks but was still a rebuff to their hopes and a reminder of their isolation: their claims to Epirus, Crete and Thessaly were ignored, and although the Big Bulgaria wanted by the Russians was dismantled, the principle of Bulgarian independence was recognized in all but name. Bulgarian rivalry in Macedonia was now a new impediment to Greek expansion.

The Berlin Settlement was a sickening blow to Greek hopes, but in Crete the Turks allowed a form of popular representation under the Halepa Pact and appointed an Ottoman Greek as governor of the island. In 1881 Britain forced the Turks to give Thessaly and Arta to Greece but failed to make them give up Preveza and Janina. This did little to heal Greek bitterness over the British takeover of Cyprus during the crisis, and nationalist politicians like Deligiannis seized the opportunity to inflame the public appetite for further adventures. In 1885, copying the example of the Bulgarians, who had defied the Congress of Berlin and declared their independence, he ordered mobilization and prepared to liberate the Greeks living north of the new frontier. Bulgaria was protected from the retribution of the Powers by its geography, but Greece found itself blockaded by a fleet commanded by the same Prince Alfred whom it had once wanted to be its king; after three weeks the Greek government was forced into another climb-down by British economic pressure.

In 1897 the country was plunged into the most serious crisis since independence. The Cretans set up an independent government in the Akrotiri peninsula and once more proclaimed enosis. All the pent-up frustrations of Greek nationalism exploded in a torrent of support which swept even the cautious royal family into a national crusade. The warnings of moderate politicians and the advice of foreign governments were ignored. A fleet commanded by Prince George set sail for Crete; Greek volunteers landed on the island; and on the mainland the Greek army crossed the frontier and began to occupy Turkish territory. This northern advance ended in catastrophe: in the west the drive into Epirus was checked and repulsed, and in the east Prince Constantine's army was defeated and driven southwards beyond Larissa. By May of 1897 the Turks were poised within a few days' march of Athens.

At this juncture the Powers came to the rescue, preventing further disaster by imposing an armistice and showing clearly their determination to prevent the recurrent crises of Greek nationalism from disturbing the status quo. The Greeks were forced to pay an indemnity to the Sultan and to surrender recently-won territory. In Crete a six-nation peace-keeping force bombarded the Greek rebels in Akrotiri into submission and proclaimed an international protectorate over the island. The imposition of an international commission to supervise the Greek economy and ensure regular payments of its huge foreign debt caused further national frustration and humiliation.

Confrontation in Macedonia

At the same time Greece was facing a growing confrontation with the Slavs over the future of the Turkish province of Macedonia. This huge region, stretching from Lake Okhrid in the west to the River Nestos in the east and from the shores of the Aegean to the Shar and Rhodope mountains in the north, was a rich prize for the newly independent nations pressing around its borders. It contained the fertile plains of Thrace, the important communications corridor running down the Vardar/Axios valley, and above all the great port of Salonika. In Macedonia the ethnic and cultural claims of Greece were far more dubious than elsewhere. The word 'macédoine' used to describe a pudding of many ingredients, came from the region's rich ethnic mixture of Greeks, Serbs, Bulgars, Albanians, Vlachs, Jews and Turks. In 1910, when a British official asked a peasant his nationality, he replied – in Albanian – 'I am Greek'.

By setting up an independent Bulgarian Exarchate, the Turks had deliberately called into question the predominance of Hellenism in the

Balkans since Byzantine times. In the 1890s, a violent contest began for the allegiance of Macedonian Christians. The Bulgarian government and the newly independent Bulgarian Church sought to wrest them away from their traditional loyalty to the Greek Church by a campaign of propaganda and intimidation. In 1893 Greek claims were challenged by the Interior Macedonian Revolutionary Organization (IMRO), a socialist group seeking to establish an independent Macedonian state by force. IMRO partisans (*komitadjis*) began a campaign of terror directed both at the Turks and at any Macedonian villager who claimed allegiance to the Greek Church. Both the Bulgarian government and IMRO staged armed uprisings in 1902 and 1903. It placed yet another strain on the tottering Greek government at a time when it could least afford to meet it. Hellenism and the Great Idea demanded a response and both the government and unofficial nationalist groups took strong action. By 1894 the Greek Ethniki Etairia (National Society) was disseminating Orthodox and nationalist propaganda to 80,000 Macedonians; Greek guerrillas, often commanded by regular army officers, fought a long and debilitating struggle with the *komitadjis* in the villages of Macedonia which further drained Greece's slender resources.

The defeat of 1897 began a period of deep disillusionment in Greece, and brought home the appalling cost of constant foreign adventures in pursuit of the Great Idea. The frustrated hopes of Greek nationalism were destroying the fragile economy and killing the tender growth of political consensus that Trikoupis had tried to nurture. When he had died in 1896, most of his work lay in ruins. Servicing of foreign debt took up one-third of the state's income; imports outweighed exports by 44%; and a disastrous fall in the price of currants crippled state revenue and weakened the currency. New roads and railways exposed the peasants to the forces of the international market, and the division of farms caused by the growing population led to an increase of underemployed and landless peasants. Thousands of Greeks were forced by declining living standards to emigrate. In 1893 Trikoupis had declared the state bankrupt.

The Rise of Venizelos

Not surprisingly, frustrations led to fundamental criticism of the existing order. On the Right, politicians like Ion Dragoumis asked whether western democratic institutions were relevant to Greek traditions and raised the spectre of authoritarianism. Officers' organizations openly expressed their disgust with the politicians in Athens. The Left, no less wedded to nationalism, sought to create an efficient state more capable of pursuing the Great Idea. The return to sterile political manoeuvring after the death of Trikoupis, and the king's cynical manipulation of the system, encouraged Republicanism. There were demands for a revision of the constitution, for lower taxation, and for the confiscation of large estates. Disaffection with the old ways showed itself in an enthusiasm for literature written in the demotic language rather than in *kathourevousa*, leading to riots in Athens over the language question in 1901.

The resentments simmering beneath the surface came to a head in 1908. The Powers had decided that the persistent instability and conflict in Macedonia required international action. In 1903 emperor Franz Josef II and Tsar Nicholas II proposed an international police force to supervise the region: British, French, Russian and Italian officers arrived in Drama, Serres, Salonika and Monastir respectively. In 1908 King Edward VII and the Tsar pressed a further programme of reforms upon the Turks. This latest example of interference led to an uprising in the Turkish army in Salonika and the seizure of power in Constantinople by the Young Turks, a group determined to defy foreign interference and build a modern Turkish nation state on the ruins of the Ottoman Empire.

The impact of the Young Turk revolution was profound. Turkish nationalism posed a new threat to the non-Turkish peoples of the Empire; the partiality of many of the Young Turks for Imperial Germany brought the Balkans into the forefront of the growing confrontation between the Great Powers. In the short term, the events of 1908 seemed to present an opportunity for surrounding states and subject peoples to take advantage of the confusion in Constantinople to grab a share of the spoils. King Ferdinand of Bulgaria severed all links with the Sultan; Russia spelled out her designs on the Straits; and the Austrians took the fateful step of annexing the provinces of Bosnia and Hercegovina.

The Greek response came, predictably, from the Cretans, who on 7 December 1908 again raised the Greek flag and proclaimed their allegiance to King George. After so many false dawns, it seemed inconceivable that on this occasion they would fail to secure their goal, but the government in Athens, paralysed by memories of 1897, refused to recognize them. In August 1909 Athens acquiesced when an international force of marines landed at Chania and forced the nationalists to haul down the Greek flags from public buildings and submit to the Turkish authorities.

This unherioc response, combined with the multiplicity of grievances that had accumulated since 1897, caused an explosion of revolutionary fervour on the streets of Athens. Radical hunger for reform and nationalist impatience came together to pose a formidable threat to the existing order. In August the Athens garrison, led by officers loyal to the Military League, staged a coup at Goudi on the outskirts of Athens. For the next few months the Military League ruled the country by manipulating a puppet government and introducing piecemeal changes aimed at satisfying the parochial grievances of the army. It was clear, even to the officers themselves, that they had neither the political experience nor the imagination to satisfy the massive public expectations that the coup had aroused. After a short period of ineffectual political fumbling they decided to call upon the Cretan politician, Eleutherios Venizelos.

Venizelos, who had made his name as a leading figure in the Cretan uprisings of 1889 and 1896, is arguably the most influential and charismatic figure of modern Greek history. Gifted with inexhaustible eloquence which, in the words of Lord Curzon, 'left not a chink for reply', he enabled Greece for the first time since independence to take the initiative in her foreign policy instead of being a helpless pawn in the hands of the Great Powers. Victorious in the elections of 1910 which followed his appointment, during the next four years he established a political consensus hitherto unknown in modern Greek history, inaugurated a foreign policy that nearly doubled the size of the country, and set in motion a massive programme of domestic reform.

With his party holding 80% of the seats in parliament, Venizelos was able to free himself from the dubious embrace of the Military League and proceed with radical reforms. Progressive income tax provided much-needed revenue and eased the unfair burden of indirect taxes on the poor. Civil servants were given security of tenure that freed them from political influence. Education was made free and compulsory at elementary level. Repressive legislation against trades unions was repealed, and the activities of 'yellow' unions controlled by employers curbed. The principles of a minimum wage for women and children and employers' liability for accidents at work were established. A start was made on provision of sick pay and pensions. The constitution of 1864 was amended to allow the expropriation of land, opening the way for land reform and the break-up of the huge, unproductive *chifliks* of northern Greece.

A landslide victory by Venizelos's new Liberal Party in the election of March 1912 confirmed the enormous support for the first Greek politician since Trikoupis to attempt to break the mould. But domestic reform ran second to foreign policy in the minds of almost all Greeks, and Venizelos had made his name as a crusader for the Great Idea in the pursuit of Cretan enosis. It was inevitable that the pursuit of the Great Idea would outweigh even the demands of domestic reform in his scheme of things.

The Balkan Wars

In 1911 war broke out between Turkey and Italy, ending after threats of Italian landings at Salonika in a treaty which 'temporarily' ceded Rhodes and the Dodecanese to Italy. It was clear that the Italians had joined the predators who were gathering to pick the bones of the Ottoman Empire and that a new competitor now stood in the way of the Great Idea. A further threat came from King Ferdinand of Bulgaria, who claimed that Bulgaria, rather than Greece or Russia, was the true heir of Byzantium. In 1912 he concluded a defence treaty with Serbia by which the two countries planned to divide Macedonia and exclude the Greeks. There was a real danger that Greece would find its national birthright usurped in a scramble to take advantage of Turkey's temporary weakness.

Fortunately for the Greeks, history had presented them at this critical moment with a statesman who was capable of profiting from the growing international anarchy. Venizelos concentrated his efforts on military reforms and preparations for a diplomatic coup. Military reform had always been hampered by factionalism within the army and the financial restraints imposed by the International Commission. The Greek navy had been reduced to accepting the gift of a cruiser, the *Averoff*, from an expatriate millionaire. Under Venizelos revenue from taxation allowed military expenditure to be constituted on a rather more formal basis. French and British officers were imported to staff military and naval missions, and training and equipment were improved. Legislation was introduced to prevent officers standing for parliament, and the wounds of the Military League coup were healed by the reinstatement of officers. Crown Prince Constantine was given a military command.

In 1912 Venizelos visited London and won a powerful ally in the chancellor of the exchequer, Lloyd George, whose uncritical support for the Greek cause would be a key element in the events of the next ten years. British hostility to growing German influence in Turkey made her much more sympathetic to Greek aspirations and served to oil the wheels of Venizelos's diplomacy, enabling the components of a Balkan League to slide rapidly into place. Aided by the Balkan correspondent of *The Times*, Venizelos concluded a 'defensive' treaty with the Bulgarians, tacitly accepted as a preliminary to a joint attack on the Turks. In the summer of 1912 he secured verbal agreements with the Serbs and Montenegrins for joint action. The scene was set for the long-awaited onslaught upon the Turks by the united forces of their former Balkan provinces.

On 8 October 1912 the Montenegrins launched an attack on Turkish positions in northern Albania. Within ten days they were joined by the Serbs, the Bulgarians and the Greeks. The Turkish position was hopeless; disrupted and demoralized by revolution and outnumbered two to one by their enemies, they were quickly forced back to the Chatalja Lines forming the last defences of Constantinople. The Greek fleet, bolstered by the *Averoff*, secured control of the seaways, but the bulk of the fighting was done by the Bulgarians who pursued their designs on Constantinople at great cost, and to the detriment of their more realistic claims in Macedonia. On 8 November a Greek army under Crown Prince Constantine made an unopposed entry into Salonika only hours before the Bulgarians arrived, establishing control over what was in fact a Jewish, rather than a Greek or Bulgarian, city. Meanwhile, Venizelos had proclaimed the union of Crete with the Greek kingdom and summoned Cretan deputies to sit in the Greek parliament. A Greek army advanced into northern Epirus, and when the Young Turks staged another coup and resumed the war, Greek soldiers were at last able to enter Janina, the city that they had for so long coveted. By May of 1913 the Young Turks were forced to sign the Treaty of London which ended the First Balkan War.

The Balkan League had been forged out of fear, suspicion and, above all, a desire not to be excluded, and none of its members were satisfied. Although Bulgaria had borne the brunt of the fighting, Greece, Serbia and Rumania were resentful of the gains she had made. Venizelos was determined that Bulgaria should not keep western Thrace and, within weeks of the ending of the First Balkan War, he signed a treaty with the

The Spirit of Greek Independence

Serbs as a prelude to forcing the Bulgarians to give up the fruits of their victory. Threatened from all sides, the Bulgarian army foolishly made a pre-emptive strike against the Serbs in Macedonia and the Second Balkan War began. The Bulgarians, attacked from all sides and exhausted after two years in which they had suffered proportionately more casualties than Britain in the First World War, were swept aside by a Greek army which drove them out of Thrace and advanced rapidly eastwards along the Aegean coast, occupying Kavalla, and stopping only when they encountered Turkish forces who had retaken Adrianople.

Achievements and Expectations

The Treaty of Bucharest, which ended the Second Balkan War, would have been regarded by most nations as a triumphant conclusion of decades of struggle. By opportunistic diplomacy and with minimum loss of life, Venizelos had thwarted the Bulgarian threat and nearly doubled the size of the Greek kingdom, which now encompassed southern Epirus, Macedonia, western Thrace, the islands of Samos and Crete, the great port of Salonika, and the important commercial centres of Janina and Kavalla. The population of the country was increased from 2.75 million to 4.75 million. The fertile northern plains of Macedonia and Thrace brought Greece a productive agricultural region, with a well-established tobacco-growing industry to provide much-needed exports. For the first time the country had sufficient territory and resources to make an escape from economic backwardness and underdevelopment. The domestic reforms initiated by Venizelos had only scratched the surface of Greece's internal problems, and logic dictated a period of consolidation and regeneration.

Such was the power of the Great Idea, however, that there was no possibility that Greeks would be content with this limited fulfilment of their national destiny. For Venizelos himself, nationalism far outweighed the impulse for domestic reform. The successes of the Balkan Wars merely whetted the national appetite to complete the task and turned the spotlight more intensely upon the millions of Greeks yet unredeemed. The creation of the new state of Albania stood in the way of Greek northward expansion; the British occupation of Cyprus, and determination to retain Turkish rule in the islands of Imbros and Tenedos excluded more Greeks from the motherland; the continuing Italian occupation of the Dodecanese raised justifiable doubts about her future intentions. Above all, the defeat of Turkey raised to a frenzy the hope that the greatest prize of all might soon be attainable.

The euphoria engendered by victory masked the fact that the region had become the cockpit of international conflict. The victory of the Serbs had been a disaster for Austrian interests, and supported by her ally, Imperial Germany, she actively sought an opportunity for revenge. The Russians, having fostered Pan-Slavism in the region, now found themselves propelled into conflict with Austria by forces they could no longer control. The losers in the Balkan wars, Turkey and Bulgaria, reacted to defeat by drawing closer to the Central Powers and raising for Greece the prospect of facing a war of revenge backed by German bayonets.

On 18 March 1913 King George was murdered by a mad assassin while visiting the newly conquered city of Salonika. His death, coming as it did on the eve of a great national crisis, was a disaster for Greece. However distasteful he found the radicalism of Venizelos, the king had seen the need for change and was prepared to back a man who he realized was an outstanding statesman. The new king, Constantine I, was a far more abrasive and authoritarian character. His very name proclaimed for Greeks the imminent fulfilment of old prophecies. Just over a year later, in July 1914, the First World War broke out.

CHAPTER FIFTEEN

From Triumph to Catastrophe
1914–1922

The Dilemma of Neutrality

Greece was not a part of the pre-war alliance systems and could have remained honourably neutral during the First World War, but it soon became clear that Venizelos was determined to bring her into the war on the side of the Triple Entente of Britain, France and Russia. He believed that British seapower would eventually win the day, and that commitment to the Entente would establish overwhelming moral credit with the victors when it came to a peace settlement. He would then be able to secure the national goals of Greece from a position of strength.

On 18 August 1914 Venizelos offered to give the British 'all the military and naval forces of Greece', but Sir Edward Grey, the British foreign secretary, not wishing to provoke the Turks, refused his offer. Turkey's entry into the war on the German side in November caused the British to reassess their attitude, but their courtship of Greece was still held back by the belief that it could push Bulgaria onto the German side. British annexation of Cyprus showed Venizelos the dangers of remaining neutral, and he even responded favourably to British suggestions that Greece might give up the recently conquered towns of Kavalla, Serres and Drama in order to buy Bulgarian neutrality and free the way for Greek entry into the war on the side of the Entente. The Entente had begun to dangle before Venizelos a prize so rich that it would make the loss of recently won territories in Macedonia relatively painless: in January 1915 he received from the British a vague but exciting promise of 'important concessions on the coast of Asia Minor'. What could this mean but the liberation of the Ottoman Greeks?

This vague and irresponsible promise to Greece should be seen in the context of the war for survival that was now being waged in Europe. Realization that there would be no quick end to the war had pushed the Powers into making reckless promises that they would be unable to make good even if they won the war. In April 1915 the Entente made a secret treaty with Italy promising her territory in Asia Minor in return for joining the war; later in the same year, in an attempt to keep the tottering Russian Empire in the war, they promised it a dominant role in Constantinople and the Straits. These promises, embarrassingly revealed by the Bolsheviks in 1917, were much more specific than the vague hints given to the Greeks, and if they were implemented they would deny Greece any possibility of redeeming the Greek population of Asia Minor.

Venizelos was aware of the Entente's promises to Italy, but he retained a naïve conviction that the moral right of Greece's legacy in Asia Minor would prevail over Italian opportunism or Allied *realpolitik*. But it was becoming clear that the king and his advisers were deeply opposed to his pro-Entente policies, and their differences soon provoked a furious debate over fundamental constitutional questions about the role of the king and his elected ministers. This was the origin of the 'National Schism', a division so profound that it would poison Greek politics for the next twenty years and lead to a major national catastrophe.

The 'National Schism'

The King and many of his advisers were profoundly shocked by Venizelos's willingness to concede Greek territory for mere promises of future reward at the whim of foreign powers. They believed that the prime minister was putting the great gains of the Balkan Wars at risk by giving Turkey and Bulgaria a chance to wage a war of revenge in alliance with the military might of the German Empire, in return for ill-defined gains in Asia Minor that would strain Greece's meagre resources to breaking point.

Events in Athens now moved towards a destructive crisis which tore apart the fabric of the state. The acting chief of staff of the army, Colonel Metaxas, resigned rather than accept the prime minister's

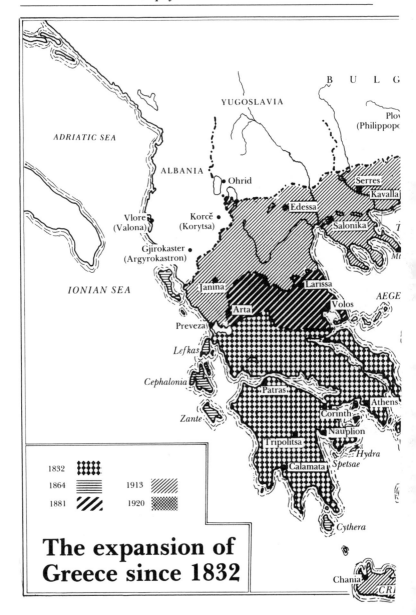

The expansion of
Greece since 1832

I   A

Marica

BLACK SEA

● Edirne
(Adrianople)

1920–1922

Istanbul
(Constantinople)

Alexandroupolis
(Dedeagatch)

Sea of Marmara

● Izmit
(Nicomedia)

● Iznik
· (Nicaea)

Gallipoli

ros

Tenedos

nos

EA

● Bursa

T U R K E Y

● Aivalik

Mytlini

1920–1922

ra
Chios

● Izmir
(Smyrna)

● Aydin

ros

Samos

Naxos

Cos

DUODECANESE
ISLANDS
to Italy 1912;
to Greece 1947

Rhodes

Scarpanto

eraklion

```
0        50        100    miles  150
|——|——|——|——|——|——|——|
0    50   100   150   kms
```

orders; the king defied public opinion by choosing to support Metaxas rather than Venizelos, who had been recently re-elected with a large majority. While enraged crowds surged through the streets demanding war, Venizelos resigned. The king then ignored the tradition established by Trikoupis in 1875 and appointed a prime minister, Gounaris, who had no majority in parliament. Throughout the spring of 1915 the king and his advisers continued to defy public opinion and resisted all pressure to join the war. Britain and France, frustrated at Constantine's obduracy, began to woo Bulgaria with promises of territory, raising once again the spectre of a 'Big Bulgaria' on Greece's northern borders.

The June 1915 elections again showed that the majority of Greeks supported Venizelos, and he redoubled his efforts to get Greece into the war. He agreed to help the shattered Serbian army retreating southwards through Albania, and accepted the Entente's plan to land troops at Salonika. The British and French wasted no time: claiming their rights under the Treaty of Protection of 1833, they began to land troops in Salonika on 5 October, the day after Bulgaria declared war. Venizelos obtained a clear mandate in parliament to join the war and for a short time it seemed as if his policies, for good or ill, had triumphed over the king's caution and pro-German inclinations. This was an illusion: the day after the elected representatives of the Greek people had given their verdict King George ordered Venizelos to resign.

Whatever the merits of the king's assessment of Greece's real interests, he had chosen to act in defiance of the popular will and had incurred the lasting enmity of the British and French governments, which became determined to unseat him. His position became increasingly untenable as the defiant Venizelists began to operate as a virtual alternative government and the Entente used its overwhelming military strength to override Greek sovereignty. They occupied and used any portion of Greek territory which suited their interests. Bases were arbitrarily set up in Suda Bay on Crete, on Lesbos, and at Mudros on the island of Lemnos, where a large facility was established by the British navy in defiance of the king's wishes. Allied forces occupied Corfu and built extensive reception facilities for the Serbian army that was evacuated there by the allied fleets. In defiance of the Greek army, the allied armies in Salonika requisitioned Karabouzou Fort, controlling the harbour, and disrupted the communications network of Greek Macedonia by blowing up bridges that might have assisted a Bulgarian offensive. All this might have been more acceptable if the allied force at Salonika had shown a capacity to protect Greek soil, but the 'Gardeners of Salonika' were badly led, poorly equipped and, until the last weeks of the war, completely lacking in any spirit of aggression. Their presence seemed more of a provocation than a shield.

Meanwhile Greece was becoming ever more deeply divided. After Venizelos boycotted elections on the grounds that the country had already twice given its verdict, his supporters were removed from all positions of responsibility in the civil service and the army and a violent persecution began. The high-handed attitude of the Entente pushed many Greek politicians and officers into collusion with the Central Powers. The Serbian army, now recovering in Corfu, was forbidden to cross overland to link up with allied forces in Salonika. By the spring of 1916 it was apparent that the war issue had become an arena for bitter internal rivalries. At the moment of greatest crisis and opportunity, the Great Idea had become yet another issue that divided Greeks. For many Royalist officers the feud with their Venizelist opponents became more significant than national defence. Rupel Fort, controlling the natural invasion route through the Struma valley, was abandoned to German and Bulgarian forces, and Kavalla to the Germans by an anti-Venizelist officer in September 1916. This seems to have been the last straw for the allies and for Venizelos himself. Taken home to Crete by a French warship, he proclaimed open revolution against the king, and in October established an alternative government in Salonika. Greece was now divided into two separate states along political and geographical lines. The king retained support for his neutralist stance in the 'Pre-1913 Kingdom', while 'New Greece' leaned towards the reformist and interventionist government of Venizelos in Salonika.

In retrospect it is easy to dismiss the attitude of the king as short-sighted and reactionary, but from the perspective of late 1916 it was far from certain that the interests of Greece would best be served by throwing in its lot with the Entente. Stalemate on the Western Front, huge losses at sea, and the imminent collapse of Rumania, Russia, and even Italy, made the prospect of taking on the Central Powers, supported only by the inadequate allied army vegetating at Salonika, a far from attractive one. But by the end of 1916 the Entente decided to force the king's hand.

In November the French issued a series of humiliating demands: 'enemy agents' were to be expelled; Greek naval vessels were to be disarmed; control of the main rail line to the north was to be surrendered; artillery batteries were to be handed over to the allies. Not surprisingly, the king regarded these demands as insulting and unacceptable; they evoked a strong sense of national pride and anger when they became known. British and French troops, landed at Piraeus to enforce the diktat, were forced back to their ships with heavy casualties, causing the French to bombard the royal palace from their ships anchored off Piraeus. The rebel regime of Venizelos in Salonika was recognized by the allies, and a blockade of southern Greece and the Peloponnese was mounted to force Royalist Greece to capitulate. Terrible hardship was inflicted on the civilian population but the Entente was determined to use its overwhelming naval power to force the king to capitulate. After three months of blockade he was faced with the alternatives of surrender or abdication.

Greece Enters the War

On 16 January 1917 the allied ultimatum was accepted and the blockade lifted. Royalist units were ordered to withdraw from Athens to the Peloponnese, and under pressure from the allies Constantine announced that he was willing to leave Greece and accept the succession of his second son, Alexander (his eldest son, George, was not acceptable to the allies). In June Venizelos came back as prime minister and the 'Lazarus Parliament', originally elected in June 1915, was reinstated. Some constructive reforms, including distribution of land to the peasants, were introduced, but in a mirror image of the purge of Venizelists in 1915, all supporters of the previous regime were hounded out of office. Many leading figures thought to be pro-German were sent into exile in Corsica. Ominous precedents were being set for the future of Greek politics.

After generating such division and bitterness by forcing Greece into

Venizelos

the war, the allies seemed oddly reluctant to make use of them. In the spring of 1917 Greek troops took part in an offensive which achieved little at the cost of many casualties, but it was not until May 1918 that they were again seriously involved, in a successful offensive against the Bulgarians which held out some prospect of salvaging some military glory and national honour from the sorry events of the previous few years. Hopes of joining a triumphant allied advance upon Constantinople seemed remote, however, and only the arrival of the dynamic French general, Franchet D'Esperey, in June raised the prospect for Greek troops of serious fighting.

On 14 September the long-awaited offensive was launched against the Bulgarian army. British and Greek troops, many of them Cretans, advanced up the Vardar valley and fought an engagement with the Bulgarians near Lake Doiran, near to the point where the road linking Belgrade and Salonika crosses the Greek–Yugoslav border. After heavy fighting, during which the allies made little progress against strong Bulgarian defences, the Bulgarians abandoned their positions and retreated in disorder.

In October the Allied High Command ordered Greek and British troops under General Milne to advance eastwards against the Turks. The Turkish army was exhausted and prostrate; Greece's historic rivals, Bulgaria and Russia, were eliminated by defeat and revolution; the prospect of Greek soldiers entering Constantinople for the first time since 1453 seemed to be a real possibility. Unfortunately for Greek hopes, Milne's force was ordered to halt at the border town of Alexandroupolis when news arrived that the Turks had signed an armistice aboard the British battleship *Agamemnon*, anchored off Port Mudros. For Greece the war was over almost as soon as it had begun; the real battles would be fought around the conference tables rather than on the plains of Thessaly or in a glorious assault upon the Chatalja Lines before Constantinople.

The Triumph of Venizelos

Venizelos's faith that Britain and France would be the ultimate victors had been triumphantly vindicated. In terms of casualties Greece had suffered less than any of the belligerents, but the political cost of his stand could only be justified if he succeeded in winning the extravagant prizes that he had promised the nation. He had raised expectations to such a pitch that nothing less than complete fulfilment of the Great Idea would compensate the losers in the National Schism for the humiliations that they had suffered. The end of the war was only the beginning of the real battle for Venizelos.

As soon as hostilities had ceased, he began a tour of European capitals to lay the groundwork for the Paris Peace Conference, due to meet in January of 1919. With all his eloquence, charm and persuasiveness, as well as a mass of dubious statistics about the balance and distribution of the Greek and Turkish populations in Asia Minor, he expounded the Greek case at endless meetings with key politicians and journalists. By the time the Conference convened he had good reason to hope that at last the ambitious goals of the Great Idea would quickly be achieved. Despite

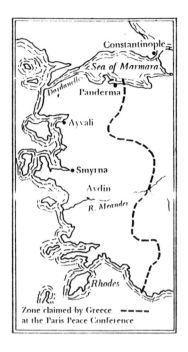

Zone claimed by Greece — — —
at the Paris Peace Conference

being the representative of a minor power, he managed to establish himself as one of the major figures at the Conference. The young British diplomat Harold Nicolson noted his 'strange mixture of charm, brigandage, *welt-politik*, patriotism, courage, literature . . .', and made the surprising claim that this 'large muscular smiling man, with his eyes glinting through spectacles,' stood with Lenin as 'the only two great men of Europe'. Lloyd George, who had already been captivated by him in 1912, was a consistent supporter of Greece throughout the Conference. Woodrow Wilson, the American president, had made it clear that the achievement of self-determination for all peoples was a primary goal of American foreign policy. Above all, there lay at the centre of Venizelos's diplomacy the belief that the Ottoman Empire was now so helpless that she was incapable of resisting the claims of the victors.

At the beginning of February 1919 Venizelos appeared before the Council of Ten to present his initial demands. He claimed Greek

Greek battleship patrolling the Bosporus

sovereignty over northern Epirus, Bulgarian and Turkish Thrace, the Turkish islands of the Aegean, and the Dodecanese Islands that had been occupied by the Italians since 1912. By far the most radical Greek claims related to Asia Minor, where he wanted Greece to have virtually the whole coast of western Turkey, stretching inland along a line joining Panderma on the Sea of Marmara and the Island of Kastellorizo about 116 km east of Rhodes. He proposed that the large Greek population of Pontus bordering the Black Sea should be incorporated in a new Armenian state, which he hoped would become an American protectorate. He accepted that the city of Constantinople and the Straits would be internationalized, but there is little doubt that he had high hopes that eventually they would fall into Greek hands as the centrepiece of a new Hellenic Empire.

During the next few months it was the attitude of Italy that provided the greatest danger to Greek hopes and the best opportunity for Venizelos to practise his diplomatic skills. The Italians had made sacrifices in the war far outstripping those of Greece, on the understanding that they would be rewarded. The promises made to them by the allies in April 1915 were very specific, and directly conflicted with the vague offers made to Greece at the same time. The lesson for Venizelos should have been clear: the victors, having made rash promises in wartime, were quite incapable of fulfilling them at the Conference. In

April 1919 the Italian representatives walked out and prepared to act unilaterally to achieve their goals in Asia Minor. Soon news began to arrive that Italy had sent warships to Smyrna and was preparing to occupy by armed force the region that Greece was claiming for herself.

It was now imperative that Greece should act swiftly to prevent a *fait accompli*. By skilful manipulation of the Italian threat, Venizelos persuaded the Conference to let him land Greek troops in Smyrna to protect the Greek population and to forestall any unilateral action by Italy. It was on this casual basis that the fateful Greek expedition to Asia Minor began. On 15 May 1919, before any agreements had been concluded defining their status or zone of occupation, Greek troops began disembarking on the quayside of Smyrna amidst scenes of hysterical enthusiasm. This was a momentous step for Greece; thereafter the destiny of the large Greek population of Asia Minor would lie not in conference resolutions and international action, but in the capacity of the Greek army to defend them.

With the establishment of what amounted to a Greek government in Smyrna, events seemed to be moving relentlessly towards the conclusion of Venizelos's grand strategy. After Italian claims had been successfully thwarted by a Greek army acting in the name of the victors, the Turks, under enormous international pressure, were forced to sign a treaty at Sèvres on 10 August 1920 which conceded to the Greeks almost everything they had been striving for since independence. Greece was to receive Smyrna and a large surrounding area in Asia Minor for five years (followed by a plebiscite that would certainly make the occupation permanent); the northern coast of the Sea of Marmara and the Gallipoli peninsula, with an international commission to administer the Straits; the whole of Bulgarian and Turkish Thrace, right up to the Chatalja Lines; the Aegean Islands, including Imbros and Tenedos, which even Venizelos had not hoped to secure; and the Dodecanese, subject to a separate agreement with the Italians.

In the summer of 1920 it must have seemed to the Greeks that their centuries-old dream of national regeneration was at long last about to reach a triumphant conclusion. But within a matter of months, a nightmare began in Asia Minor that would deal Greek aspirations a blow almost as crippling as the disaster of 1453.

Intimations of Disaster

The confidence with which Venizelos expounded the Greek cause impressed all who listened to him, but even sympathetic observers were beginning to express serious doubts about the practicality of his schemes. In retrospect, it appears that the apparently inexorable logic of his arguments rested upon foundations of sand.

During the debate over Greece's entry into the war, the acting chief of staff, Colonel Metaxas, had presented a memorandum to Venizelos setting out the extreme difficulties that a Greek occupation of territory in Asia Minor would entail. His arguments centred upon the great problem of establishing a viable eastern frontier for the new Greek state. Any defensible frontier would push the Greek zone of occupation deep into areas where the population was overwhelmingly Muslim. Greece, Metaxas argued, a small, poor and undeveloped state, would find herself engaged in an endless struggle to maintain her position, drawn ever deeper into the hostile Asian hinterland. The boundaries proposed were not defensible; even Greek propaganda figures showed that Greeks would be in a minority even within the 'Greek' zone, and Venizelos persisted in deluding himself that the Turkish population, after centuries of enmity and recent humiliations, would accept and even welcome Greek rule.

The greatest weakness of Venizelos's position, however, was a massive overestimation of the willingness and capability of the Great Powers to support the Great Idea. Like most Greeks fed on a diet of nationalist propaganda, it was difficult for him to accept that, despite the fund of goodwill for Greek culture, his was a small country of peripheral importance in the scheme of international politics. He remained convinced that his special relationship with Lloyd George together with British seapower would carry the day. But Lloyd George's philhellenism was based upon emotion rather than upon any real understanding of the realities in Asia Minor; Harold Nicolson tells how he mistook a physical map of the area for one which showed population distribution, believing 'that the green means Greeks instead of valleys, and the brown means Turks instead of mountains'. President Wilson's commitment to the rights of small nations was only equalled by his complete naïvety about international affairs and his inability to persuade the American people to play a world role. The French prime minister, Georges Clemenceau, sympathized with Greek goals, but only if they fitted in with France's own considerable plans in the Near East.

Catastrophe

Within hours of the Greek landings at Smyrna many of Metaxas's premonitions began to be fulfilled. Thirty unarmed Turkish prisoners were massacred when a shot was fired at the Greek forces parading triumphantly through the town; Greek civilians plundered and looted Turkish houses, attacked and humiliated prisoners, and released pent-up religious and racial hatreds upon Turks living in the surrounding countryside. The determination of the Greek population to drive Muslims out made a nonsense of Venizelos's sanguine belief that they would welcome Greek 'liberation'. No administrative machinery or trained personnel existed. Attempts to deal fairly with the Muslim population stirred up resentment amongst the Greeks, while the Turks were outraged by the excesses of Greek officials. Greek rule was under constant scrutiny from journalists and representatives of the Great powers, whose often hostile reports eroded European goodwill.

As Metaxas had predicted, the Greek army was forced to push deeper and deeper into Asia Minor to consolidate its position, resulting in atrocities on both sides that further embittered communal relations. Above all, the arrival of a Greek army in Asia Minor had stimulated the development of a dynamic Turkish national movement. Even as the Greeks were disembarking at Smyrna, a young Turkish officer was rejecting the Sultan's subservience to foreign demands and calling for a national regeneration based upon a modern Turkish nation state. Unfortunately for the Greeks, this officer proved to be one of the most energetic, able and determined statesmen of the century, Mustafa Kemal, better known as Kemal Atatürk. The new spirit of Turkish nationalism that he unleashed was all the more devastating to the plans of Venizelos because it was completely unexpected.

In September 1919 Kemal had told the Powers that he regarded the Sultan's regime as an illegal tyranny which had no right to speak for the

Turkish people. It was becoming clear that unless his national movement could be crushed, the treaties and agreements that were being laboriously negotiated with the Sultan would be useless scraps of paper. In January 1920 the new Turkish parliament confirmed a national pact which pledged rejection of all foreign impositions and proclaimed a new Turkish national state. Allied attempts to coerce the nationalists resulted in the establishment of an alternative government at Ankara, and the Sultan's acceptance of the crippling terms of the Treaty of Sèvres destroyed any lingering authority his regime retained. Kemal declared that he had no intention of allowing the treaty to be enforced.

For the Greeks these developments quickly dispersed the euphoria that followed the landings at Smyrna and the signing of the treaty. With the Ottoman Empire replaced by an infinitely more dynamic and hostile force, how was it to be enforced? Western governments now began to turn their backs on Greece and, in the case of France and Italy, to negotiate secretly with the Turkish nationalists. The Greek army in Asia Minor, striving to sustain what now seemed like a Greek colony on a hostile continent, was dangerously isolated and vulnerable. At the beginning of 1920 the nationalists defeated the French occupying forces in Cilicia and captured large quantities of military supplies; support for them was growing daily. Venizelos still placed his hopes in Britain and tried to persuade Lloyd George to mount a joint expedition to destroy the nationalists and enforce the treaty. The offer was refused; it seemed that even the Turkophobe Lloyd George was beginning to question the wisdom of his previous ill-considered policies.

In the midst of this mounting national crisis for Greece, there came two completely unexpected domestic shocks: the death, in bizarre circumstances, of King Alexander, and the completely unexpected defeat of Venizelos in the elections of November 1920. Dizzy with success over the signing of the Sèvres Treaty, the prime minister decided to capitalize on what he believed would be a landslide of popular enthusiasm. His confidence was partly based upon his success in converting the young king from a potential enemy into a puppet: a measure of Venizelos's power was his insistence that the king conceal his marriage to the commoner, Aspasia Manas, and even to accept her exile in Paris until Venizelos judged the announcement to be politically opportune. In the event, Alexander was never able to enjoy the company of his new bride. On 30 September 1920, walking in the grounds of the summer palace as Tatoi, he rescued a pet monkey from the jaws of his dog, Fritz, only to receive a bite from the monkey's ungrateful mate which proved fatal. He died of blood poisoning on 25 October.

The King's death was a disaster for Greece and for Venizelos. The constitutional wounds that had been slowly healing since the fall of Constantine were at once reopened. Anti-Venizelists began to press for the return of the exiled Constantine, and the election campaign was transformed into a contest over the future of the monarchy. The results, announced on 14 November, showed that Venizelos had been clearly defeated. Like Churchill in 1945, he overestimated the appeal of foreign success and undervalued the material cost of these adventures to ordinary people. High taxes, shortages, the seemingly endless mobilization – all played a part in disenchanting many voters. The long supremacy of the Venizelists had created an army of discontented officials, army officers and functionaries whose only way to regain their jobs and influence was by overthrowing the existing order.

To the new regime, united only by a desire to share in the spoils of office, winning the war in Asia Minor was less important than revenge. All those associated with Venizelos, whether in local government, the judiciary, the civil service or education, were ruthlesly purged and replaced. Venizelos himself left in disgust for exile in Nice, and throughout Greece there were violent clashes between his supporters and the Royalists. Officers who had been removed or demoted by the Venizelists were reinstated, causing confusion, bitterness and conspiracy in the ranks of the hard-pressed armies in Asia Minor. Against allied wishes a referendum was organized to settle the question of Constantine's return. After a heavy vote in his favour, he returned to Greece in December 1920.

The most damaging impact of the fall of Venizelos lay in its international implications. The return of Constantine, raising memories of the shooting of French marines in 1916, destroyed any lingering scruples the French may have felt in leaving the Greeks to their fate. In Britain the General Staff advocated a complete readjustment of the country's position in the Near East. Winston Churchill, obsessed by the

'Bolshevik threat', argued that a revitalized Turkey would be a far more effective barrier to Communism than a Greece ruled by the 'traitor' Constantine. Lloyd George alone still contended that the best guarantee of Britain's interests was the establishment of a Greek Ionian empire. The international tide was now running strongly in favour of a sell-out of Greece's interests and a complete revision of the Treaty of Sèvres.

With foreign support ebbing away, the new regime in Athens decided to try to break out of the trap that was closing around it by means of a great military offensive against the Turkish nationalist capital, Ankara. Launched on 23 March 1921, it turned out a costly and crippling disaster that destroyed any possibility of Greek survival in Asia. In two great battles at Inonu, guarding the road to Ankara, an army of 200,000 Greeks, despite great bravery and persistence, failed to break through the Turkish positions and was forced to retreat with 20,000 casualties to the positions it had held at the beginning of the offensive. It had by no means been disgraced and it remained an effective fighting force, but the essential hopelessness of its situation had been exposed.

Few Greeks now believed that their position in Asia Minor was sustainable, but could they extricate themselves from the maze of difficulties that now enclosed them? Faced with the intractable problem of holding down a hostile population the army of occupation was forced to adopt harsh measures of repression. 'There is a systematic plan of destruction of Turkish villages and the extinction of the Muslim population,' reported an Inter-Allied Commission of Enquiry. A withdrawal of the Greek army would leave one and a half million Greek inhabitants exposed to the inevitable Turkish retribution. The delicate balance between religious groups that had grown up over the previous four centuries of ramshackle but tolerant Ottoman rule had been blown to pieces by three years of twentieth-century nationalism.

The Greek government cast wildly around to find means of escape from the impending catastrophe. Attempts to ease the crushing financial burden of the campaign foundered when the British government refused to underwrite a loan. At the beginning of 1922 the Greeks were even prepared to accept the restoration of Turkish sovereignty in Smyrna in return for guarantees for the local population, but the Turks were now so confident that they refused to accept any conditions. In July, hoping to undermine the relentless Turkish build-up against their extended front in Anatolia, Greece massed its forces in Eastern Thrace for an assault upon Constantinople itself, but the Powers forced them to abandon the one strategy that might have forced the Turks to negotiate. 'We are defending the capital of one of the parties against the other,' Lloyd George complained to the Commons on 4 August. '... We are not allowing the Greeks to wage the war with their full strength.'

Such sentiments from their only international friend were of little comfort to the Greek army when, after a secret build-up behind the lines, Mustafa Kemal launched fourteen divisions against the Afyon Karahisar salient on 26 August. Within hours the Greek armies were in desperate retreat to the coast. While dozens of ships thronged the harbour at Smyrna, a terrible massacre ensued amongst its smoking ruins. It marked the death and incineration not only of the unfortunate inhabitants of the city, but of thousands of years of Greek occupation of Asia Minor and of the dream that had excited the Greek nation since independence.

CHAPTER SIXTEEN

The Road to Dictatorship and Defeat
1922–1941

The End of the Great Idea

The territorial settlement that Greece was forced to accept under the Treaty of Lausanne (July 1923) was far less onerous than might have been expected following her comprehensive defeat in Asia Minor. Turkey recovered eastern Thrace and the islands of Imbros and Tenedos; northern Epirus returned to Albania; the Italians retained Rhodes and the Dodecanese, and in August took advantage of Greek prostration to seize Corfu; the British continued to control Cyprus. Greece had been forced to give up the possibly unrealistic gains obtained at Sèvres, but she kept all the territory won in the Balkan Wars plus western Thrace.

Perhaps more important that the redrawing of the map were the huge population exchanges resulting from agreements with Turkey and Bulgaria. In the next few months nearly 400,000 Turks and over a million Greeks were forced to give up their homes and set off for an uncertain future in a country that most of them had never seen; only the 100,000 Greek inhabitants of Constantinople were exempt from deportation. The decision to make religion rather than language the criterion of nationality caused particular hardship. Thousands of Cretan Greeks, many of them substantial landowners, who had converted to Islam centuries before but who regarded themselves as Greek, were forced to give up everything for a life of poverty in Asia Minor. Many Orthodox Christians from Asia Minor who spoke Turkish found themselves consigned to the squalid shanty towns, like Nea Smyrna, that sprang up on the outskirts of Athens and Salonika, surrounded by an often resentful local population that was alien in all but religion.

In the longer term, despite the tragic human consequences, certain benefits accrued from this draconian solution. The arrival of the Ottoman Greeks, steadily reinforced by refugees from Istanbul, brought a much-needed infusion of skills. Many Greeks who have made their mark in the twentieth century, like Aristotle Onassis and Elia Kazan, were of refugee origin. There was an infusion of talent into the professions, the academic and scientific world, and into business. Land previously farmed by the Turkish population was made available for Greek resettlement, and Anatolian immigrants built up the tobacco industry that was essential to the Greek balance of trade. With the removal of Turkish and Bulgarian minorities, Greece became for the first time an ethnically heterogeneous state with few of the problems of national minorities that plagued her northern neighbours. The 'coming home' of the Anatolian Greeks removed the festering problem of a hostage Greek population in Asia Minor constantly demanding attention from Greece, and killed for ever the irredentist ambitions that had for so long absorbed her meagre resources.

The Political Aftermath

The events of 1923 were far more destablizing than mere military defeat. The economic and political balance of forces that had existed was permanently altered: for 150 years Greeks had focused obsessively on a goal that had been suddenly and irrevocably snatched away at the very moment when it seemed within reach. A purely military defeat would have focused the national will upon preparations for a war of revenge, but the removal of the Greek population from Asia Minor had destroyed the Great Idea with a crushing finality. For the next twenty years Greek politics were poisoned by bitterness, recrimination, and an endless debate over responsibility for the débâcle which nullified any attempt to bring about unity and reconciliation. During a period when the country, with virtually no industry and a chronic shortage of good agricultural land, was forced to absorb an additional population equivalent to a quarter of its pre-war total, politics reverted to a sterile pursuit of advantage by individuals and privileged interest groups.

The pattern for the future was set even as the ships carried the exhausted Greek army homeward from Asia Minor in September 1922. A revolutionary committee was set up by two colonels, Nicholas Plastiras and Stylianos Gonatas, representing officers who were determined to seek retribution for the mismanagement that had led to defeat. King Constantine was forced to abdicate and leave the country (he died the following year), and his eldest son, who succeeded as George II, had to agree to the court-martial of eight ministers and generals (including the prime minister, Gounaris) who were made scapegoats for the national humiliation. Amidst a hysterical atmosphere of recrimination six of them were executed by firing squad on 28 November 1923, thus adding further bitterness to the feud between the monarchists and their enemies, and ensuring that the political divisions of the Great Schism would continue long after their original cause had been eliminated.

The revolutionary government of Plastiras and Gonatas set ominous precedents for military involvement in politics and the seizure of power by armed force. Having revenged itself upon the hapless scapegoats and been forced to accept the unpalatable Lausanne peace settlement, the revolutionaries had few solutions to the huge social and economic problems of the country other than to bring an end to the monarchy. In April 1924, in an atmosphere of militarist intimidation, Greece voted for the establishment of a republic. The precedent had been set for constant military interference in politics and the establishment within the officer corps of a 'state within a state' that defied governments of which it disapproved and intervened in domestic politics whenever its interests were threatened.

Hopes that a republic would bring political stability were quickly dashed. Venizelos, who was briefly prime minister again in January 1924, withdrew from politics in disgust. Within eighteen months of the establishment of the republic there had been six changes of administration, a mutiny in the navy, and numerous ill-organized military coups. In June 1925 General Theodore Pangalos began a period of military rule, the main achievement of which was legislation defining the length of women's skirts. In August 1926 he was overthrown by Colonel Kondylis, whose chief attribute seems to have been the tailoring of his political principles to any shape required to secure power for himself. After elections in November 1926, held for the first time under proportional representation, the brief promise of a 'Government of National Reconciliation' was swiftly undermined by the refusal of interest groups to make any concessions in the national interest.

THE RETURN OF VENIZELOS

It was at this juncture that Venizelos decided to return and use his political skills in an attempt to halt the slide towards chaos. In the four years between 1928 and 1932 he strove to rekindle the fires of national unity that his reforming administration of 1911 and his apparent international triumph at Sèvres had briefly lit. Building upon the foundation of his previous land reforms, he introduced a series of measures designed to raise agricultural production: loans were raised for ambitious drainage projects which brought much-needed new land into cultivation; an agrarian bank was set up to provide peasants with capital for improvements; new strains of cereals were introduced to boost crop yields. He tried to stimulate industry by erecting protective tariffs, and reorganized the educational system to promote the growth of much-needed practical skills.

In 1929 Venizelos's efforts were thwarted by the beginning of the Great Depression, which had a particularly crippling effect upon the Greek economy, dependent as it was upon the export of a few semi-luxury crops. Unemployment in the United States cut deeply into the remittances of Greek immigrants, whose numbers had already been reduced by severe immigration curbs. As the economy ground to a halt payments of interest on foreign loans absorbed two-thirds of state expenditure, and led to the humiliation of a default on debt repayments reminiscent of 1893. Falling living standards had an appalling effect on the poor, who at the best of times lived only a few degrees above starvation.

The world depression highlighted not only the inadequacies of the Greek economy, social structure and political system, but also the limitations of Venizelos's political ideas and methods. No one had done more to create the fragmented peasant agriculture in which 90% of farms were less than twelve and a half acres, making the introduction of modern farming methods impossible. His protectionism had encouraged the growth of small, inefficient businesses and helped to create a situation where only 15% of the population was employed in industry. His previous neglect of the national economy in favour of expensive foreign adventures had diverted resources needed to escape from underdevelopment, and one suspects that his ideal of a Greece of small proprietors and family businesses was designed to create a loyal political following rather than to encourage a modern agricultural and industrial economy. His commitment to the republic, and indeed to democratic freedom if it threatened his authority, must also be doubted. His treatment of opposition further embittered and polarized political life; the intense pressure he put upon Constantine Tsaldaris, leader of the Populist (Monarchist) Party, to compromise himself by accepting the republican constitution, forced the Populists into 'internal emigration' and destroyed any hope of a settled two-party system. The persistence of Venizelist agents in continuing the traditional methods of patronage and monopoly of public offices did nothing to reconcile the warring factions, while his rehabilitation of figures from the past who were hateful to the monarchists drove them deeper into extra-parliamentary conspiracy.

The treatment meted out by Venizelos to the small but growing Greek Communist Party (KKE) was to have a significant effect upon future Greek history. The KKE was founded in 1918 and built up its organization in the 1920s based almost entirely upon refugees from Asia Minor, like the Party Secretary, Nikos Zakhariadis. Inhibited by the absence of an industrial proletariat of any size, and by an obsession with the establishment of a separate Macedonian state that offended nationalist susceptibilities, the KKE began to gain adherents in the economic crisis following the slump, but it remained very small. None the less, in 1929 Venizelos introduced the notorious 'Idonym Law' against 'attempts to undermine the social order'. It was aimed, not at the military adventurers who constantly threatened the stability of the state, but at the tiny Communist Party. It began a process whereby Communists and Socialists were hounded out of political life, driven underground, and invested with a cloak of martyrdom.

The Drift to Dictatorship

In April 1932 the economic crisis and the suspension of interest on international loans began a four-year crisis which culminated in the collapse of democracy and the dictatorship of John Metaxas. After attempts to form a government of national unity had again failed, politics quickly declined into a power struggle between Venizelos and the Monarchists. On 5 March 1933, having fought and lost an election on the issue of 'the Republic in danger', Venizelos acquiesced when his supporter General Plastiras staged an abortive coup to overturn the verdict of the people. This enraged the extreme Monarchists and increased their determination to crush the Venizelists and overthrow the Republic. Venizelos miraculously emerged unscathed from his bullet-riddled car when extremists tried to kill him on the Athens–Kifissia road, but moves by Monarchists to tamper with constituency bound-aries, reintroduce proportional representation and sack Republican officers, led him to adopt violent tactics himself. On 1 March 1935 he led a revolt against the government which ended in defeat and his flight to Rhodes. In March 1936 he died in exile in Paris. His attempts to achieve national unity had foundered upon his own ambivalence towards democracy when it worked against his interests, and the intractable problems of a country which was now rapidly moving towards dictatorship. The failure of the coup led to a wholesale purge of Venizelists from the army, the judiciary and the civil service, and to numerous trials and executions. The extreme Monarchists were again in the ascendant. In October a group of officers led by General Papagos used physical force to intimidate the prime minister, Tsaldaris, and after his resignation a rigged referendum restored the monarchy. On his return, George II faced a parliamentary crisis in which fifteen Communist deputies held the balance between an almost equal number of Monarchists and Republicans. An ultimatum from Papagos pro-claimed that the army would not accept Communist participation in government, and the king made the fateful decision to appoint General Metaxas as commander-in-chief to bring the army to heel.

With the authoritarian Metaxas only a step away from power, the politicians were still incapable or unwilling to act to preserve democracy. On 13 April 1936 the king appointed Metaxas prime minister, and parliament tamely voted 241 to 16 for its own dissolution. It would not meet again until after the Second World War.

The only resistance to the rising tide of dictatorship came from the Communists who, in May 1936, organized a series of strikes culminating in a great demonstration led by tobacco workers in Salonika. This gave Metaxas the opportunity to persuade the king, who was terrified of communism and social disorder, to approve the suspension of certain articles of the constitution, to introduce press censorship, and to extend the dissolution of parliament indefinitely. Thus, on 4 August 1936, began the personal regime of John Metaxas, a ruler without a party and with virtually no popular following, whose only claim to legitimatcy was the support of the king.

Metaxas

The chief characteristic of Metaxas' regime was the contrast between its grandiose pretensions and its negligible achievements. Although racialism, antisemitism and aggressive foreign policies played no part in his programme, he adopted the fashionable trappings of fascism. Styling himself 'First Peasant', 'First Worker' and 'Leader', he sought to sweep away the failed parliamentary democracy that had proved irrelevant to the country's needs, and to eradicate communism, which he saw as the greatest threat to its values. He aimed at nothing less than the creation of a 'Third Greek Civilization', incorporating all that was best in the Ancient and Byzantine past. To attain their destiny, Greeks must become more disciplined, purposeful and 'Germanic'. A central role in this undertaking would be played by the Youth Movement (EON) which, through a rigorous programme of nationalist propaganda, route marches and songs around the campfire, would reconstruct the national psyche. Rival organizations like the Boy Scouts were banned, and the young were protected from such revolutionary propaganda as Perikles' funeral oration, which was purged from the textbooks.

Far more serious than Metaxas' fantasies of a Greek cultural revolution were the concrete measures he took to curb civil rights. Strikes were banned, compulsory arbitration was imposed on workers, which in practice meant the enforcement of employers' terms, and opponents of the regime were exiled to remote islands. To reinforce the half-baked fascist concept of a 'corporate state', and to foster the

Metaxas

impression that the new order had the interests of all the people at heart, peasant debts were cancelled and a national minimum wage, adhered to largely at the whim of the employer, was decreed. At the very time when people were turning to the Communist Party as the only organization that had resisted Metaxas and which offered an alternative to the endless and sterile machinations of traditional politicians, it was declared illegal; its leaders were arrested and forced to sign 'declarations of repentance', and its newspaper was subjected to government 'dirty tricks'.

As the 1930s drew to a close it seemed unlikely that Metaxas' schemes would be allowed to run their course. Despite his efforts to isolate Greece from the world and buy time to fulfil his grand design, the greed and resentment of Greece's neighbours were propelling her inexorably towards a war of survival.

Foreign Policy and the Coming of the Second World War

Not surprisingly, Greek foreign policy was completely disoriented after the sudden collapse of the Great Idea in 1922. Her relations with all her neighbours were embittered, even leading to brief hostilities with Bulgaria during the military rule of General Pangalos. It was only with the return of Venizelos in 1928 that the country began to adjust itself to the new realities. Venizelos realized that the collapse of the Great Idea had freed Greece from many of the constraints that had previously governed her international position, and that she was no longer obliged to court the Great Powers. As the hopelessness of domestic politics engulfed him after 1929, he turned his attention more and more to foreign affairs in an attempt to redefine Greece's position in the world and defuse possible areas of conflict with her neighbours. In 1930 he signed a treaty of friendship and commerce with Turkey. Later in the same year the first of four Balkan Conferences was held, in which Greece, Yugoslavia, Rumania and Turkey developed a close relationship, culminating in the signing of a defensive Balkan Entente in February 1934. Given the troubled history of the region the Balkan Entente was a great achievement, but it failed to solve the most pressing dangers to peace – the territorial ambitions of Mussolini's Italy and the continuing resentments of Bulgaria.

Despite the utopian illusions of Metaxas in the realm of domestic politics, his assessment of Greece's international situation was realistic. He had no faith in Venizelos's Balkan Entente, and while he hoped to maintain Greece's neutrality in a European war, he believed that if she was forced to become involved, geography dictated that it must be on the side of Britain and France. His achievements in improving the organization, discipline and logistics of the Greek army must be set against his exclusion of hundreds of able officers who were tainted with Venizelist or Republican sympathies.

Even though Italy had invaded Albania in April 1939, when the Second World War broke out in September it seemed as if Greece would be able to maintain the neutrality that Metaxas so deeply desired. Despite a guarantee of her security given by Britain and France, her best hope lay in the possibility that the tide of war might pass her by. As in the First World War, however, geography and economics made neutrality extremely difficult to sustain: Britain complained about the continuing trade with Germany which had become a mainstay of the economy under Metaxas; Germany complained about the use of Greek ships to carry enemy supplies. Neither side could ignore the strategic importance of the Greek islands and eyed them covetously.

In May 1940 Mussolini, having gained little but contempt for his cowardly attack upon the prostrate French, turned his attention eastwards, hoping that an easy victory against the Greeks would bolster his sagging prestige. Metaxas, while preparing for the worst, did everything in his power to ignore Italian provocations. Even the sinking of the Greek cruiser *Elli* while she lay peacefully in harbour at Tinos failed to obtain the required response from him. But Mussolini was determined to have his war: after accusing the Greeks of violating the Albanian frontier, an ultimatum was delivered to Metaxas on 28 October 1941. His reply was unequivocal: 'This means war.'

Mussolini's dreams of easy pickings against the Greek army rapidly turned into a nightmare. Whereas many Italian soldiers had been dragooned into what they regarded as a pointless foreign adventure, the Greeks rallied to the cause in a rare display of national unity. After surrounding and defeating the 3rd Alpine Iulia Division in the rugged terrain north of Metsovo. Greek forces went on to the offensive, capturing the Albanian town of Koritsa and driving along the coast to cut the Italians off from their supply routes. In December Argyrokastron and the port of Santi Quaranta were taken, before deteriorating winter weather and stiffening Italian resistance induced a stalemate. Not an inch of Greek territory had fallen to the enemy.

The involvement of the Greek army in Albania did not inevitably mean that Greece would be drawn into the wider conflict. If the Greeks had confined their effort to holding the Albanian front against Mussolini, it is possible, as Hitler hinted, that they would have been left alone as an irrelevant distraction from Germany's forthcoming invasion of the Soviet Union, although prolonged neutrality might have only postponed the onslaught. However, by successfully resisting Mussolini, Greece had become Britain's only ally against Axis aggression, and Churchill was determined to persuade the Greeks to accept British support and enlist her in the British cause. Anthony Eden, the British foreign secretary, took a more cynical view, encouraging the Greeks in order to persuade Turkey and Yugoslavia to join a common front against Germany.

Metaxas, realizing the provocation that a British force on Greek soil would be to Hitler, refused to allow the British to land troops in Salonika. But on 29 January 1941 he died suddenly, and General Alexander Papagos, now the most influential of the king's advisers, agreed in principle to accept a British expeditionary force, which began landing early in March. British troops in Greece posed a threat on Hitler's southern flank that he could not ignore, and he became convinced that the Balkans must be cleared before he could safely unleash his assault on the Soviet Union.

It is possible that, with sufficient organization and preparation, an Anglo-Greek force might have been able to hold up Hitler's advance long enough to force him to abort his plans for the invasion of Russia, but unfortunately the preparations of the new allies were marked by a lack of urgency and unity of purpose that doomed their efforts from the outset. On 22 February, when Eden and Generals Dill and Wavell had discussions with the Greek High Command, both sides came away with completely differing interpretations of their joint strategy.

Eden believed that Papagos had agreed to withdraw Greek forces to the so-called Aliakmon Line to form a more easily defensible front, while Papagos believed that only 'preparations to withdraw' had been agreed. Both men subsequently gave different versions of their negotiations, but it is likely that the Greeks were understandably reluctant to abandon national territory, while the British were more concerned with how the Greek front would fit into their overall war effort. As a result, nothing had been done to co-ordinate strategy or prepare a defensive line by the time the Germans launched their attack on Yugoslavia and Greece on 6 April.

The Invasion of Greece

Within days the invading armies of General List exposed the confused strategies of the Anglo-Greek forces. Three columns of German troops swept into Greece following the historic invasion routes. In the west a column pushed through the Babuna pass and drove southwards towards Monastir (Bitolj), isolating the army of General Tsolakoglu. In the east a two-pronged assault was mounted upon Salonika: one column advanced down the Vardar/Axios valley along the railway line running from Gevgelija southwards; another, sweeping aside a Greek force fighting in the Rupel pass to erase the memory of the surrender of 1916, drove towards Salonika from the north-east; on 8 April German tank columns entered the city. The Greek army manning the strongly fortified Metaxas Line in Thrace against the Bulgarians was bypassed and cut off, making a joint strategy between Yugoslav, Greek and British forces impossible, with allied forces hopelessly strung out in the mountains of northern Greece.

British troops lay far to the north of the natural defensive line running along the Aliakmon river linking the Albanian mountains with Mount Olympos. By 12 April they were overwhelmed by German armoured forces thrusting down their left flank towards Klisura and cutting them off from the Greek army in Epirus, which suffered a severe defeat in the Metsovon pass, scene of their recent triumph against the Italian Alpine division. On 20 April, defying instructions from Athens, General Tsolakoglou surrendered his army. British, Australian and New Zealand forces fought desperate delaying actions in the passes around Olympos and the vale of Tempe, before making a last stand in the pass of Thermopylai. Against barbarian hordes in tanks there could be no re-enactment of the ancient epic: by 21 April Commonwealth forces were in full retreat across the Isthmus of Corinth.

There was to be no easy withdrawal. On 6 April a huge explosion had destroyed the port of Piraeus, making it impossible for the British fleet to use its facilities. On 26 April a bold German parachute assault secured the Isthmus of Corinth, cutting off the remnants of the retreating forces and driving them northwards into the inhospitable mountains of Rumeli. But the bulk of the 50,000 Commonwealth troops were able to make their way in reasonable order to beachheads in the Peloponnese to await evacuation to Crete, which, well within range of enemy aircraft and surrounded by seas teeming with enemy submarines, provided a dubious haven. Already on 26 March the Italians, in a daring raid using frogmen and inflatable boats, had sunk the cruiser *York* and three supply ships in

Suda Bay. British retaliation was swift: in a naval battle off Cape Matapan (Akri Tenaro) at the tip of the southern Peloponnese, the Royal Navy sank three Italian cruisers, crippling the Italian Mediterranean fleet.

THE FALL OF CRETE

Even before the last Commonwealth soldiers had left the windswept beaches of mainland Greece, Hitler, concerned at the threat posed to his position in the Balkans by the excellent harbour of Suda Bay and the airfields at Herakleion, Rethymnon and Maleme, ordered an invasion of Crete. Despite Churchill's earlier orders to make the island 'an impregnable fortress', little had been done. General Freyberg's 30,000 defenders were dispersed amongst a series of strongpoints along the north coast of the island, linked by the inadequate coastal road. No attempt had been made to improve links between the north and south of the island, and all supplies had to be sent from Egypt to the vulnerable northern coast. There were only thirty-six serviceable aircraft and virtually no armour; wireless and communications equipment was obsolete and in short supply. Nothing had been done to train and arm a Greek population eager to avenge the Cretan division that had suffered heavy casualties on the mainland.

The German assault began at dawn on 20 May with an aerial bombardment by over 400 bombers and dive-bombers, followed by one of the greatest parachute assaults of the war. A prime target was the airfield at Maleme, where glider-troops destroyed the anti-aircraft positions at the mouth of the Tavonitis river and captured the bridge. By the next day the defenders were forced to retreat, leaving the airfield in German hands. Elsewhere, German parachutists landing on the Akrotiri peninsula and near Galatas encountered fierce resistance from inadequately armed Greek soldiers and villagers. The Germans had been told the local population would welcome them; instead, hundreds were killed even before they reached the ground or cut to pieces while entangled in their parachutes.

General Student, installed amongst the potted palms of the Hotel Grande Bretagne in Constitution Square in Athens, was shocked and surprised at the German losses, but it was obvious that the position of

Commonwealth forces on Crete was unsustainable. Complete command of the air enabled the Germans to build up their forces with impunity. On 25 May they took Galatas after ferocious fighting, and were able to link up in a continuous front, making the position of the defenders of Chania and Suda Bay untenable. The Navy managed to evacuate the Herakleion garrison, but most of the men were forced to retreat southwards through the exhausting defiles and passes of the White Mountains to Sfakia. Many Commonwealth troops were taken off under cover of darkness, but virtually the only Greeks to escape were King George and his prime minister, Emmanuel Tsouderos, who crossed the mountains by night from their temporary homes near Chania and were evacuated from the village of Ayia Roumeli at the foot of the Samaria gorge by a British submarine.

Thus ended the formal military resistance to the Axis onslaught on Greece. However uncoordinated and brief it was, the effort seriously impaired the German war effort. 'Goering', wrote Churchill, 'gained only a Pyrrhic victory in Crete; for the forces he expended there might easily have given him Cyprus, Iraq, Syria, and even perhaps Persia.' The Greek people had again become the victims of their geography. The efforts of Venizelos and Metaxas to secure Balkan co-operation had been frustrated by parochial rivalries. Metaxas' hopes of neutrality were destroyed by Mussolini's greed. The very success of the Greek army against the Italians in 1940 had served to bring the crushing weight of the German army down upon them. Churchill's determination to support Greece was not matched by an ability to organize an effective military collaboration and only provoked the Wehrmacht into greater excesses. For the next three and a half years the Greek people passed under a regime of ruthless oppression, as helpless victims of a conflict beyond their control.

The Occupation

Conquered Greece was divided up between German, Italian and Bulgarian zones of occupation. Bulgarian rule in western Macedonia was deeply resented, reopening the struggle that the Greeks had won thirty years before, and reintroducing Slav settlers who threatened the hard-won Greek cultural dominance in the region. Italian rule in western Greece and the Islands was relatively humane, but memories of the invasion of 1940 poisoned the relationship between Italian officials and the people. The Germans held only those areas strategically important to them – Athens, Salonika and the Turkish border – but they dominated the country through a succession of puppet governments, starting with that of General Tsolakoglu, whose surrender had been so convenient to the success of their invasion.

It was in German-occupied Greece that the civilian population suffered most. The Germans intervened whenever they believed their security was threatened, and imposed the brutal system of repression that was their hallmark. The pattern was set in May 1941 when 200 villagers were shot in reprisal in the Cretan village of Kastelli; in 1943 over 1400 people were massacred near Kalavryta. Anyone who challenged the Germans ran the risk of arbitrary arrest, torture and deportation. Greek Jews suffered the greatest disaster: in Salonika, home for centuries of a huge Jewish population, 50,000 people were shipped off to the concentration camps within weeks of the German occupation; in Kavalla and Janina the story was repeated. By 1942 the Jewish community that had existed in Greece since the Middle Ages had ceased to be.

The occupation was a terrible burden to a country that was dependent upon imports for 25% of its cereals and for many other essential foodstuffs. The allied blockade caused such hardship in the winter of 1941–2 that King George's government in exile appealed for it to be lifted. Raging inflation made the drachma worthless by 1944. However, despite the horrors of occupation, it was the Greek tradition of resistance to foreign domination, and the equally traditional tendency to transform resistance into internal strife, that would cause most suffering over the next three years.

CHAPTER SEVENTEEN

Resistance and Civil War
1941–1948

The Divided Resistance

From the moment the Axis powers entered Greece, a spontaneous popular resistance began in the mountains. The tradition of resistance to foreign domination, and the rugged and inaccessible nature of much of Greece, were formidable barriers to enemy occupation. In the summer of 1941, Athanasios Klaras, alias Aris Veloukhiotis, became the leading figure in the 'people's war' that was breaking out spontaneously in the mountains. He was an outstanding leader who also possessed the ruthlessness to weld Greek mountain warriors into a disciplined resistance army. Largely through his leadership, the National Popular Liberation Army, known by its initials ELAS, quickly grew into the most significant and effective instrument of resistance. Although organized and led predominantly by communists, ELAS attracted a wide range of people because of its wholehearted commitment to fighting the occupation; in the spring of 1943 the experienced non-communist, Colonel Stafanos Sarafis, became its overall commander.

In September 1941 the National Liberation Front (EAM) was founded. Its aim was not merely the liberation of Greece but radical post-war reform, and its popularity was based as much upon its promise to lead Greece into an era of real change as upon its active leadership of the resistance. EAM made it clear that overthrowing the German yoke was only the preliminary stage in a long-overdue restructuring of Greek society. Such was the general disenchantment with the pre-war order that large numbers of Greeks – most of them non-communists – felt that, for all the dangers of Stalinist manipulation, coalition with the

227

Communists within EAM provided the only hope for effective resistance and change.

The right-wing resistance groups were mainly offshoots of discredited pre-war political organizations, whose activities were as much aimed at the Left as at the enemy. Some, like the fascist 'X' organization of Colonel George Grivas, collaborated with the Germans; others seemed paralysed by caution. The National Republican Greek Army (EDES), under Colonel Napoleon Zervas who had been closely associated with the Pangalos dictatorship of 1926, owed its ultimate allegiance to General Nicholas Plastiras, architect of the military coup of 1922. For a year after the fall of Greece EDES seemed more concerned with manoeuvring against ELAS than engaging in guerrilla activity, and armed clashes between the two over demarcation of territory became frequent. Virtually no impetus for armed resistance came from the royal government in exile, which advised Greeks that it would only provoke German reprisals against innocent civilians and was deeply suspicious of the activities of ELAS and EAM.

The Communists and the Resistance

The Greek Communist Party (KKE) was alarmed and excited by the spontaneous appearance of EAM and ELAS. The party organization, forced underground by the repression of Metaxas, was the ideal basis for a resistance movement, and although its leader, Nikos Zakhariadis, was captured and sent to Dachau, his successor, George Siantos, was able to maintain the party machine virtually intact underground in Athens. Unfortunately for those who looked forward to a reforming 'broad left' regime after the war, the KKE leadership was made up of men whose formative years had been spent in Moscow in the 1930s and whose loyalty to Stalin and his broad revolutionary strategies usually overrode the 'narrow' interests of Greece.

The KKE leadership shared Stalin's suspicion of any left-wing movement not under Moscow's control, and viewed the spontaneous development of ELAS in the mountains with alarm. But in 1941 Stalin had decreed that Communists should co-operate with any organization opposed to fascism, and said that their eventual route to power should be within a coalition of the Left. The KKE therefore saw EAM as an organization to be used to attain power legally. The next few years were dominated by the KKE's determination to control and manipulate the diverse elements of the Greek resistance with a view to obtaining a dominant position in a post-war government of the Left.

Siantos believed that Athens was the key to both resistance and the party's eventual rise to power. He resisted pleas by both Aris and the British SOE (Special Operations Executive) to take to the mountains. In 1942 an SOE mission was sent to organize the destruction of the vital Greek railway line carrying supplies for Rommel's forces in North Africa. It brought together Aris and Zervas, each of whom was eager to take part and become the recipient of British support. The deep hostility that existed between ELAS and EDES soon became clear, but on the night of 25 November 1942 they co-operated to blow up the Gorgopotamos railway viaduct. In one of the most spectacular and effective acts of sabotage of the war, German supply routes through Greece were cut for weeks and their North African campaign seriously disrupted.

The success of the Gorgopotamos project did little to heal the rift between the resistance groups. Within weeks fighting had broken out between ELAS and the right-wing groups, marking the beginning of the struggle for control of post-war Greece. Members of the anti-Communist resistance joined the 'security battalions' set up by the Greek collaborationist government, and a virtual civil war began which was to inflict more suffering on the Greek people than the occupation itself.

Churchill and the Resistance

Winston Churchill was opposed to supporting EAM/ELAS and determined to restore the monarchy. The King's support for Metaxas in 1936 and his reluctance to encourage resistance to the occupation had discredited him in the eyes of most Greeks, but although Greek public opinion had become strongly anti-monarchist, Churchill remained blindly committed to King George. He found great difficulty in reconciling his anti-Communism with the fact that it was ELAS that was making the running in the resistance, and he made little distinction between the non-Communist supporters of EAM who wanted radical reforms and the revolutionary Communists of the KKE. To him anyone who opposed the monarchy was a communist.

The British mission in Greece strove in vain to bring home the realities of the situation to Churchill but their assessment, formed from first-hand experience on the ground, was extremely unpalatable to him: ELAS and EAM, although they intended to establish socialism and abolish the monarchy, must be supported because they were the only effective resistance group. What was more, the popularity of the king had waned to such an extent that to continue to back him and his government in exile, and to support only the monarchist resistance groups, would simply undermine the war effort in Greece.

Churchill ignored this advice. In April 1943 he gave instructions that only monarchist resistance groups should be supplied with arms and intelligence by British agents. Zervas, the leader of EDES and a long-standing republican, was persuaded to make an opportunist declaration in favour of the monarchy. British forces suppressed an anti-monarchist rising amongst Greek soldiers in Egypt, and Churchill continued to make the royal government in Cairo the focus of his Greek policy. The end result was that the British forfeited the trust of non-Communists in EAM, pushing them closer to the KKE, and compromised the anti-Communist cause by associating it with foreign interference and the discredited monarchy.

In the summer of 1943 allied plans for the invasion of Sicily and the need for a diversionary campaign in Greece forced Churchill briefly to temper his suspicion of ELAS. The 'National Bands Agreement' acknowledged its predominance in the resistance and allowed British agents to arm and supply its partisans. In August a delegation of resistance leaders came to Cairo. Believing they had been invited to clarify the constitutional arrangements when the war ended, they asked the king to make a statement that he would not return to Greece before a plebiscite was held, and for a coalition government in which EAM would have the portfolios of war, justice and the interior. The representatives of the right-wing resistance groups did not oppose these demands, and SOE supported them as representing the wishes of most Greeks, certainly of those who were actively opposing the occupation.

The demands were rejected out of hand. The king was urged by

Churchill and Roosevelt to stand firm, and the delegation was packed off to Greece bearing only the vaguest of concessions to their supporters. This finished all hope of a peaceful end to the occupation. EAM now believed that the British and the Americans were determined to force them to accept the return of the monarchy. The hard-liners in ELAS became convinced that they would have to fight to retain the influence they had won in the resistance, or victory would be snatched from them by foreign intervention and right-wing intrigue.

The 'First Round' of the Civil War

During the visit of the resistance delegation to Cairo, Italy signed a separate peace with the Allies, bringing down a terrible revenge on Italian troops in Greece: 4000 were massacred in Corfu. For ELAS, the Italian surrender meant a rich harvest of captured equipment, which fell into their hands at the very moment that the rebuff from Cairo had stiffened their resolve to fight. Their partisans began a campaign against the right-wing resistance groups, accusing them of plotting to exclude the Left after the liberation, and of colluding with the German occupying forces against them. Throughout the winter of 1943–4 bitter fighting, later called the 'First Round' of the Civil War, raged in the mountains, causing terrible suffering to innocent civilians already groaning under the weight of German occupation. By February 1944, when the Plaka Agreement was signed by the warring factions, virtually the whole of Greece was under the control of EAM and ELAS.

In March EAM was in such a strong position that it set up an 'alternative government' in Greece, PEEA (Political Committee of National Liberation), headed by the non-communist academic Alexander Sovolos. Its workers' organization mounted strikes against the collaborationist government, and scotched German plans to introduce compulsory work drafts; its relief organization, Mutual Solidarity, helped the victims of famine; and its youth organization kept alive the spirit of resistance amongst the young. In the large area of 'Free Greece' controlled by EAM an efficient and relatively incorrupt administration was introduced under PEEA. Schools were reopened, and health facilities developed and made available to all; a system of popular justice replaced the élitist and expensive machinery of pre-war years. These improvements were perforce rudimentary, but for many Greeks, communist and non-communist, they heralded an exciting possibility of economic and political progress for the future, under a popular socialist government in which the KKE had only a minor role.

In 1944 it seemed that a popular government, forged in the resistance to foreign occupation, and legitimized by a programme of radical reform, would soon come to power in the wake of the German retreat. But during the next few months events conspired to dash these high hopes.

EAM's Revolution Thwarted

In April a mutiny amongst the Greek forces in Egypt demanded recognition of PEEA. The British authorities, still determined to support the government of King George, threatened to fire on Greek warships in Alexandria harbour, and dispersed Greek army units to far-flung postings. But from this crisis a new leader of the royal government in exile emerged. George Papandreou was a subtle politician, a liberal and, above all, anti-communist, who was destined to be a major force in post-war politics. Determined to outmanoeuvre EAM and to create an opening for his own political ambitions with British support, in May at a conference in the Lebanon he and the British pursued a policy of 'battering delegates of PEEA, EAM and KKE into a mental daze'. The left-wing delegates were induced to sign a document, known as the Lebanon Accord, by which they agreed to surrender their forces to a 'Government of National Unity' headed by Papandreou, and in which EAM was only offered minor posts.

Not surprisingly, news of this agreement was received in disbelief by EAM representatives in Greece who repudiated it out of hand. They could not believe, given their almost total military predominance in the resistance and the large measure of popular support that they enjoyed both in the towns and the countryside, that their representatives had conceded so much. They believed that their military superiority, the wide popularity that they had earned, and the support of the Soviet Union, must ensure their victory over the pretensions of émigré politicians and their foreign backers. But supporters of EAM and the KKE had not realized that Greece had become a pawn in the game being played by the Allies for control of the post-war world. In October 1944 Churchill travelled to Moscow to settle the future of the Balkans. He presented Stalin with what he called a 'naughty document' setting out, in percentage terms, the spheres of influence for the Powers after liberation. Russia was to have a '90%' interest in Rumania and a '75%' interest in Bulgaria; both sides should have a '50%' interest in Hungary; Greece was placed '90%' under the control of Great Britain. After a cursory perusal of the scrap of paper Stalin placed a large tick against Churchill's proposals.

In this atmosphere of casual *realpolitik* the fate of millions of people in central and southern Europe was decided. For the next eighteen months the 'naughty document' symbolized the informal understanding between Stalin and Churchill which governed the international position of Greece. Churchill felt free to pursue his personal obsession with re-establishing the monarchy and crushing the Greek Left, in the knowledge that Stalin would probably not interfere. In July Stalin's emissary, Colonel Popov, had arrived from Moscow for consultations at ELAS headquarters. On 2 September, in an extraordinary volte-face, EAM suddenly reversed its opposition to the Lebanon Accord and accepted six portfolios in a government of national unity headed by Papandreou. On 7 September, as German forces were beginning to leave Greece, the EAM ministers agreed at Caserta to place their forces under the control of the Papandreou government; in practice, this meant under the British general, Robert Scobie, who was appointed commander-in-chief on the 18th.

These bewildering changes of direction by EAM reflected the different goals of the groups that made it up, and the influence that Moscow held over the KKE. The bulk of EAM supporters were non-communists, willing to support any government that offered progress and reform; for these people the Lebanon Accord and submission to Papandreou were acceptable compromises if they led to national regeneration. Many ELAS *kapetanios* in the mountains, like Aris Veloukhiotis, wanted to use force to maintain the power they had already won. The Stalinist leadership of the KKE followed Moscow's instructions to co-operate with the 'legal government' of Papandreou and wait for the 'correct' historical moment for the Greek revolution.

The instructions that Popov had presumably conveyed from Stalin caused the Left, under the influence of the KKE, to abandon the position of enormous strength it had won by resisting Metaxas and Hitler, and tamely accept the reimposition of a regime that was only supported by a handful of émigrés and Winston Churchill. If EAM had chosen to resist the return of the king while its partisans still retained their arms and organization, Britain did not have sufficient forces available to impose its will. Many Greeks still believe that Stalin's interference and British intervention robbed them of an opportunity to establish an independent socialist Greece that would not recur until the 1960s.

The 'Second Round': Liberation or Intervention?

On 4 October 1944 British troops landed at Patras and began advancing along the Gulf of Corinth. On the 13th, in a move aimed as much against ELAS as against the Germans who were now leaving Greece far to the north, British commando units secured Megara airport on the outskirts of Athens. On the 18th Papandreou's government arrived at Piraeus aboard the ancient cruiser *Averoff*, which came to rest at last after its epic voyage through the history of modern Greece.

The coalition was immediately faced with a series of intractable problems that threatened to blow apart its fragile unity. The streets of Athens were filled with homeless and starving people whose expectations had been raised by liberation; the price of a kilo of bread was 122 million drachmas; collaborators walked free, waging war against leftists in the streets; monarchist soldiers of the Rimini Brigade and the Sacred Company were threatening violent action to ensure the return of the king. In these uncertain conditions ELAS partisans showed an understandable reluctance to lay down their arms, while many of their leaders regretted their lost opportunities and still believed that they could seize power.

In November there was complete rift between the Left and Papandreou's government. When General Scobie threatened to use force to compel ELAS units to disarm by 10 December, the EAM ministers resigned from the government amidst strikes and demonstrations. On 3 December serious fighting broke out in Athens after police fired on a demonstration in Constitution Square. The next day vicious street-fighting took place between General Scobie's troops and demonstrators mobilized by the KKE. The same day Churchill sent a telegram to Scobie: 'We have to hold and dominate Athens. It would be a great thing to succeed in this without bloodshed if possible but also with bloodshed if necessary.' Against the advice and wishes of his foreign office advisers and of most British representatives in Athens, Churchill had committed himself to a full-scale intervention in Greek affairs.

The Americans, discovering the contents of Churchill's aggressive telegram, remained neutral and uncooperative. Throughout December vicious street-fighting continued in the centre of Athens, as the forces of the Left were gradually overcome. Siantos, the KKE leader, still obsessed with urban revolution, forbade ELAS fighters from the mountains to come to the city, whereas large numbers of well-equipped and battle-hardened British troops arrived from the Italian front. On 24 December Churchill himself landed in Greece; after the discovery of a huge bomb in the cellar of the Hotel Grande Bretagne, he stayed aboard HMS *Ajax* in Piraeus harbour and negotiated with the factions in the British embassy.

The attempts of Siantos to secure a coalition government were now doomed by the desperate situation of his fighters. Over 11,000 people had died and large areas of Athens had been destroyed. At the end of the year Papandreou resigned; more significantly, the king, now in London, agreed not to return until after a plebiscite, and Archbishop Damaskinas was appointed regent. After a ceasefire and long negotiations, an agreement was signed at Varkiza, on the coast between Athens and Sounion, on 12 February 1945. The British-backed government, now headed by General Plastiras, agreed to guarantee democratic freedoms, to conduct a plebiscite on the monarchy, and to hold a general election under international supervision. Plastiras promised a vigorous purge of collaborators, a national amnesty, and there was to be no attempt to persecute members of left-wing organizations. In return for these guarantees, ELAS agreed to surrender its arms and withdraw its fighters 240 km from Athens.

The Terror against the Left

The amnesty promised at Varkiza never came into force, and the Left believed that it was merely a trick to persuade them to lay down their arms. Over the next year a large-scale 'Terror' began, not only against ELAS but against anyone remotely connected with the left-wing Resistance during the war or associated with the pre-war opposition. In the spring of 1945 thousands were arrested by the army and the new gendarmerie, largely made up of collaborators and right-wing activists from the days of Metaxas. Hundreds were condemned to death for their wartime activities, and thousands imprisoned for membership of Left-wing organizations, or for such offences as 'making an unpatriotic speech'. Right-wing gangs, such as the 'X' militia of George Grivas, roamed the countryside with impunity, attacking and intimidating political enemies. Newspapers were full of the names of people who had disappeared, or who were found murdered in towns and villages all over Greece. By the summer nearly 50,000 former partisans were imprisoned in island camps like the one at Makrinoras, where conditions resembled those of wartime concentration camps.

Three former prime ministers and a noted liberal politician signed an open letter alleging that 'terrorist organizations of the extreme right, which had been armed by the Germans, have not been disarmed or prosecuted but have openly allied themselves to the security forces in order to strangle all democratic thought'. Such an appeal to the government had little value; ministers were able to uphold the Varkiza agreement by protecting the leaders of EAM, but they had no power to influence events in the countryside where local officers, administrators and warlords were able to institute an uncontrolled terror. The British authorities found themselves responsible but powerless: Churchill had established what amounted to a protectorate over Greece at a time when it was impossible to provide resources to fulfil the obligations that this entailed. The wealthy Athens district of Kolonaki became known as 'Scobia' and the ministries of 1945–6 as 'the governments of the English'. Many Greeks continue to believe that Britain could have done more and prevented the suspension of civil rights, the publication of authoritarian decrees, and the blatant activities of right-wing gangs in the capital.

The Greek Left set great store by the election of Attlee's Labour government in July 1945, believing that at last Britain would use its influence to restrain the excesses of the Right. But one of the first acts of the new British foreign secretary, Ernest Bevin, was to assure King George that British policy would continue unchanged. Greece was now completely dependent on Britain for a whole range of essential supplies; and in the absence of an elected parliament, British missions supervised the administration, finance and defence. The cost to Britain of this huge commitment, at least £400 million, at a time of great austerity made the government desperate to ease the burden on British resources. In September 1945 they agreed that elections should be held *before* the plebiscite on the future of the monarchy. This decision, contrary to the terms of the Varkiza agreement, further shook the confidence of the Left in the validity of elections which they believed had no chance of being conducted fairly in the atmosphere of intimidation and violence. Defying Stalin's wishes for once, the KKE made the disastrous decision to boycott the elections of March 1946, opening the way for a right-wing victory by Constantine Tsaldaris in a poll in which only 49% of the voters took part.

The Tsaldaris regime was even more repressive than its predecessors. Elected trades-union officials were deposed and replaced with government nominees. The plebiscite on the monarchy, held in September 1946, was conducted in circumstances which made a mockery of democratic processes: four-fifths of the country was in the hands of right-wing gangs, who intimidated voters by resting sten guns on the ballot boxes; Allied observers confirmed that ballot-rigging took place on a massive scale. The result – a vote for the return of the monarchy – was a travesty of democracy and a confirmation that there could be no justice under the existing system.

By the summer of 1946 80,000 people had been forced to flee the Terror. For those who had been associated with ELAS in the resistance the choice lay between remaining in their homes to await arrest, or going to the mountains to defend themselves. By the time King George II returned to Greek soil on 27 September 1946 (he died six months later and was succeeded by his brother Paul), the 'Third Round' of the Civil War, which threatened to outstrip in its ferocity anything that had gone before, was under way.

The 'Third Round': Defeat of the Democratic Army

Even before the election of 1946 the KKE, perhaps encouraged by Stalin's demand for the withdrawal of British troops into believing that he would now back a seizure of power, called for preparation for an 'armed struggle'. Throughout the summer fighting between left-wing guerrillas and government forces gradually escalated. On 26 October Markos Vafiadis, the new leader in the mountains, announced the establishment of a 'Democratic Army'; by the end of the year he had recruited some 7000 guerrillas into a force that at its peak consisted of about 30,000 men. Until the end of 1949 the Democratic Army defied the government, using traditional guerrilla methods and taking control of large areas along the Albanian and Yugoslav border.

The Democratic Army's success depended upon factors that were largely outside the control of the partisans in the mountains. Could Britain, facing a grave economic crisis, continue to sustain the Greek government? Would Stalin and Tito's Yugoslavia help the Left? Would the KKE allow the Democratic Army to mobilize their potential recruits from the cities, and continue to use the guerrilla tactics that held out the best chance of success in Greek conditions?

In March 1947 Britain suddenly informed the United States that it could no longer afford its role in Greece. The US response was immediate and dramatic: on 12 March President Truman proclaimed the Truman Doctrine, which inaugurated a US commitment to 'fight Communism wherever it might appear in the world'. It marked the beginning of the Cold War and the end of Stalin's reluctance to support the Greek Left. For the Greek government it meant an immediate and huge influx of American aid, both economic and military, which completely changed the balance of forces within the country; US missions and advisers moved in on a scale that dwarfed previous British efforts. The size of this effort inevitably had a great impact upon every aspect of Greek life. Much of the aid found its way into the pockets of black-marketeers, speculators and opportunists. 'Athens today', wrote an American journalist, 'is a kingdom of intrigue, hatred, wickedness and corruption, challenging the standards of the Middle Ages.' The Americans had no more success than the British in restraining the excesses of the Terror, now organized by the enthusiastic minister of public order, Napoleon Zervas: camps and prisons continued to swell with victims (the British *Daily Mirror* published a picture of government 'bounty hunters' delivering severed heads to the authorities).

As the Civil War grew more bitter, repressive measures were intensified. In October 1947 newspapers published by KKE and EAM were banned; in December the Communist Party itself was made illegal and the right to strike restricted. In 1948 martial law was introduced and, despite protests in the West, hundreds of prisoners executed; in the mountains, atrocities by both sides became commonplace. In military terms the Americans transformed the prospects of the government army. In November 1947 a joint US–Greek general staff was established, and the experienced General James Van Fleet given a co-ordinating role. Decent roads were built for the first time, and existing ones widened for military use; the government obtained tanks and aircraft, including the latest Curtiss Helldiver ground-attack fighters. Greece was seen by the state department as a testing ground for its new policy of confronting the 'Communist Menace', and by the Pentagon as its 'laboratory experiment' – for napalm, for the strategy of evacuating the civilian population, and, as some claim, for defoliants. In the autumn of 1947 the government introduced conscription, swelling the ranks of the regular army to over 200,000 men, many of them reluctant ex-ELAS partisans.

Despite the massive power deployed against him, Markos Vafiadis was relatively untroubled by the offensives launched against him during 1947 (subsequent history has demonstrated the ability of experienced guerrillas to thwart massive conventional forces). But at the end of the year the KKE leader, Nikos Zakhariadis, decided to demand a change in tactics by the Democratic Army.

A hard-line Stalinist, Zakhariadis had dramatically reappeared in Athens in March 1945 after surviving years in Dachau concentration camp. The policies he followed after his reinstatement as party leader were a major reason for the widening split between the Communists and the wartime EAM coalition. A bomb outrage at Litochoron on the eve of the 1946 election and the futile boycott of that election alienated liberal opinion. By the time the Democratic Army was formed, the majority of moderate leftists no longer supported an armed struggle that was clearly a prelude to Greece becoming a satellite of the Soviet Union.

The KKE's subservience to Stalin's instructions in October 1944 had prevented the Left from retaining the power by popular acclaim, and it is possible that even if EAM had been able to take power then Stalin would have used 'salami tactics' to eliminate non-communists and independent socialists 'slice by slice', as he did subsequently all over Eastern Europe. In the 'third round' of the Civil War the Democratic Army was cut off from mass support, and seen by many previous supporters as the agent of Soviet imperialism.

Any chance that the Democratic Army may have had of fighting a successful guerrilla war was sabotaged by Zakhariadis' doctrinaire interference in its strategy. His authoritarian instincts were disturbed by the bearded freedom fighters in the mountains, whom he longed to bring under the discipline of the Party. In Athens the Communist secret police, OPLA, crushed any sign of dissidence, and in June 1945 the severed head of Aris Veloukhiotis was put on display in Trikala after his death in a mysterious grenade explosion. Hundreds of other 'Trotskyists', 'mensheviks' and 'anarchists' were purged in an atmosphere that reminded many observers of the Spanish Civil War. In addition, throughout 1946 and 1947 Zakhariadis' dreams of staging an urban revolution in Athens prevented ex-ELAS fighters leaving the city, making them sitting ducks for the security police: mass arrests in the summer of 1946 filled the prison islands of Makrinoros, Aegina and Ikaria with trained and experienced officers, severely weakening the Democratic Army.

In September 1947 Zakhariadis himself took to the mountains. Confident in the support of the Soviet Union, Yugoslavia and Bulgaria, he proclaimed that henceforth the Democratic Army would give up guerrilla tactics and begin a conventional 'positional war': towns would be captured and territory secured and held. Markos and the other *kapetanios* were totally opposed to this strategy, believing that their only hope lay in guerrilla tactics, but none the less he accepted the position of head of a new provisional government, and was forced to bear responsibility for the subsequent disasters. In June 1948 70,000 government soldiers launched Operation Coronis against 12,000 partisans entrenched on the slopes of Mount Grammos on the border of Greece and Albania. It was a battle far more suited to the tanks and aircraft of the regular army than to the lightly equipped partisans. After eight weeks of bitter fighting, the Democratic Army was forced to disperse or flee across the border to avoid annihilation. In the recriminations that followed Vafiadis was deposed and replaced by a Supreme War Council dominated by Zakhariadis.

A more serious blow was the split that occurred in July 1948 between Tito and Stalin. The extent of aid given to the Greek Communists from outside is still hotly debated, but it is certain that the KKE looked ultimately to Stalin to save them. Ever since 1944 they had been trying to dance to Stalin's tune, but unfortunately this was a melody often heard dimly from behind closed doors. On the whole Stalin had stuck by the informal agreement he had made with Churchill in 1944, and discouraged Yugoslav and Bulgarian Communists from helping Greece. Early in the Cold War in 1947 he gave some support, but the Soviet Union had no common border with Greece and any material assistance had to come through Yugoslavia or Bulgaria. After the Stalin/Tito split Zakhariadis was forced to choose between Stalin, who was still reluctant to help him, saying at the beginning of 1948 that the 'Greek Revolution should be stopped immediately', and Tito, who had the means to help him but was now 'excommunicated'. Zakhariadis seems to have continued to keep faith, against all the evidence, with Stalin.

Despite his defeat on Mount Grammos, Zakhariadis was determined to carry on fighting a conventional war against the Greek army and to secure a major town as a base of operations. In the winter of 1948 there were unsuccessful attempts to take Serres, Edessa and Naoussa; Karditsa was held for two days; and in January 1949, in the only success of his strategy, Karpenision was captured for eighteen days. But government forces began to push the Democratic Army relentlessly back to the killing grounds in the extreme north-western mountains. On 10 July Tito formally closed the border with Greece; a month later a second battle of Mount Grammos ended in another defeat for the Democratic Army, which swept its remnants into exile and defeat in Albania. In October 1949 the KKE proclaimed a 'temporary halt' to the Civil War.

It was the misfortune of progressive Greeks that their best opportunity to take power coincided with a vast global upheaval. Churchill's determination to intervene in Greek domestic politics, the manipulation of EAM by the KKE for its own ends, and Greece's position in the cockpit of the Cold War had doomed her to be the plaything of wider historical forces. What is more, the nature of the 'third round' of the Civil War enabled the Right to label any progressive Greek who had supported EAM during the war as a Communist, an agent of Russia, and an associate of the atrocities that marked the last phase of the conflict. It would be 1962 before the Greek government announced an end to its continuing vendetta against the Left.

CHAPTER EIGHTEEN

Post-War Greece
1949–1985

The Ascendancy of the Right

Nearly ten years of fighting had left a legacy of material, political and psychological damage in Greece, and attitudes are still profoundly coloured by the savage divisions that it engendered. Relatively, Greece had suffered losses almost as grave as the Soviet Union in the Second World War. Half a million people (7% of the population) had been killed; 700,000 (10%) were refugees; thousands had been forced into an exile that in some cases was to last for over twenty years; 30,000 children, evacuated to Communist countries by the Democratic Army to avoid the fighting, were believed by the right to have been kidnapped for indoctrination. Thousands remained in prison and executions continued for long after the Civil War ended. Many remained in hiding for years to avoid persecution, or because they lacked the 'Certificates of Civic Loyalty' demanded by the police until 1962, which enabled people to register to vote, move house, or obtain even the most menial jobs.

Greek politics had been profoundly distorted. At least half the people believed that the post-war system had been imposed on them by the West, while the rest were convinced that they had narrowly escaped a communist conspiracy. The chief legacy of the war was to ensure the dominance of the Right in Greece until 1962. The KKE remained illegal until 1974, and the only legal party of the Left was the EDA (Union of the Democratic Left). The Centre was also a victim of the polarization of politics: radicals, still dreaming of the lost promise of EAM, tended to move to the left or opt out of politics, while more cautious liberals sought security in anti-Communist parties that would ensure prosperity through American support.

At the height of the Cold War the Americans were determined to support anti-Communist forces in Greece by military and economic aid, which by the end of the Civil War already amounted $2 billion. They were quite prepared if necessary to interfere directly in Greek politics. Between 1947 and 1952 a bewildering succession of governments succeeded one other. The election of March 1950, for instance, was contested by forty-four parties, no less than ten of which were represented in the eventual government. Continuity of policy was impossible in such chaos, and the Americans believed that it increased the threat of a Communist resurgence. In 1952 the US ambassador announced that his government 'did not approve' of coalitions, and that Greece should change from proportional representation to simple majority voting.

The election of November 1952 was a triumph for American pressure, imposing a new simplicity on Greek politics but also emphasizing its distortions. At the head of his new 'Gaullist' party, Greek Rally, Field Marshal Papagos won 82% of the parliamentary seats with less than 50% of the votes. Despite its 11% support in 1951 the 'Left front' party, EDA, won no seats; but the most dramatic casualty of the new system was EPEK, a laboriously constructed centre coalition, which won only 51 out of 300 seats with 34% of the vote. The Left was disenfranchised, the Centre crippled, and the Right assured of power for the next ten years.

The governments of Alexander Papagos and his successor Constantine Karamanlis were committed to the free market, with little emphasis upon social reform or spending, and to integrating Greece into the Western Alliance. This ensured the financial and military support of the United States. The drachma was devalued by 50% and foreign investment encouraged; American aid built roads and bridges and public works projects generated an impression of progress. As Greece benefited from the world boom of the 1950s national energies were turned towards the huge task of reconstruction.

The importance of Greece to US strategy in the Cold War was reinforced by her new role in securing the southern flank of NATO, which she had joined in 1951. In October 1953 a military agreement gave the Americans the right to build and operate sovereign bases and to make extensive use of the Greek transport system. This agreement, which secured massive American aid for Papagos's regime, reminded many Greeks of previous infringements of their sovereignty, but prospects for a steady advance within the American orbit looked set fair. However, in a scenario reminiscent of an earlier age, the hopes of Greek Rally were thrown into the melting pot by the problems posed by a demand for union (*enosis*) by the Greeks of Cyprus.

The Cyprus Problem

Although it technically remained part of the Ottoman Empire, the island of Cyprus had come under British rule in 1878. When Turkey entered the First World War on the side of the Central Powers this was transformed into a formal annexation by Britain, later confirmed in the Treaty of Lausanne of 1923. In 1931 there was serious rioting on the island in favour of enosis, but because of Greek disenchantment with foreign adventures at the time this found little echo in the motherland.

In 1950 Archbishop Makarios was elected Ethnarch, traditionally the political as well as spiritual leader of the Greek Cypriot people who comprised 80% of the population. Immediately a powerful drive for union with Greece began. An unofficial referendum showed 96% of the Greek majority were in favour of enosis. In 1951 Makarios and George Grivas, the Cypriot-born nationalist who had played a dubious role in the Greek resistance, formed a revolutionary committee to further the cause of enosis. For the next twenty-three years there was a destructive interaction between Cypriot and Greek politics which was reminiscent of the Cretan Question in the nineteenth century.

In July 1954 Britain outraged Cypriot and Greek opinion by stating that Cyprus could 'never' become independent, and the following spring Grivas's organisation EOKA (National Organization of Cypriot Combatants) began attacks on British installations. A spiral of violence began which, given the irredentist traditions of the Greek state, made the involvement of Athens inevitable. In 1953 Papagos had been rebuffed when he tried to discuss Cyprus with Britain, and several Greek attempts to raise the problem in the United Nations were frustrated. In an attempt to broaden his support by attracting nationalists of the Centre, Papagos became more and more deeply involved with the issue and it soon began to threaten Greece's relationship with the Western Alliance.

At a conference in London in August 1955 the Turks demanded that, if Britain left Cyprus, it should revert to Turkish rule. After violent anti-Greek riots in Istanbul, it became clear that the Cyprus issue could re-open old wounds and destroy Greece's co-operation with Turkey in NATO. American condemnation of Turkey was lukewarm and the UN refused to discuss the Cyprus issue. Public opinion in Greece, fuelled by deep-seated resentments and memories of past injustices, began to demand a foreign policy that was more independent and less servile to American interests.

In October 1955 Papagos died and his successor, Constantine Karamanlis, led a new right-wing party, ERE (National Radical Union), into the election of February 1956. Supported by America, he won after the electoral rules were changed yet again, but the result showed that cracks were beginning to appear in the dominance of the Right: the fragmented opposition with 44% of the votes would soon be able to mount a serious challenge. Two years later, although Karamanlis won again, support for ERE had fallen to 41% and the leftist EDA became the largest opposition group with 25% of the vote. EDA's appeal was enhanced by admission of 'errors' of strategy during the resistance and civil war; Zakhariadis was expelled and Markos Vafiadis temporarily rehabilitated. Stefanos Sarafis, the respected leader of ELAS, briefly became head of EDA but was killed in a car crash involving an American serviceman. There was now intense pressure on politicians of the Centre like Sophoklis Venizelos and George Papandreou to combine in order to meet the twin threat from the Right and the resurgent Left.

Meanwhile the deteriorating Cyprus situation absorbed most of the nation's energy. In January 1956 both Karamanlis and Makarios were quite prepared to consider conciliatory moves by the British, but elements in the British government and in EOKA blocked agreement. In March Makarios was exiled to the Seychelles, and the mood in Greece swung violently against NATO, the UN, and the United States which had failed to support the Greek position. Even Karamanlis began to flirt with non-alignment and strove to improve relations with the Communist bloc, while rumours that the Americans were planning to install ICBMs on Greek soil and that Khrushchev had threatened to 'vaporize the Parthenon' in retaliation made the Left's neutralism suddenly very attractive.

In March 1957 Makarios was released and allowed to resume negotiations with the Turks, but not to return to Cyprus. Ominously the hardliner Grivas had returned, and the Turks began to raise the possibility of partitioning the island. Greeks suspected that Britain, mainly concerned with the security of its bases and in the larger questions of the Cold War, secretly favoured this solution and was prepared to sacrifice the Greek Cypriots in the interests of *realpolitik*. Stalemate was followed by more vicious fighting between EOKA and the Turkish minority. By the end of 1958 all the parties wanted a solution. For Karamanlis, the opposition's use of the Cyprus Question to mobilize public support was becoming a strong incentive to abandon enosis and seek a settlement with Britain.

In February 1959, after protracted negotiations in Zurich, agreement on an independent republic of Cyprus was reached, with a complicated and probably unworkable constitution safeguarding the rights of Greeks and Turks. Makarios was allowed to return to Cyprus and in August 1960 became the first president of the new republic.

The Rise and Fall of George Papandreou, 1960–67

The Cyprus Question, which had originally been taken up by the Right as a populist issue, had in fact provoked a strong desire for change within Greece itself. The election of May 1958, pushing the Centre into second place behind the Socialists, had shocked the leaders of the divided centre parties into the need for unity. The spirit of compromise and concession has never come easily in Greek politics, which has always been a battlefield for rampaging egos, but in September 1961 George Papandreou announced the formation of the Centre Union Party, a coalition stretching from Tsirimokos, who had flirted with EDA, to Venizelos, whose politics overlapped with the left wing of Karamanlis' ERE. It was a broad and perhaps opportunist conglomeration, made formidable by its determination to end the long ascendancy of the Right and by the exceptional quality of its leader, George Papandreou.

The rise of the Centre Union, amidst hints that the Kennedy administration might welcome it, posed a real threat to Karamanlis. There was much to be proud of in the economic progress achieved under successive right-wing governments: average incomes had more than doubled since 1951; tourism and remittances from migrant workers had eased Greek finances; industrialization had for the first time balanced the urban and rural populations – Athens had grown hugely since the war and contained nearly a quarter of the population. Karamanlis believed these beneifts would outweigh the urban sprawl, decay of village life and inequalities of wealth that were their counterpoint. Hoping to capitalize on this, and on Greece's pending associate membership of the EEC, he decided to call an election in October 1961.

The result seemed to be conclusive. ERE won 51% of the vote and 176 seats; Papandreou's Centre Union obtained 33% and 100 seats; the EDA lost ground with 15% of the vote and 24 seats. Foreign observers remarked on the great success of the new party, but Papandreou and his supporters furiously rejected the outcome. Claiming that the government had used intimidation, ballot-rigging and jerrymandering, that thousands of bogus votes had been cast, and that right-wing thugs and the army had been used to sway the result, he declared a 'relentless struggle' to overturn the verdict. (Hindsight has shown that most of these claims were justified: although Karamanlis himself did not order excesses, right-wing interest groups, particularly in the army, fearing that their long ascendancy might be ending, had been driven to desperate measures.)

After eighteen months of unabated political ferment, the lowest point of which was the assassination in Salonika of the left-wing deputy Grigorios Lambrakis in May 1963, Karamanlis resigned. Ostensibly he went because of King Paul's defiance of his objections to a visit to London by Queen Frederika, but observers suspected a deeper disenchantment with the system. It would be eleven years before he returned to Greece from his self-imposed exile in Paris.

New elections were held in November 1963, supervised by the President of the Supreme Court. On this occasion there was no hint of malpractice and Papandreou's Centre Union won 138 seats, six more than ERE, with the left-wing EDA holding the balance with 28 seats. However, Papandreou refused to rule with the support of EDA, and after struggling on for 55 days resigned on Christmas Eve. In the ensuing election in February 1964 he triumphed, winning 53% of the votes, representing an overwhelming mandate for reform.

Papandreou's first act was to bring to an end the long vendetta against the losers in the Civil War. Although the KKE remained an illegal organization, political prisoners, some held since the war, were released and exiles were at last able to return home. Ambitious social and economic reforms followed. Legislation raised the school leaving age, introduced demotic Greek in primary schools, and lessened the obsession with the classical past. Papandreou's son Andreas, an American-educated economist, cut income tax by 10%, increased public spending and initiated welfare legislation; minimum prices were established for farm produce, and banks encouraged to make borrowing easier. There were inflationary dangers in these policies, and they were dependent upon continuing growth of the world economy for their success, but the accession of the 23-year-old Constantine II in March 1964 on the death of his father seemed to herald a period of internal harmony and progress for Greece.

However, Papandreou's reforms were soon threatened by the persistent problem of Cyprus. The complex constitution had proved unworkable. Greek Cypriots who still wanted enosis and Turkish Cypriots who desired partition sabotaged the settlement to further their own ends, and military confrontation between Greece and Turkey was a constant threat. Serious intercommunal fighting broke out on the island during 1963, and on Christmas Day Turkish planes dramatically menaced Nicosia. The following summer EOKA attacked the village of Kokina, through which the Turks were infiltrating weapons, and with the Turks besieged in enclaves and with extremists from both communities rejecting all solutions, the problems of the island continued to demand attention and to blight any internal Greek reforms.

The confrontation with Turkey caused Papandreou to question Greece's position in the Western Alliance. Although the United States had probably deterred the Turks from invading Cyprus in 1964, disenchantment with the West and bitter historical memories of foreign interference led him to make advances to the Eastern block, alarming both the army and the Americans. The Right hated his economic policies, which caused inflation and setbacks during 1965, and feared that his tolerance of the left would lead to growth in support for EDA, which polled 30% in Athens local elections. By 1965 the air was thick with rumours of right-wing conspiracies against the elected government.

In May 1965 a plot by Aspida (Shield), a subversive group of left-wing army officers, was uncovered, and it was claimed that Andreas Papandreou, frustrated by his father's caution, was part of the conspiracy. At the same time Colonel George Papadopoulos claimed falsely that Communists were planning violence on the Bulgarian border and confidential information was leaked to the right-wing press by supporters in the army. Papandreou decided on a purge of disloyal officers which was regarded by the Right as a mortal attack upon its domination of the army that had lasted since 1935. The minister of defence, Garoufalias, who had the confidence of the king, refused Papandreou's orders to dismiss certain officers, and then refused to resign when he was sacked. On 15 July, when King Constantine refused his prime minister's appeal to remove Garoufalias, Papandreou himself resigned, precipitating a major constitutional crisis.

During the next two years the king refused to allow elections, and undermined the Centre Union and the parliamentary system by asking individual politicians, some of them 'apostates' from the Centre Union, to form governments which had no majority in parliament. Enough politicians were lured by the spoils of office to co-operate, but Papandreou began another 'relentless struggle' to defend democratic rights. Speeches, strikes, demonstrations, posters and graffiti proclaimed the disgust of the 53% who had voted for the Centre Union and found their wishes brushed aside. The hysterical atmosphere was maintained by a vast demonstration addressed by Papandreou at Kastri in July 1966, and by trials of Lambrakis killers and of the Aspida group which provided constant revelations about the corruption of the system. King Constantine and his advisers, the most important of whom was his mother Queen Frederika, seemed to have done little but provoke anarchy by their high-handed actions.

Eventually Papandreou joined with Kanellopoulos, the leader of ERE, to demand elections for the spring of 1966. The king, believing perhaps that ERE stood a chance of winning, cautiously gave his approval and, against all precedent, appointed Kanellopoulos to oversee the campaign, during which there were calls for Andreas Papandreou to be prosecuted over the Aspida affair, and rumours that the king and senior generals, using a NATO contingency plan, had made preparations to act if the Centre Union won.

In fact neither the election nor the royal coup took place. In the small hours of 21 April 1967 a group of unknown army officers staged an efficient and unexpected coup d'état of their own.

The Colonels

The *putsch* of the 'Colonels' took both Greek and international observers completely by surprise. The leading figures in the new regime, Papadopoulos, Pattakos and Makarezos, were virtually unknown. Their actions seem to have been motivated as much by the need to protect themselves from a Centre Union victory, and by the low pay and status of the officer class, as by any high political ideals. They were men from peasant or lower middle-class backgrounds, with little education and no experience of civil administration or international affairs, whose crude and vulgar demeanour soon alienated them from the traditional right-wing élites. Having seized power by force, largely to protect their careers, fear of retribution prevented them from giving it up, and compelled them to justify their actions by cobbling together a half-baked political philosophy.

At its centre was obsessive anti-communism – a blunt instrument with which even George Panandreou was bludgeoned. Beyond this the new regime spoke, in similar terms to Metaxas, about the need to create a new Greek Christian civilization and return to traditional values. Confusing references to Ancient Greece and Byzantium figured repeatedly and often interchangeably in their speeches. Papandreou's educational reforms were torn up, and confused schoolchildren found their textbooks rewritten to accommodate the new barrack-room version of Greek history. The revival of *katharevousa* fortunately made many of the outpourings of the new order incomprehensible to most Greeks. Hatred of long hair and mini-skirts formed an important part of the Colonels' political philosophy, to the great detriment of the Greek tourist trade. Like most regimes of this type, it was prepared to take irresponsible short-term measures to generate a temporary economic boom, and for a while was able to take credit for rising living standards.

By far the most efficient aspect of the regime was its repressive apparatus. An immediate decree, falsely claiming the king's signature, proclaimed martial law, set up military courts, abolished political parties, and withdrew the right to strike. Rigorous press censorship was introduced and the most unlikely books condemned as subversive. The recently emptied prison camps on Leros, Yioura and Makrinoros filled up again with opponents of the regime; independent reports soon confirmed that torture and brutal treatment took place there. Anyone who opposed the regime felt the hand of the security police. In January 1968 eighteen generals and fifteen colonels were dismissed; a purge of senior air force and naval officers followed a month later. In March, 900 civil servants lost their jobs, and in 1969 twenty-one senior judges and public prosecutors. Thousands of oridinary people were dismissed on suspicion or their past record, or for no reason at all.

The regime rapidly evolved into the personal dictatorship of Colonel George Papadopoulos. Although the king had wanted to block the return of the Centre Union, he regarded the unexpected coup with contempt and embarrassment. In December 1967 he staged a counter-coup, which ended in failure and exile in Rome, and later in London, and gave the Colonels an excuse to carry out a purge. Civilian politicians were dismissed from the cabinet and a regent appointed to replace the king. In a derisive referendum held under martial law, an illegal 'constitution' was confirmed which in November 1968 legitimized the new regime, at least in its own eyes. Papadopoulos, who clearly had great confidence in his own administrative genius, became prime minister, education minister, defence minister, and later regent. To describe the elevation of this grey and nondescript reactionary as a cult of personality would be a contradiction in terms, but by 1972 he appeared to have convinced himself that the job was his for life. In June 1973 he formally abolished the monarchy, declaring Greece a republic with himself as president.

However, in less than six months Papadopoulos had been ousted by Ioannides, the brutal head of the secret police. The subsequent excesses compromised the regime with even the most pragmatic 'cold warriors' in Washington and London. In July 1974, in a gamble that nationalism still had the power to outweigh the growing disgust of the Greek people, the Colonels made the disastrous decision to play the Cyprus card.

THE END OF THE DICTATORSHIP AND
THE RETURN OF DEMOCRACY

Like most post-war Greek governments, the Colonels had been immediately confronted with a crisis over Cyprus, which they had handled with characteristic ineptitude. When attacks on Turkish Cypriot villagers in November 1968 led to Turkish threats of invasion, they first adopted a belligerent attitude, and then made a humiliating climb-down in the face of overwhelming Turkish military superiority. They were forced to recall their agent, Grivas, and withdraw the Greek army contingent from the island. This began a process of alienation from Archbishop Makarios, whom they regarded as a dangerous leftist, that was to lead to their downfall.

In July 1974 the Colonels plotted to kill the Archbishop and replace him with a former hard-line member of EOKA, Nikos Sampson. Presumably it was then intended to proclaim enosis and save the dictatorship in a torrent of nationalist fervour; perhaps they also hoped that the Americans, who regarded Makarios as a fellow traveller, would reward them for replacing their *bête noire* with a man who would not conceivably do deals with the Russians. The resulting fiasco was a disaster both for Cyprus and for the Colonels. On 15 July 1974 Makarios survived an attempt on his life and escaped to the safety of the British base. The Americans *did* come close to recognizing the thuggish government of Nikos Sampson, but the Colonels, like many a Greek government before them, had underestimated the resolve and capacity of Turks to respond to their challenge.

On 20 July Turkish forces began a huge invasion of Cyprus by sea and air to protect their people from Sampson's terrorist regime. The Colonels had given the Turks an opportunity to impose a brutal and perhaps final solution to the Cyprus Question, in circumstances in which the British, having seen one of the guarantor Powers of the Republic of Cyprus attempt to subvert it and put in power one of their enemies, would be very unlikely to act.

Having provoked the Turks and wrecked the Greek economy with their expenditure on arms, the Colonels none the less found themselves incapable of resisting. An attempted mobilization against Turkey in Thrace was a disorganized farce. And having demonstrated their ineptitude in the one area in which they might have shown at least average competence, the regime now slunk tamely from office. On 24 July 1974 Constantine Karamanlis was summoned from Paris to assume the role of elder statesman and saviour of democracy.

The Second Ministry of Karamanlis, 1974–81

The comprehensive disintegration of the Colonels' regime had wiped the political slate clean and exposed the inadequacies of post-war politics. It provided another opportunity to confront Greece's perennial problems. The shock of their brutalities made change inevitable; whether this would come about as a result of Karamanlis's drive towards full membership of the EEC, or from the radical socialist restructuring envisaged by Andreas Papandreou, are questions that have not yet been answered. What is certain is that both Right and Left had been shocked into seeking new ways to escape the legacy of the past.

Capitalizing on the desire for stability and upon his stature as a familiar 'elder statesman', Karamanlis wasted no time in calling elections for 17 November – only four months after the fall of the dictatorship – and announcing a referendum on the future of the monarchy. Both resulted in decisive mandates: in the sixth vote on the monarchy since independence 69% of the people voted for its demise; while Karamanlis's conservative party, New Democracy, won a decisive victory with 54% of the votes. However, despite this victory for conservatism, the election heralded a break with the past in two significant ways: the Communist parties were allowed to campaign openly for the first time since the war, and Andreas Papandreou unveiled his new radical party, PASOK (Panhellenic Socialist Union).

The incompetence of the previous regime meant that Karamanlis was confronted with massive problems. The economy had been shattered by extravagance and corruption, and the public was demanding that all vestiges of the old regime should be swept away and its leaders punished. But the repressive machinery remained largely intact, and there were still weapons in the hands of those who remained loyal to the Colonels. In addition, the national humiliation suffered over the Cyprus affair had turned to violent anti-Americanism and a disenchantment with the Western Alliance which made it impossible for Karamanlis to pursue the traditional policies of the Greek Right.

It is not surprising therefore that his natural pro-Western and free-market instincts were modified by a need to proceed cautiously. He showed remarkable flexibility in trying to balance conflicting aspirations, pursuing his major goal of bringing Greece into the Common Market while appeasing popular demands for domestic reform and an independent foreign policy. A series of trials of the leading figures of the previous regime, and purges of the civil service and army, weakened the militarist clique that had for so long manipulated Greek politics. Educational reforms were introduced, and the government intervened in the economy to control some of the more blatant excesses of Greek capitalism. Despite these efforts, reform was often frustrated by the unfavourable world economic situation, by huge expenditure on armaments to counter the perceived Turkish threat, and above all by continuing tensions in international affairs which absorbed most of the prime minister's energies.

Within weeks of the Colonels' fall the Turks carried out further advances in Cyprus that brought nearly half the island under their control. There followed what amounted to a population exchange, with 200,000 Greek Cypriots forced out of the north of the island and Turkish Cypriots fleeing northwards or to the safety of the British bases. The powerlessness of Athens to prevent this – and the historical echoes it invoked: frustrated nationalism, foreign interference, and the uprooting of Greeks from their ancient homelands – made the events in Cyprus particularly wounding to Greek pride. In February 1975 the creation of a 'Turkish Federated State of Cyprus' lessened still further any chance of reconciliation. Numerous initiatives by Karamanlis and by the international community failed to achieve any solution to the division of the island, and as in the past the priorities of the government in Athens were distorted by the demands of the overseas Greeks.

The festering crisis over Cyprus had poisoned relations between Greece and Turkey. Greek complaints about the treatment of their minority in Istanbul (now less than 10,000, compared to 70,000 in 1960, 100,000 in 1920, and nearly 300,000 in 1820) were matched by Turkish anxieties about the Turks of eastern Thrace. Complex geographical problems over ownership of mineral rights in the Aegean, which could only be solved by compromise, led instead to military confrontations. In July 1976 the two countries nearly went to war over the activities of the Turkish survey vessel *Sismik* in the Aegean. Disputes over air traffic control, which at other times would have been solved by quiet diplomacy, became front-page news in Athens and Istanbul. Not for the first time in Greek history, the huge effort of keeping the Greek army on constant alert diverted resources from domestic reform.

Feelings of helplessness in the face of Greece's ancient enemy often turned into violent anti-Americanism, disenchantment with the West in general, and a revival of the Greek obsession that all her problems stemmed from foreign interference. Rightly or wrongly it was believed that the United States had connived at, and even welcomed, the rule of the Colonels and the partition of Cyprus. The US–Turkish Defence Agreement of 1976, and the resumption of US arms shipments to Turkey in 1978, intensified anti-American feeling. In the aftermath of the Cyprus crisis several American officials paid with their lives for their country's apparent hostility to Greek interests. Even Karamanlis, in sharp contrast to his pro-Americanism of the 1950s, was swept along in the reaction and, despite his enthusiasm for European integration, sought a new alignment in foreign affairs. The status of the vital American bases at Herakleion, Suda Bay, Nea Makri and Elleniko was called into question, and relations with the United States remained cool. At the same time efforts were made to improve relations with the Eastern bloc and to pursue independent initiatives with Middle Eastern and non-aligned countries.

There is no doubt, however, that Karamanlis remained at heart wedded to the Western Alliance and convinced that the most effective way to prevent a repetition of dictatorship and to shock Greece into modernization and change lay in entry into the Common Market. On 28 May 1979, in what may well turn out to be the most fundamental change in her national status since the collapse of the Great Idea in 1922, Greece signed the Treaty of Accession to the European Economic Community.

Andreas Papandreou and the Triumph of PASOK

The victory of George Papandreou's radical Centre Union Party in 1962 had signalled a clear desire for fundamental change. But after his death and in the insecure aftermath of the dictatorship, it was not surprising that Greeks had turned to Karamanlis, the surviving charismatic leader of the post-war era, rather than Papandreou's son, the young, exciting but unpredictable Andreas, to re-establish democracy. It was certainly safe in the hands of Karamanlis, but it remained to be seen whether he could satisfy national expectations once the shock of dictatorship had subsided. Many people questioned whether, despite the more tolerant and popularist policies he now embraced, Karamanlis was too deeply imbued with traditional Greek political ways to lead Greece into a new age.

The radical coalition of the sixties had been thrown into confusion by the dividing tactics of the monarchy and by the persecution of the Colonels, but after 1974 a large section of the electorate was waiting for the reappearance of a party that would express their aspirations. The radical opposition was not dead but merely regrouping, and within weeks of his return Karamanlis faced a vigorous opposition, which accused him of stealing an unfair advantage by holding elections before the country was ready, and imposing the Constitution of 1975 which enhanced the power of the presidency at the expense of the legislature. Andreas Papandreou called it 'totalitarian' and claimed that a constitutional crisis would occur if the president and the ruling party were ever of different political persuasions. The opposition demanded withdrawal from NATO and the removal of the American bases, and claimed that Karamanlis' foreign-policy initiatives and 'openings to the Balkans' had achieved no more than those of Venizelos in the 1930s, and were only a smoke-screen for his EEC ambitions – which, they claimed, would only serve the interests of big business and civil servants, and would be detrimental to the living standards of ordinary people. Above all, the opposition believed that Karamanlis was unwilling to use the power of the state to bring about change, and relied on Greece's entry into the Common Market to do the work for him.

For several years after 1974 it seemed that the opposition was too fragmented and disorganized to mount a serious challenge. In September 1977 Karamanlis again won a comfortable victory with 42% of the vote and 172 parliamentary seats. The Communists, who had marked their readmission to political life by splitting into 'Eurocommunist' and Moscow-oriented factions and renewing their post-mortems on the Civil War, made no headway. The liberal Union of the Democratic Centre, natural heir to the Centre Union, was also crippled by internal crisis. It was Andreas Papandreou's PASOK that showed the most significant rise in support, increasing its share of the vote to 25% (93 seats) from only 14% three years before. Papandreou was emerging as a powerful and responsible politician, no longer wedded to revolutionary Marxism and the obvious heir to the radical traditions of the broad Left and of EAM. Many now looked to him to provide a way forward based upon radical domestic reform.

PASOK was helped by the decision of Karamanlis to lay down the leadership of New Democracy and stand for the presidency. At the party conference in Khalkidiki in May 1979 – the first true conference of a non-Communist party – he attempted to establish a modern party organization to replace the traditional Greek conglomeration around a charismatic leader. The decision that future ND leaders should be elected paved the way for him to resign and stake his claim to the presidency, which he won by a very narrow majority later in the month. After a damaging power struggle George Rallis became leader of ND, which was inevitably weakened by the loss of its founder.

On the first day of January 1981 – an election year – Greece became the tenth member of the European Economic Community. The nation was divided between those who saw this as a great opportunity, and those who believed that the Community represented an infringement of national sovereignty and a threat to living standards. PASOK boycotted the debate on ratification and claimed that the visit of President

Karamanlis to Moscow, Prague and Budapest in October 1981 merely gave the illusion that the country could still pursue an independent foreign policy. Later in the month Papandreou led PASOK into the election under the slogan 'Allaghi' (Change). Promising to use the state to bring about radical reform, PASOK undertook to renegotiate the EEC Treaty, to withdraw Greece from NATO, and to demand the closing down of American bases.

The response was decisive. PASOK won 48% of the votes (172 seats) against ND's 36% (112 seats), with 11% for the Communists (13 seats). The electorate had placed its confidence in the first Socialist government in Greek history.

CHAPTER NINETEEN

The Decade of Papandreou
1981–89

Change (*Allagi*) was the slogan under which Andreas Papandreou won the election of 1981. In the euphoria of victory, PASOK followers believed that they could break the stranglehold of social conservatism that, since Independence, had defied the efforts of reformers as diverse as Capodistrias, Trikoupis, Venizelos, and George Papandreou. But the next few years were to prove that *'Allagi'* would be easier to promise than to achieve.

Because of their history, the Greek people needed to feel that their country was pursuing a proud and independent foreign policy, but from the start, Papandreou faced foreign criticism. Greece was accused of harboring anti-Israeli sentiments and pilloried for her handling of a series of accidents and natural disasters. Anyone who understands Greek history will grasp the special bitterness that such 'interference' provoked. Many Greeks believed that the Great Powers had always treated their country like a colony; imposing an alien monarchy after Independence; and frustrating the dream of Greek unity throughout the nineteenth century. The Powers had encouraged Greece to enter the First World War and to pursue unrealistic ambitions in Asia Minor, and had then abandoned her to the tender mercies of Mustapha Kemal. They had pushed her into war against Hitler to further their own war efforts, and then proved incapable of protecting her from invasion and occupation. After the war, they had imposed a regime that was repugnant to large sections of the Greek population, and had then acquiesced in the Right Wing Terror. For the next twenty years they had interfered in Greek politics, and then kept silent while the people suffered under the heel of the Colonels.

It is not surprising therefore that when Andreas Papandreou at last asserted Greek independence, he was as popular at home as he was infuriating to Greece's critics. Over the next few years, he regularly outraged his partners in the Western Alliance and the Common Market by his failure to conform to common positions. He refused to support EC sanctions against Poland, to condemn either Libyan intervention in Chad, or the shooting down of a Korean airliner by the Russians. Disentangling Greece from both the superpowers, he pursued an independent line in the Middle East. He ruthlessly used the EC to further Greek national goals, blocking, for instance, the entry of Spain and Portugal until Greek interests were safeguarded. But although Papandreou could deliver an occasional rebuff to America that satisfied public opinion, in matters of real substance the road to change remained blocked. The unequal struggle with Turkey continued. There was no realistic alternative to the Western Alliance. The economy remained weak. The political system still depended upon charismatic individuals rather than modern party organisations.

The promised restructuring of Greek society also proved very difficult in the face of entrenched interest groups and bureaucratic inertia. Some progress was made in modernising the educational system, although most people continued to supplement state education with private tuition. The status of women was improved, and in 1987, amidst great controversy, abortion was legalised. A start was made in the creation of a welfare state, but Greece lacked the resources to do much more than build its foundations. The economy resisted change stubbornly, leaving Greece at the bottom of the European league according to almost all economic indicators.

It was not long before Papandreou's abrasive style of leadership reactivated the political instability that had been the dominant theme in modern Greek history. In the spring of 1985, Constantine Karamanlis resigned the Presidency and went into exile, claiming that Papandreou had tricked him into believing he would support his re-election as President, whereas in reality the Prime Minister was secretly backing Sarzetakis (a hero of the Lambrakis Trial).

When Sarzetakis was elected President, the opposition refused to recognise him; shattering the fragile constitutional consensus, and further embittering the relationships between PASOK and New Democracy, whose leader Mitsotakis was already reviled for his part in undermining George Papandreou in 1965.

Papandreou retained power with a slightly reduced majority in the election of June 1985, but he was forced to introduce an economic austerity package that strained the loyalty of his supporters to breaking point. Strikes, demonstrations, and fierce press criticism heralded the end of PASOK's honeymoon with the people. In the autumn of 1985, the death of a young left-wing demonstrator provoked a crisis in the party and the resignation of a minister, Constantine Laliotis. The stringent 1986 budget was a further shock to those who still hoped for a more equal society.

PASOK's promises to nationalise key sectors of the economy and to reform the tax structure particularly infuriated its opponents. In April 1987, in one of PASOK's few successes in controlling private wealth, Church estates were confiscated and measures introduced to broaden the ownership of land. Henceforth, debt repayments, inflation, a negative trade balance, and the highest relative expenditure on arms of any European state, forced Papandreou to turn his mind to economic survival rather than restructuring.

By the end of Papandreou's second term in June 1989, the outlook was clouded by uncertainties and unresolved problems. After eight years of power, much of PASOK's programme remained unfulfilled. Greece was still part of the European Community, taking a full part in its organisational structures and benefiting greatly from its financial support. She also remained a member, if an eccentric one, of NATO. The Americans still enjoyed substantial military facilities in the country, and huge arms deals confirmed Greece's dependence upon US military technology. Relations with Turkey had gone from bad to worse, and the two countries came very close to war in March 1987 over mineral rights in the Aegean. There had been no progress on the Cyprus Question, and every year that passed served to confirm the status quo on the island.

By the summer of 1988 Papandreou had carried out no less than

14 government reshuffles since coming to power and PASOK was threatened by rising support for rejuvenated Left Wing parties and trades unions. In February 1986, dissidents formed a new Socialist Trades Union Movement in opposition to the government. Some opinion polls showed that only 25% of the electorate still supported him. Adverse publicity over the ageing leader's affair with ex-air-hostess Dimitra Liani emphasised PASOK's unhealthy reliance upon the fortunes of its charismatic founder. Revelations of corruption in high places and a scandal over the affairs of the Bank of Crete led to calls for the Prime Minister himself to be put on trial.

Stalemate and Scandal June 1989–April 1990

In the elections of 18th June, 1989 PASOK's share of the vote fell to just over 30% (from nearly 50% in 1985) and its parliamentary representation from 161 to 125. Nonetheless, the opposition New Democracy party did not have an overall majority, and was not able to form a government on its own. After its leader Mitsotakis, and then Papandreou failed to form governments, the balance of power in the Greek Parliament was held by a collection of small parties and splinter groups, giving the Communists their first chance to wield power since the Second World War. Eventually, after tortuous discussions, an extraordinary coalition of opposites emerged, held together only by their determination to exclude the Communists from power. Tzannis Tzanetakis (New Democracy) became the head of a joint administration comprising representatives of the Left Coalition and the hitherto staunchly anti-Communist New Democracy. Clearly, such a combination stood little chance of agreeing on anything, apart from a determination to prosecute Andreas Papandreou for his alleged involvement in corrupt dealings. With the announcement on 27th September that Papandreou would be brought to trial there was nothing left to hold the caretaker government together.

The elections of November 5th 1989 were again inconclusive. New Democracy (148) was still three seats short of an overall majority; PASOK (128) had gained a little ground; the Left lost seven seats. Greece seemed to be locked into the stalemate that occasionally afflicts countries with a system of proportional representation, where disproportionate power can be wielded by small groups holding the balance of power. On November 22nd, 1989 responsible politicians of all parties backed an all-party caretaker government led by 85-year-old Zenophon Zolotas, former Governor of the Bank of Greece.

The Zolotas government was in no position to provide decisive leadership. Workers began a series of 24-hour general strikes demanding 19% pay raises that would merely match the rate of inflation. This forced the collapse of the government's pay policy, and caused yet another government reshuffle. At the same time there was no agreement about who should be the next president. The deadlock was finally broken on April 8th, 1990, when a weary Greek populace yet again went to the polls after nearly a year of instability and paralysis. This time, New Democracy won 150 seats and with the support of another small party, Mitsotakis was at last able to form a government.

CHAPTER TWENTY

New Democracy
1990-1993

New Democracy was as determined to break the mould as had been the PASOK government a decade before, and the victory of Mitsotakis heralded a radical switch of direction towards a free market economy. There was to be a far-reaching privatisation programme, a drastic pruning of the social security system, educational reform, and the adoption a more co-operative relationship with the EC and the United States. Various developments spelt out the new orientation. On May 4th, 83-year-old Constantine Karamanlis finally became President. On May 21st, full diplomatic recognition was given to the state of Israel. A few days later a new defence agreement allowed the United States to retain military facilities in Greece.

Economic and Social Reform

The new government was unfortunate that its attempts at economic and social re-structuring coincided with a series of world problems over which it had no control: a global recession, the collapse of communism in eastern Europe, and the Gulf War.

In the Spring of 1990 inflation in Greece was 17.8%, the highest rate in the EC. Greece had escalating government spending, a huge external debt, and a hugely expensive programme of arms purchase that consumed a greater proportion of national income than that of any other European state. In October 1992, a new contract was signed to buy the enormously expensive American F16 fighter aircraft. After the collapse of communism in the Soviet Union and the Balkans, there was a huge influx of Greek refugees and illegal immigrants. In December 1990, thousands of Albanian Greeks crossed the border following the collapse of the communist dictatorship. More unexpectedly, hundreds of thousands of Pontic Greeks, whose ancestors had lived in southern Russia and the Ukraine since ancient times, began to 'come home' to Greece in scenes reminiscent of the aftermath of the debacle of 1922. Their arrival, at a time of economic depression and restructuring, posed major problems of resettlement, housing, and social problems.

Unlike his predecessor, Mitsotakis was convinced that Greece's future lay in the European Community, and he believed that the economy must be reformed and institutions modernised to bring it in line with its European partners. His emergency economic package of April 25th, 1990 showed that he was prepared to tackle the country's economic and financial problems head on. He proposed big cuts in government spending, increases in the price of public utilities, and the privatisation of large sections of state owned industry. These policies provoked massive resistance from all sides, and provoked a series of general strikes that brought the country to the brink of ruin. In August 1990, inflation had risen to nearly 23%. The privatisation programme was greeted with particular hostility, not just by the Left, but also by nationalists who believed that the nation's patrimony was being sold off to foreigners. The restructuring of Greece's ramshackle educational system, essential if the country was to compete as a modern industrial nation, also met with violent resistance. In January 1991, during huge demonstrations in Athens, a teacher was killed by right-wingers, forcing the resignation of the education minister and provoking nation-wide teachers' strike. Consequently, the government's education reforms were stopped in their tracks, making private schools and foreign universities the only recourse for ambitious parents, and condemning the economy to a continuing shortage of trained personnel.

The polarisation of Greek politics meant that any attempt at reform provoked violent divisions and recriminations. Nothing illustrated this more than the long-awaited trial to uncover the truth about the Bank of Crete scandal, which began in March 1991. No one questioned the fact that bribery, fraud, and dishonesty had taken place, but guilt or innocence became secondary as the trial developed into a political battlefield. The Left were convinced that the charges, however justified, were motivated by political vindictiveness, and the Right were equally determined to use it as a weapon against their enemies. The most important figure in the scandal, the former Bank of Crete chairman, Koskotas, continued to resist extradition from the US, and never appeared in court. Witnesses disappeared, and Papandreou's ex colleague, Agamemnon Koutsogioras, actually died in the courtroom. Papandreou himself refused to answer charges or recognise their validity, and at the beginning of 1992, proceedings against him were withdrawn.

The Gulf Crisis of 1990 was very damaging to Greek interests. Her international position was weakened, and the economy suffered from a massive drop in tourism. In March 1991, an American serviceman was killed, and a month later a bomb killed several people in Athens. Although Greece sent off a frigate to the Gulf, this could not compare with the massive strategic support Turkey gave to the American bombing campaign, and there were fears that the Americans would reward Turkey by supporting her in future territorial dispute. The links that successive Greek governments had forged with the Arab world were weakened, while initial hopes that the post war 'new world order' would benefit Greek interests by leading to a settlement of the Cyprus problem came to nothing.

THE FALL OF MITSOTAKIS

No sooner was the Gulf War settled than a new set of crises surrounding the collapse of communism on Greece's northern borders led to New Democracy's downfall. In March 1992, the Yugoslav republic of Macedonia declared its independence after the withdrawal of troops of the Yugoslav National Army. Over the next year, the new state was recognised by the United States, Russia, China and most EC members. It was admitted to the United Nations in April 1993 under the name 'Former Yugoslav Republic of Macedonia', [F.Y.R.O.M.]. Shortly afterwards American troops arrived as part of a UN force to guarantee its borders. In February 1994, the World Bank and the I.M.F. announced loans to develop the Macedonian economy.

These developments had a profoundly disturbing and divisive impact on Greek politics, and quickly brought Greece into conflict with the United Nations and the European Community. Greece had lived for forty years alongside the Yugoslavian region calling itself 'Macedonia', but Greek nationalists whipped up an extraordinary hysteria over the name and flag adopted by the newly independent state. 'Skopje' as they called it, had stolen a name that was sacred to the Greek past. It had put on its new flag the sun symbol of Alexander the Great, and instituted a constitution that seemed to lay claim to Salonika and parts of Northern Greece. It was as if they believed that this tiny impoverished state was poised to march southwards, seize Salonika, and redraw a frontier that had lasted for eighty years and survived two world wars.

The rest of the world, preoccupied with the bloodletting in Bosnia, could only look on with frustration and bewilderment. In the summer of 1992, when some Greek students were arrested for calling for compromise, 169 leading Greek intellectuals signed a protest. In December, on the eve of the Edinburgh European Summit, a million Greek people took to the streets in protest against concessions to the Macedonians by the EC. Foreign tourists were bombarded with the slogan 'Macedonia is Greek'. The names of Alexander the Great and other heroes of the distant past were invoked, bringing back memories, on the seventieth anniversary of the Debacle of 1922, of previous nationalist hysteria and of the bloodshed and national humiliation to which this had led.

The national obsession with Macedonia placed the Mitsotakis government in a difficult position. Already faced with intense opposition to its economic programme, it now faced accusations of lack of patriotism if it adopted a moderate stance over Macedonia. In April 1992, the Prime Minister sacked his Foreign Minister, Samaras, indicating that there were serious disagreements within the government over the issue. In December Mitsotakis went further and dismissed his entire Cabinet, which could not agree over economic policy or the Macedonian question.

By the beginning of 1993, it seemed as if the government, purged of hard-liners, was edging towards compromise. In February, international arbitration was accepted over the Macedonia 'name issue', a month later an accord pledging co-operation was signed with Bulgaria, and the Government narrowly won a vote of confidence in Parliament for its Macedonian policy. In May, after the new Republic had been admitted to the UN as 'Former Yugoslav Republic of Macedonia' [FYROM], Greek and Macedonian officials held discussions.

However, it was clear that powerful forces in Greece were determined to obstruct this compromise, despite the dangerous situation in the Balkans. In June 1993, the youthful and ambitious former Foreign Minister Samaras set up a new Party, Political Spring (POLA) pledged to pursue a hard line over Macedonia, and to break the strangle-hold of the 'dinosaurs' of Greek politics. With his tiny majority, the position of the Mitsotakis was now very precarious. Problems seemed to press in on all sides: The budget for 1992 envisaged a reduction of 3-4% in real incomes. The lifting of currency controls in May 1993 caused a flight of capital. In June, the promising discussions in New York on the future of Cyprus broke down. Relations with Greece's other small neighbour, Albania, began to rival those with Macedonia in their rancour. In August a controversial visit by ex-King Constantine re-opened old wounds. If all this was not enough, allegations were made about the involvement in corrupt practices of Prime Minister Mitsotakis himself.

The storm broke on September 6th 1993 when Samaras called upon those New Democracy deputies who disagreed with Government policy to withdraw their support. Three days later, Mitsotakis submitted his resignation and called for early elections, the result of which, declared on 10th October, was a clear victory for PASOK, which polled 46.9% of the vote (170 seats), leaving New Democracy with 39.3% (111 seats) and the smaller parties with 12.3% (19 seats).

CHAPTER TWENTY-ONE

New Challenges, Old Problems

On 13th December 1993, 75-year-old Andreas Papandreou, whose health had allowed only four public appearances during the election campaign, announced his last government. To universal astonishment, it included his new wife, Dimitra and his personal physician. Papandreou's programme held few surprises: PASOK now regarded itself as a Social Democratic rather than a Socialist Party, and despite increased spending on welfare and a halt to the privatisation campaign, there was to be no return to the radicalism, anti-Americanism, and Euro-scepticism of the '80s. The new challenges would come from the continuing deterioration in Greece's relations with her neighbours, and the demands placed upon the Greek economy by the approach of the Single European Currency.

Some Greek political tradition had not changed: Within weeks of PASOK's return to power, thirty-five senior Army officers resigned over the reinstatement of 'socialist' colleagues, and a wholesale replacement of officials associated with the previous government soon began. In a mirror image of the N.D.'s treatment of Papandreou three years before, Constantine Mitsotakis was accused by Merlina Mercouri, the new minister of culture, of profiting from illegal archaeological excavations. In May, 1994 it was announced that he would be put on trial for telephone tapping, and in September, new charges relating to the privatisation of the state cement company were laid against him. In another settling of old scores, ex-King Constantine was deprived of his Greek citizenship, and in April 1994, Royal property in Greece was confiscated.

In June 1994, Andreas Papandreou stood at the height of his long career, hosting the Corfu Summit during Greece's presidency of the European Union, but in November 1995 he was admitted to hospital with what proved to be a terminal illness. His incapacity plunged the Party into crisis. For the rest of the year, while the aged leader clung to life and office, his colleagues seemed incapable of agreeing on a successor. Papandreou had been the founder and driving force of the ruling Party since its inception, and had conquered illness, personal scandal and corruption scandals to win victory against all the odds. In his absence, domestic and international problems piled up as Greece drifted aimlessly. At last, in January 1996, Papandreou resigned. His death later in the year, together with those of actresses Merlina Mercouri [1994] and Aliki Vougioklagi [July 1996], Greece's beloved 'national star', marked for the older generation of Greek people a sad passing of familiar national icons. Under its new leader Constantine Simitis, PASOK won the elections of September 1996 comfortably, but it faced an unenviable catalogue of domestic and international problems.

The Threat from the North

Simitis inherited the problems that flowed from the disintegration of Yugoslavia and the collapse of the Albanian state. The violent civil war in Bosnia dragged on despite UN intervention, sanctions on Serbia, and endless diplomatic initiatives. Historically Greece had related to fellow Orthodox Christians in the Balkans. Many Greeks felt an affinity with Serbia, and identified with the Bosnian Serbs in their war against the Muslims. There were suggestions that Greek companies were secretly breaking the UN sanctions against Serbia. Diplomatically, the Greek government kept up informal connections with Belgrade, and joined with Russia in trying to soften the position of the international community towards the Bosnian Serbs. In September 1995, Athens criticised the continued bombing of Bosnian Serb targets, but the subsequent NATO imposed cease-fire allowed Athens to escape from its ambivalent position. In December 1996, Greek soldiers joined the international peacekeeping force in Bosnia, and Greece established diplomatic relations with Bosnia.

ALBANIA AND KOSOVO

No sooner had the Bosnian conflict been settled than an even more dangerous situation arose, this time just across the frontier. Throughout the nineties, relations with Albania had continued to deteriorate. Greek nationalists made inflated claims about the numbers of ethnic Greeks in Albania, rekindled Greek claims to 'Northern Epirus', and encouraged the activities of Greek extremists in Albania. In April 1993, after the 'Northern Epirus Liberation Front' killed two border policemen, Albania banned Greek Orthodox Easter processions, leading to Greek claims of persecution. In May 1994, after an abortive Greek-Albanian meeting in Zurich, six Greek Albanians were charged by Tirana with subversion. Greece claimed that the Greek minority was being 'terrorised', and Andreas Papandreou threatened to close the Albanian border if Greece did not approve the verdict of the impending trial. Eventually Albania released four of the Greeks who had become known as the 'Omonia Five' and constructive discussions between Athens and Tirana began.

However, in February 1997, Albania suddenly dissolved into chaos after millions lost their savings in a government-backed pyramid savings scheme. Within weeks, the whole of Southern Albania had fallen into the hands of local warlords, and the country was awash with stolen arms. The anarchy threatened to spread into ethnic Albanian regions of Serbian Kosovo and Macedonia on Greece's northern borders. Greece had already absorbed 300,000 Albanians since 1991, and the situation not only posed a threat to the Greek minority in Southern Albania, but the possibility of hundreds of thousands of fresh refugees swamping Greece's welfare resources and crippling her economy.

In 1998, the deteriorating situation in the Yugoslav province of Kosovo faced Greece with the possibility of an even greater catastrophe. The Yugoslav assault on separatist Albanian K.L.A. and the Albanian civilian population, raised the possibility of hundreds of thousands more refugees, and the prospect of a regional catastrophe if the conflict spread to into the ethnic Albanian regions of Macedonia. When NATO air strikes against Yugoslavia began in

March 1999, the Greek government found itself in a familiar dilemma. Public opinion was strongly sympathetic to the Orthodox Serbs and hostile to American intervention, but sympathy for the suffering of Serb civilians became overlaid with anti-Americanism and the national obsession with foreign interference. The opponents of NATO bombing held vast anti-western demonstrations, and blockaded NATO supply routes to Macedonia, while extremists placed bombs in the Athens Intercontinental Hotel, Citibank, and the Dutch embassy. When President Clinton visited Athens in the autumn, he was greeted with violent anti-American protests, despite his attempt to appease his hosts by apologising for America's support for the Colonels' dictatorship 20 years before. In the last analysis, Greece had to choose between an alliance with the bankrupt gangster-states of the old communist block, or solidarity with the western democracies. By the end of the conflict in June 1999, Prime Minister Simitis had succeeded in pursuing a statesmanlike and humanitarian course without betraying Greece's historical solidarity with her Balkan neighbours. From the outset, he announced that Greece would play no military role in the war, but Greece would not prevent NATO from using its bases on Greek soil. Simitis tried to play a mediating role, maintaining a strong line against the brutal Serb treatment of Kosovar civilians and allowing NATO to use its facilities on Greek soil, but keeping the door open to Belgrade by calling for a halt to NATO bombing and sending aid to Serbian civilians. A few weeks later Greek troops joined the international force in Kosovo.

At least the Kosovo conflict provided the opportunity to end Greece's long impasse with the republic of Macedonia. In February 1994 Greece had closed the Macedonian border, imposed a unilateral trade blockade, and prevented the release of EU funds to Macedonia until it agreed to change its name, flag and constitution. This brought Macedonia close to economic and social collapse. In September 1995, the two countries agreed to try to normalise relations, but the 'name issue' still festered, with Greece protesting strongly at Serbia's recognition of the new state, under the name 'Republic of Macedonia'. At a meeting in Skopje in December 1998, the Greek Foreign Minister refused to accept that there was a

Macedonian minority in Greece, and branded the 'Rainbow' organisation, which represented it, as a group of 'Stalinists, homosexuals and Slavo-Macedonians'. However, the stresses and potential dangers of the Kosovo war had the effect of making both countries recognise their shared economic and strategic interests. Border restrictions were eased. A high-speed rail link began to run regularly between Salonika and Skopje. In December 1999, the two states signed an agreement on military co-operation in which Greece pledged support for Macedonian entry into NATO and other EU institutions.

RELATIONS WITH TURKEY AND THE CYPRUS PROBLEM

On May 19th 1994, Greece declared a Day of Remembrance to mark the 'Turkish genocide' of 1919. It was not lost on the Turks that this was also the date of Atatürk Commemoration Day, one of their most sacred national celebrations. This gratuitous reopening of old wounds reminded the world that the perennial conflicts between Greece and Turkey remained a serious threat to the peace of the region. Over the next few years, explosive territorial disputes in the Aegean and rival Turkish and Cypriot ambitions to enter the European Community added fuel to the centuries old Greek-Turkish vendetta. The result was a ruinous arms race in the eastern Mediterranean and the constant possibility of an all out war.

The complex question of sovereignty over the waters around the coasts of Greece and Turkey had been dealt with by the Lausanne Treaty of 1923 and the Montreux Convention of 1936. Until the 1970's, these arrangements had proved acceptable to both sides, but the question of mineral rights on the continental shelf upset the status quo. UN pressure and the agreement at Berne in 1976 temporarily defused the crisis, but it flared up again in 1987.

The Law of the Sea Conference of November 1994 allowed states to extend their coastal waters from six to twelve miles, but in the case of Greece and Turkey this would be almost impossible to implement. In many places the Greek and Turkish coastlines were tightly mixed together and far less than 12 kilometres apart. The coastlines were dotted with thousands of uninhabited rocks and tiny islets, the sovereignty of which neither side had previously bothered to clarify. To bring in a twelve-mile limit in these circumstances could only be negotiated with good will, compromise, and moderation, but it soon became clear that both sides intended to use the situation as a weapon in their ongoing battle for Aegean mineral rights. Scarcely a week went by without Greece or Turkey claiming its waters or airspace had been violated. The scene was set for yet another round in the long contest that had begun in 1453.

Even before the Law of the Sea came into effect, the Greek navy fired on Turkish fishing boats, leading Turkey to claim that they could 'settle the matter' militarily in 48 hours. When the Greek Parliament ratified the Law of the Sea in June 1995, Turkey threatened war if Greece attempted to implement it. In the skies over the Aegean Greek and Turkish warplanes fought 'mock dog-fights' amidst mutual claims of violated air space. Turkey complained that Greece was installing missiles on islands demilitarised under the 1924 Treaty of Lausanne. Greece used her position in the EC to block the release of funds to Turkey, and to obstruct Turkish entry into the EU. At the beginning of 1996, there was a serious escalation when Turkey fired on Greek fishing boats that had entered disputed waters off the coast of Thrace. Greek ministers were vilified in parliament and the press for not asserting the national interest. A visit by the American mediator Richard Holbrooke was cancelled at short notice when a US official stated that America had no view on the sovereignty of rocks in the Aegean. Germany was excoriated for its attempt to maintain an even-handed approach to Greece and Turkey. Britain was vilified for proposing face to face talks to solve the dispute.

In May 1996, the Greek President toured American cities to drum up support for her cause in the Aegean. The run-up to American presidential election in November 1996 put the powerful American Greek lobby in a strong position to wield influence. The electoral success of the Turkish Islamic Party in December 1995 was used to portray Turkey as an Islamic 'terrorist' state. Turkey's poor human rights record, and its attempts to improve relations with Iraq and Iran, were used to good effect in the battle for American support. However in the aftermath of Bill Clinton's victory, American enthusiasm for involvement in the Aegean and Cypriot disputes suddenly slackened, leading to Greek accusations in July 1998 that Clinton had lied to gain electoral advantage.

A further crisis exploded in the summer of 1996, over the question of divided Cyprus. A cavalcade of motorcyclists had ridden overland from Berlin to dramatise the division of the island. By the time they arrived, saturation coverage of their progress on Cypriot and Greek television had whipped the public into a frenzy of expectation that somehow the events of Berlin in 1989 would be re-enacted, and the island would be re-unified in a wave of euphoria. What could have been a peaceful headline-catching demonstration ended in tragedy when a young Cypriot zealot who was exchanging insults and missiles with the Turks in the neutral zone was beaten to death by them. Two days later his cousin, ignoring the pleas of UN soldiers, attempted to pull down a Turkish flag, and was shot to death in front of the world's TV cameras. The Cypriots had deliberately engineered a confrontation to force their grievances to world attention, and the Turks, predictably, had overreacted to the provocation.

Consequently, the promising discussions over the island's future collapsed. Greek politicians, manoeuvring ahead of their September elections, lined up to visit Cyprus and make inflammatory speeches. In the autumn, under a new defence agreement, Greek and Cypriot armed forces held joint manoeuvres. At the turn of the year, Cyprus announced that it intended to install a Russian-made air defence system on the island, and began to build military facilities to support it. Turkey declared that it would not allow the system to be installed, and threatened to invade the south if Cyprus was allowed to join the EU before an overall settlement of the Cyprus problem was agreed. In December 1997, relations hit a new low when Turkey's bid to join the European Union was rejected. An infuriated Turkish president blamed this setback on Greek machinations and the threat by Athens to use its veto to block Turkish entry.

For the next two years relations between the two states hit new depths, with Cyprus providing a theatre for aggressive posturing and tit-for-tat escalation. Greece blocked Turkey's entry to the EU until the Cyprus question was solved. Turkey blocked the entry of Greek Cyprus because it saw it as Enosis by the back door. In June 1998 Turkey responded to a visit of Greek warplanes to Greek Cyprus by sending its own planes to the north. Later in the month the Greek president made a first official visit to Cyprus, followed a few weeks later by the first Turkish presidential visit to its own enclave. Greece and Cyprus had committed themselves to the installation of the Russian built air defence system, and as the deadline of their delivery approached, they seemed to have locked themselves into a course that would lead inexorably to a war. In July, Turkey said that it would deploy its own missiles in North Cyprus if the Greeks persisted with installing the Russian system. In October thousands of Greek troops took part in joint exercises on the island, but with overwhelming Turkish forces poised only 40 miles from the Cypriot coast it seemed as if the Hellenic partners had once more bitten off more than they could chew. Under American and Turkish pressure, cash-strapped Russia found excuses to delay delivery of the promised missiles, and on December 29th, after a meeting of Greek and Cypriot leaders to discuss the crisis, it was announced that Cyprus had decided not to deploy the missiles after all.

Greek and Cypriot newspapers berated their politicians for giving way to Turkey, and Greek Cypriots were bitter that Athens had let them down. War had been avoided, but the decision to relocate the Cypriot financed missiles to the island of Crete meant that the crisis would continue into the next year. Greek missiles in Crete rather than Cyprus posed no less a threat to the Turks, and they threatened to respond to any attempt to install them. In February, the Turkish president described Greece as an outlaw state that sponsors terrorism, after three Greek cabinet ministers resigned over the scandal surrounding the Kurdish militant leader Abdullah Ocalan, who had been apprehended by a Turkish snatch-squad whilst sheltering in the Greek embassy in Kenya. In April 1999, two months after an EU survey had nominated Greece as the poorest country in the EU, Athens announced a further two billion dollars would be spent on re-equipping its armed forces, in addition to the $16 billion allocated in 1998. The struggle with Turkey was absorbing more and more of the country's resources. In the summer of 1999 it seemed doubtful that the two could avoid an even more ruinous war.

THE BATTLE FOR ECONOMIC REFORM

When Constantine Simitis took over in 1996, he was determined to continue the task of reforming the archaic structures of the Greek economy in order to integrate the country fully into the European Union. Certainly, Greece had benefited enormously from the huge inflow of EU development funds like the 1993 Convergence Plan that led to a rapid growth of manufacturing capacity and improvements in agricultural production. But for Greece to take the next step, and meet the criteria for the proposed Single European Currency, huge changes and sacrifices would have to take place. Greece was the poorest country in the EU, with an inefficient economy strangled by red tape, tax avoidance and over-manning. She had by far the highest rate of inflation and public spending in the Community, and her education system was completely inadequate for the needs of a modern industrial economy.

Although both the PASOK government and private industry were convinced of the benefits of the EU membership, many Greek people had seen no improvement in their lives, and resented the interference and criticism that rained down on their country from Brussels other international bodies. In 1991, the insistence by Brussels that Greece remove restrictions against individuals investing abroad had led to the rich profit by moving their money out of the country while the poor saw the value of their savings eroded. Brussels had alleged that Greece was slow to implement Community legislation, and had manipulated the figures in order to inflate the benefits she received from the Community. Her treatment of asylum seekers came under attack. She was saddled with having the worst record for pollution and ecological vandalism in Europe, and accused of harbouring cigarette smugglers, and being a centre for book and music piracy. Particularly infuriating to many people was interference by Brussels in their traditional way of life, like the ill-fated attempt to make Greece change her relaxed attitude to bar opening times and the legal drinking age. Many Greeks had grown used to living in a relatively leisurely and un-competitive society. They had become accustomed to living under a system in which many people worked in subsidised state enterprises, protected from the ruthless impact of global competition. The government was determined to change all this, but powerful groups were equally resolute in their intention to use industrial action and even violence to protect their interests and the Greek way of life.

For the next three years the government held relentless to its austerity and restructuring programme in the face of almost continuous industrial action and political agitation by almost every section of Greek society. The government's initial austerity package in the autumn of 1996 provoked an immediate backlash. A general strike crippled the country, and farmers blockaded the transport system for weeks. Greek embassies all over the world were closed down by an unprecedented strike of the diplomatic corps. By January 1997, the disruption was so severe that the British foreign office advised holiday-makers to avoid the country. The rest of the year was fairly peaceful, but in December, government plans for 1998 provoked a new general strike.

1998 proved to be the worst year yet for industrial disruption. In January, strikers shut down the city of Athens. Next month the farmers joined in, blocking the country's main north-south highway. On February 27th, the government admitted that Greece would not meet the targets for membership of the Single Currency, but it showed its determination to win eventual entry by accepting a 14% devaluation to enter the European Exchange Mechanism [ERM] and announcing an even more stringent package of austerity measures. Resistance continued with a new general strike in April, a shut down of Olympic Airways aimed at stopping its restructuring, a strike against new tests for graduate teachers, and a violent six-week strike against the privatisation of the Ionian Bank. In December there were strikes by customs officers, railway workers, doctors, taxi drivers, tax officials, school teachers, and even footballers, but the government held valiantly to its course and carried its tough 1999 budget through parliament at the end of the year. Simitis had showed great fortitude by defying industrial blackmail and holding firm to a programme that he believed was essential for the modernisation of the country.

Greece in 2000

On 17th August 1999, a massive earthquake struck western Turkey, burying tens of thousands under rubble and crippling the Turkish economy. Far from rejoicing that such a calamity had befallen her ancient enemy, the Greek people rallied to their neighbour's support in an extraordinary display of sympathy and generosity. Messages of condolence, material aid and relief workers were sent to a country against which, only a few weeks before, they seemed about to go to war. Turkish leaders expressed surprise and gratitude at this human and mature response after so many years of recrimination and distrust. On September 7th, it was the turn of Athens to experience a huge earthquake. It caused less chaos than the Turkish catastrophe, but reminded Greeks and Turks that they shared the same corner of a volatile planet. Coming at the end of the millennium, it seemed time to place the squabbles and vendettas of the previous years in a more global perspective. On September 23rd, in a demonstration of solidarity not been seen since the 1930s, the two governments set up a joint disaster response team. The Greek foreign minister said he hoped that the warming of relations would 'break down the myth that Turks and Greeks hate each other'.

In December 1999, at the EU conference in Helsinki, Greece and Turkey took a step that promised an end to five centuries of debilitating antagonism. In defiance of the predictions of experts around the world, Athens agreed that Turkey should begin negotiation for entry to the European Union. In return, Turkey agreed to bow to Greek stipulations to submit their territorial disputes to international jurisdiction, to drop objections to EU negotiations with Cyprus, and to improve its human rights record. Greek and Turkish leaders spoke of the start of a new era in their relations. As the year 2000 dawned, it seemed as if a new epoch had truly begun.

Greece begins the new millennium as a member of an expanding and forward-looking member of the European Community. The foundations of a modern economy have been laid. Social legislation has started to improve the lives of working people. The status of Greek women has been transformed by legislation on divorce, inheritance and abortion. With the passing of the great men of the post-war era, George Papandreou and Constantine Karamanlis, the rule of charismatic individuals has given way to broad-based organisations reflecting the views of a wide electorate. The crushing burden of the long feud with Turkey seems at last to have been lifted. A new spirit of confidence and optimism is in the air. A Greek film director, Theo Angelopoulos, has won the Palm d'Or at Cannes. Athletes like Olga Vasdeki and Ekaterini Thanou reflect Greece's growing impact on the sporting world. Athens will stage the Olympic Games in 2004, and a new international airport and splendid archaeological museum will enhance the city's status. Soon, perhaps, the Trans Balkan oil pipeline will run from the Black Sea to Alexandroupolis, bringing fresh development and prosperity.

For thousands of years, the Greek people have lived on the front line of battles between contending and disintegrating systems, straddling the fault-line between East and West. They have survived the clash of Persians and Aryans, Orthodox and Catholic, Christianity and Islam, Habsburg and Romanov communists and fascists. Through all this, the Greek nation has stubbornly retained its unique identity. Who would doubt that these proud, creative, and contentious people will still be there, infuriating friends and defying enemies, for at least another thousand years?

Chronology of Major Events

B.C.

Prehistory

500,000	Palaeolithic man in northern Greece
100,000	Late Palaeolithic hunters in Epiros
6500	Neolithic farmers in Greece

Bronze Age/Palace Cultures

3000	Bronze Age culture on the mainland, Cyclades and Crete
2200	Middle Minoan early Palace culture in Crete
1700	Minoan Palace culture (Linear A)
1600	Rise of Mycenaean culture in Greece
1500	Major eruption of Thera
1450	Mycenaeans at Knossos in Crete (Linear B, a form of Greek)

Dark Age/Geometric Period

1220	Destruction of Troy VIIa
1200	Widespread destruction of Mycenaean sites
1184	Traditional date for the destruction of Homer's Troy
1100	Invasion of Dorian Greeks
1050	Migration of Greeks to the Aegean islands and Asia Minor
1050	Protogeometric pottery

900	Geometric pottery
776	Traditional date for the first Olympic Games
750–00	Homer and Hesiod

Orientalizing Period

8–6th c.	Colonization to the west and north-east
730–10	Spartan conquest of Messenia
657	Tyranny of Kypselos at Corinth
632	Attempted tyranny at Athens by Kylon

Archaic Period

621–20	Drakon promulgates laws at Athens
594	Solon archon at Athens
560	First tyranny of Peisistratos at Athens
545	Persia conquers the Ionian Greeks
508	Reforms of Kleisthenes at Athens
499	Ionian Revolt
490	Battle of Marathon
480–79	Persian invasion of Greece

Classical Period

478	Formation of the 'Delian League' (Athenian imperialism)
445–26	Herodotus active
431	Outbreak of the Peloponnesian War
430	Plague at Athens
428–7	Revolt of Mytilene
421	Peace of Nikias
418	Battle of Mantineia
416	Athens attacks Melos
413	Destruction of the Athenian expedition to Sicily
411	Oligarchic revolution at Athens
410	Battle of Kyzikos
404	Fall of Athens

Fourth Century

399	Trial and execution of Socrates
396–47	Plato active
395	Thucydides' *History* published
390–54	Xenophon active
371	Thebes destroys Spartan power at Leuktra
359–336	Philip II king of Macedonia
343–2	Aristotle tutor to Alexander
338	Battle of Khaironeia
336	Assassination of Philip II

Hellenistic Period

336–23	Alexander the Great
335	Alexander sacks Thebes
334	Battle of Granikos
333	Defeat of Darius III at Issos
331	Foundation of Alexandria, Egypt; Battle of Gaugamela
327	Marriage of Alexander and Roxane
326	Battle of Hydaspes
315	Olympias, mother of Alexander, murdered
310	Murder of Roxane and her son, Alexander IV
307	Demetrios the Besieger at Athens
297–72	Pyrrhos, king of Epiros
279	Invasion of Macedonia and Greece by Celts
276	Antigonas Gonatas founds Macedonian dynasty
251–13	Career of Aratos in the Akhaian League
235–22	Kleomenes III king of Sparta
197	Defeat of Philip V
196	Romans declare Greece liberated
167	Battle of Pydna ends Macedonian kingdom
146	Romans sack Corinth

Roman Period

86	Sulla sacks Athens in the war against Mithridates
48	Battle of Pharsalos
46	Corinth refounded as a Roman colony
42	Battle of Philippi
31	Battle of Actium

A.D.

49–52	St Paul in Greece
67	Nero in Greece
c. 120	Death of Plutarch
117–38	Hadrian
c. 101–77	Herodes
c. 150	Pausanias' guide-book
306–37	Constantine the Great
c. 330	Many statues removed from Greece to Constantinople
c. 355	St Basil, St Gregory of Nazianzos and Julian the Apostate students at Athens
395	Olympic games suppressed
529	Athens' pagan philosophic schools closed
6–8th c.	Slavic settlement in Greece
9th *c.*	Byzantium reasserts control over Greece
893–927	Simeon of Bulgaria
11th *c.*	Important monastic churches, Hosios Lukas, Nea Moni on Chios and Daphni near Athens
1080–4 & 1146–9	Normans raid Greece
1204	Fourth Crusade sacks Constantinople and breaks up the Byzantine Empire
1222	Byzantines recover Salonika
1261	Michael VIII Palaeologos recovers Constantinople
1262	Byzantines at Mistra
1311	Catalan Company takes Athens
1354	Ottoman Turks enter Europe
1429	Turks capture Salonika
1430	Byzantines retake Morea from Venetians
1453	Mehmet II captures Constantinople
1460	Turks capture Mistra
1463–79	1st Turko–Venetian war; few lasting territorial changes
1466	Venetians briefly take Athens
1470	Euboia falls to Turks
1472	Tsar Ivan III marries Byzantine princess, Sophia Palaeologos
1479	Turks briefly take Ionian Islands
1480	Rhodes resists siege
1483	Last independent ruler of Cyprus bequeaths island to Venice
1499–1502	2nd Turko–Venetian war: Naupaktos, Zante, Coron and Modon fall
1520–66	Suleiman the Magnificent
1522	Rhodes captured

1529	Turks repulsed from Vienna
1537–40	3rd Turko–Venetian war; Corfu ravaged; battle of Preveza, Turks take Nauplion and Monemvasia
1566	Chios and Naxos fall to Turks
1570 Jul	Turks land in Cyprus, take Famagusta (Aug) and Nicosia (Sep)
1571 Oct 7	Battle of Lepanto
1577	Samos falls to Turks
1645	4th Turko–Venetian war; Turks attack Crete, take Chania and Rethymnon (1646)
1653–9	Venetians try to stir up revolt in the Mani
1656	Venetians crush Turkish fleet and seize Lemnos and Tenedos (recaptured (1657)
1669	Turks take Candia (Herakleion)
1683	Failure of the Turks to take Vienna
1683–99	5th Turko–Venetian war; League of Augsburg formed (Venice, Russia, Austria, Poland)
1684–1715	Venetians in occupation of the Peloponnese
1687	Parthenon damaged after Venetian cannonball blows up magazine
1694–5	Venetians briefly occupy Chios
1699 Jan	Peace of Karlowitz; Turks forced to make concessions
1709	Phanariot Greeks become hospodars of Moldavia, and Wallachia (1715)
1715 Jan	6th Turko–Venetian war; Peloponnese reconquered by Turks; Tinos captured
1716	Turks lay siege to Kerkira
Apr	Venice allies with Austria
Aug	Turks defeated by Austrians at Peterwardein; siege of Kerkira called off; Mykonos and Tinos captured by Turks
1762–96	Catherine II of Russia
1768–74	Russo–Turkish war; 1770 Orlov brothers capture Navarino
1774	Treaty of Kutchuk Kainardji gives Russia concessions in Ottoman Empire; Rhigas Pheraios publishes his revolutionary tract
1796	Napoleon sends envoy to Ali Pasha of Janina
1798 May	Rhigas executed in Belgrade
1799	Septinsular Republic in Kerkira
1800	Ionian Islands a Russian protectorate until 1807
1814	British seize Ionian Islands
	Etairia Philike established in Odessa
1816	Capodistrias refuses to become head of Etairia
1818	Headquarters of Etairia moved to Constantinople
Aug	Leading Peloponnesians recruited into Etairia

1820		Sultan launches expedition to crush Ali of Janina
1821	Feb 22	Ypsilantis crosses the Prut; War of Independence begins
	Mar 25	Germanos proclaims rising at Patras
	Apr	Hydra, Spetsae and Psara join insurgents
	Jun 19	Ypsilantis defeated at Dragatsani; escapes into Austria; Fall of Monemvasia and Navarino to Greeks
	Oct 5	Tripolitsa falls; massacres and atrocities by Greeks
	Dec	Greek assault on Nauplion fails; First 'National Assembly' at Argos with D. Ypsilantis president
1822	Feb 5	Ali of Janina defeated and killed
	Apr 18	Turks capture Chios and massacre inhabitants
	Spring	Turks mount two expeditions to crush revolt
	Summer	Turkish army massacred after failing to relieve Nauplion
	Autumn	Turks reach Missolonghi; first siege begins
	Sep 16	Canning succeeds Castlereagh
	Dec 12	Nauplion falls to Kolokotronis; massacres follow
1823	Mar 25	Canning recognizes the Greeks as belligerents; Mar/Apr 'Second National Assembly' at Astros; rival Assembly established at Kranhidhi; Civil War begins
	Jul 13	Byron arrives in Cephalonia
1824	Feb	Agreement signed for British Loan
	Apr 17	Crete captured by Egyptians
1824	Apr 19	Byron dies at Missolonghi; Apr Consignment of British gold arrives at Zante
	Jul	Psara captured by Egyptian fleet
	Oct	New Assembly meets at Nauplion
1825	Feb/Mar	Ibrahim Pasha lands at Modon; captures Navarino (May) and besieges Nauplion (Jun); Feb 2 Second Greek Loan secured in London
	Jun 30	'Act of Petition' requests that Greece become British protectorate
	Aug	Lord Cochrane's services secured by Greeks
	Oct 25	'Odysseus' killed
1826	Apr	Third National Assembly at Epidauros; 22/3 Missolonghi falls
	Aug	Turks retake Athens; Ghouras holds out in Acropolis, but killed in Oct
1827	Apr	Negotiations between Greek factions begin at Troezen; 11 Capodistrias elected president
	Jun 5	Acropolis surrenders to Turks
	Jul 6	Treaty of London; Powers recognize autonomy of Greece and demand a truce
	16	Sultan rejects demand

Oct 20	Battle of Navarino
Dec 8	Sultan rejects right of allies to mediate over Greece
1828 Apr 28	Russo–Turkish war begins
Jul 19	London Protocol allows France to evict Egyptians
1830 Feb	Crown offered to Leopold of Saxe-Coburg; he withdraws in May
1831 Oct 9	Capodistrias assassinated
1832 May	Convention between Britain, Russia, France and Bavaria confirms Otho as king
1833 Jan	Otho arrives at Nauplion; Regency begins
1834	Revolt in Mani
1835 May	Otho reaches majority
1837	University of Athens established
1838	Bavarian troops leave Greece
1843 Sep	Bloodless revolution in Athens
1844 Mar	King accepts Constitution
1850 Jan	Don Pacifico Affair; Palmerston orders blockade of Piraeus
1853	Greek irregulars cross into Turkish territory during Crimean War
May	British and French occupy Piraeus, and enforce strict neutrality on Greece (Feb 1857)
1857–9	Three Power Commission on Greek finances
1862 Feb	'Revolution'; Otho driven out
Dec	Plebiscite on monarchy won by Prince Alfred, son of Queen Victoria
1863 Mar 30	George I comes to throne; confirmed by Protecting Powers
1864 Mar	Britain cedes Ionian Islands to Greece
Nov 28	New Constitution sworn by George I; Greece a 'crowned democracy'; Powers stop attacks on Turks in Crete
1867	George I marries Russian Princess Olga Romanova
1870	Turks set up Bulgarian Exarchate; Dilessi Murders
1875 May	Trikoupis forms government
1877 Apr	'Eastern Crisis': Russia declares war on Turkey
1878 Feb	Greek troops move into Thessaly
Mar	Peace of San Stefano
Jun/Jul	Congress of Berlin
Oct	Pact of Halepa
1881	Turks cede Thessaly and Arta region to Greece under British pressure
1885	Deligiannis mobilizes after Bulgarians annexe Eastern Rumelia
1886	Three-week blockade of Greece by Powers
1889	Greek pressure in Crete; Turks suspend Pact of Halepa

1893		Major economic crisis; Trikoupis announces bankruptcy Bulgarian terrorist organization IMRO founded in Macedonia
1894		Ethniki Etairia set up to defend Greek interests in Macedonia
1895		Deligiannis wins election; Trikoupis retires to Paris and dies
1897		Riots in Crete; Deligiannis orders mobilization (Mar)
	Apr	Greeks defeated; Turks take Larisa and Epirus
1908	Jun 8	Edward VII and Nicolas II meet at Reval and agree Macedonian reforms
	Sep	Young Turk revolt in Salonika
	Oct 6	Austrians annex Bosnia; 8 Cretan Assembly proclaims Enosis
	Dec 17	First meeting of Ottoman parliament with Young Turk majority
1909	Apr	Counter-revolution in Constantinople
	Jul	'Military League' founded by Greek officers
	Aug 27	Athens garrison marches to Goudi and issues ultimatum
	Sep	Huge demonstration of support for reform of constitution
	Oct 18	Venizelos head of minority government
	Dec	New elections: Venizelos wins large majority, inaugurates reform programme
1911	Jun 11	Revised Greek Constitution
	Sep 29	Italians declare war on Turkey
1912	Mar	Elections; Venizelos wins large majority
	May	Greek–Bulgarian Agreement
	Oct 8	First Balkan War; Greece joins in (18th); Italian–Turkish treaty at Lausanne; Dodecanese restored to Turkey
	Nov 9	Greek forces occupy Salonika hours before Bulgarians
	Dec 3	Armistice; not observed by Greece
1913	Jan	War renewed; Greeks take Janina and Chios
	Mar 18	King George I assassinated in Salonika
	May 30	Turkey signs Treaty of London with Balkan states
	Jun	Greco–Serbian Treaty; 30 Second Balkan War begins; Bulgaria attacks Greece and Serbia
	Aug 10	Treaty of Bucharest
	Nov 13	Greco–Turkish Treaty
	Dec 14	Greeks formally annex Crete
1914	Jun 13	Greeks annex Chios and Mytilene; 28 Sarajevo assassination begins First World War
	Nov 5	Britain declares war on Turkey and annexes Cyprus
1915	Jan	Grey offers Venizelos 'important concessions' in Asia Minor
	Mar	Venizelos offers Greek troops for Dardanelles campaign; 6 Venizelos resigns; beginning of 'National Schism'

May	Italy declares war on Austria–Hungary and occupies northern Epirus
Jun	Election; Venizelos wins with clear majority (takes office Aug)
Sep 6	Bulgaria signs alliance with Germany and Turkey; 23 Greek mobilization
Oct 5	Venizelos resigns under pressure from king; Entente troops land at Salonika; 11 Bulgarians attack Serbia, but Greeks refuse to aid Serbs under Treaty of 1913
Dec	Venizelists boycott elections
1916 Jan	Allies seize Corfu
May 22	Rupel fort surrendered to Bulgarians
Jun 6–24	Allied blockade of Greece; Jun 23 King accepts demands of Entente
Aug 18	Greek army surrenders to Germans at Kavalla; 30 Pro-Venzelist officers launch coup in Salonika; Venizelos leaves for Crete
Oct 5	Provisional government set up in Salonika; 11 Greece accepts ultimatum to hand over fleet to Allies
Dec 1	Greeks fire on Anglo–French force in Athens; Reign of Terror against Venizelists; Allied blockade; Allies recognize Salonika regime; 19 Allies raise blockade
1917 Jun 12	King Constantine resigns, replaced by second son, Alexander; 27 Venizelos returns to Athens; resurrects 'Lazarus Parliament' (of June 1915); 29 Greece severs relations with Central Powers
Jul 2	Central Powers declare war on Greece
1918 Sep 15	Greek troops participate in Allied breakthrough against Bulgaria
Oct 30	Turkey signs armistice at Mudros
Nov 1	Anglo–French force occupies Constantinople
1919 Feb	Versailles Peace Conference begins
Mar	Italians land in Asia Minor and, in May, move towards Smyrna
May 15	Greeks land at Smyrna
Aug 5	Mustafa Kemal declares his independence of Istanbul
1920 Mar 16	Allies occupy Constantinople
May 11	Turkish National Assembly meets at Ankara
Aug 10	Treaty of Sèvres (never ratified) gives Greece huge gains of territory; Greco–Italian Treaty assigns Dodecanese to Greece
Oct	Venizelos orders Greek army to advance from Smyrna; 20 King Alexander dies from a monkey bite
Nov	Venizelos defeated in election

Dec 5	Plebiscite decides on restoration of Constantine; returns 19th
1921 Mar	Greek offensive in Asia Minor
Apr	Allies declare a policy of strict neutrality
Jun 25	Greece refuses Great Power mediation
Sep 24	Battle of the Sakkaria; Turks stop Greeks reaching Ankara
1922 Mar	Curzon proposal for compromise peace rejected by Greeks
Aug 1	Powers warn Greece against occupying Constantinople; 26 Turks launch offensive in Anatolia; Greek army routed
Sep 8	Smyrna sacked; 27 Constantine abdicates in favour of son George after coup by Plastiras and Gonatas
Oct 10	Greco–Turkish Armistice; 11 Mudania Conference: Greece undertakes to evacuate Eastern Thrace; 28 Greek officers and politicians shot as scapegoats
1923 Jan	Convention on exchange of populations between Greece and Turkey
Jul 24	Peace Treaty of Lausanne
Aug 2	Italians occupy Corfu
Dec	Elections; Venizelists win almost all seats after Royalists abstain; Dec 6 George II 'goes abroad' pending a referendum on the monarchy
1924 Jan 11	Venizelos accepts premiership, but hands over to Plastiras after a month
Mar 24	Greece proclaimed a republic; confirmed by plebiscite (Apr)
1925 Jun	Diplomatic relations resumed with Turkey; 16 Coup d'état of Pangalos
Oct	Greece invades Bulgaria
1926 Jan 3	Pangalos declares himself dictator
Aug 17	Treaty of friendship with Yugoslavia; 22 Pangalos overthrown
1928 May 31	Venizelos returns
Sep 23	Treaty of friendship with Italy
1929 Mar 27	Treaty of friendship with Yugoslavia
Oct 5	Conference of Balkan powers in Athens
30	Treaty of friendship with Turkey
1931 Oct	Disturbances over enosis in Cyprus
1932 Sep	Venizelos narrowly wins election
1933 Mar	Venizelos defeated; Plastiras stages abortive coup; purge of Venizelists
Jun	Venizelos escapes assassination attempt
1934 Feb 9	Balkan Pact between Greece, Rumania, Yugoslavia and Turkey
1935 Mar 1	Attempted Venizelist coup by Plastiras fails
Jun	Election: Populists win landslide after Venizelists abstain
Nov 3	97% in rigged vote for restoration of monarchy (George II)

1936 Jan	Communists hold balance after inconclusive elections
Mar	Death of Venizelos
Apr 13	General Metaxas appointed prime minister
Aug 4	King George agrees to suspend constitution
1937 Feb	Conference of Balkan Powers in Athens
1938 Apr 27	Greco–Turkish treaty of friendship
Jul	Pact of Salonika; Bulgaria joins Balkan Pact; allowed to rearm
1939 Apr 7	Italy invades Albania; 13th Britain and France guarantee Greece and Rumania
Sep	Second World War breaks out; Greece declares neutrality
1940 May	Reservists called up
Aug 15	Greek cruiser *Elli* sunk off Tinos by Italian submarine; 28th Metaxas refuses Italian demands; Italians invade Greece, Greeks defeat them and advance into Albania
1941 Feb 22/23	Eden, Dill and Wavell visit Athens
Mar	British expeditionary force lands; 28th Battle of Cape Matapan; three Italian cruisers sunk
Apr 6	German invasion of Balkans begins; 18th Yugoslavia defeated; 20 Tsolakoglu signs armistice with Germans at Salonika; 22nd British begin evacuation of Greece (completed May 2); 30th Germans appoint Tsolakoglu puppet prime minister
May 20	Germans invade Crete
Sep	EAM founded
1942 Sep	SOE mission parachuted into Greece
Nov 25	Viaduct at Gorgopotamos blown up
1943 Feb	Anti-monarchist mutiny in Greek army in Egypt; King goes to Egypt (Mar)
Mar	Ex-Venizelist Sarafis becomes head of ELAS; Zervas persuaded by British to state support for monarchy
Apr	Churchill orders British mission to support only monarchist groups
Jul 6	'National Bands Agreement'
Aug	Resistance delegations fly to Cairo
Sep 8	Italians surrender; arms to ELAS; 13th Resistance delegations leave Cairo after rebuff by King
Oct	'First Round' of Civil War begins
Dec 14	Germans massacre Greek villagers near Kalyvrita; 25th Stalin blocks co-operation between Bulgarian, Greek and Yugoslav resistance
1944 Feb 21	Plaka Agreement ends 'First Round'
Mar	PEEA set up to administer areas under ELAS control; 31st Second anti-monarchist mutiny in Egypt; Papandreou takes over government-in-exile

May 20	Lebanon Agreement. Repudiated by EAM/ELAS in Greece (27th)
Jul 28	Popov mission from Stalin to EAM/ELAS
Aug 15	EAM agrees to accept Lebanon Agreement
Sep 2	Six EAM ministers enter government of national unity; Caserta Agreement: Left places forces under Papandreou
18	General Scobie appointed commander of Liberation forces
Oct 4	British troops land at Patras; 9th Churchill and Stalin sign 'Percentages Agreement'; 13th British commandos take Megara airfield near Athens; 14th British enter Athens; Scobie arrives (15th); 18 Papandreou's government arrives in Greece
Nov	Scobie orders dissolution of guerrillas by Dec 10; ELAS refuses
Dec 3	'Second Round' begins: police fire on demonstrators in Constitution Square; 5th Churchill's telegram tells Scobie to use force against the Left; 25th Churchill and Eden hold All Party Conference at British Embassy in Athens; 27th Siantos' 'Six Demands' rejected
1945 Jan 3	Plastiras replaces Papandreou; 7th Scobie takes Piraeus; 15th Truce comes into force: end of 'Second Round'
Feb 2	Varkisa Agreement; Terror against Left begins
Mar 30	Zakhariadis arrives back in Greece; reappointed General Secretary of KKE
Jun	Liberals publish Open Letter criticizing the Terror; 18th 'Aris' shot
Dec	Stalin again blocks co-operation between KKE, Bulgarians and Yugoslavs
1946 Jan 21	Stalin demands British withdrawal from Greece in UN
Feb 12	Zakhariadis calls for organization of 'new armed struggle'; 17th KKE decides to abstain from elections, against Moscow's advice
Mar 30	Zakhariadis orders bomb attack on Litochoron; 31st Elections boycotted by KKE; Tsaldaris (Populist) wins Intensified Terror against Left
Spring	'Third Round' begins
Sept 1	Plebiscite decides in favour of monarchy; King George II returns
Oct 26	Markos Vafiadis unveils Democratic Army (DA)
1947 Mar 12	Truman Doctrine; huge American aid programme begins
Apr	George II dies: replaced by his brother, Paul I, and Queen Frederika
Sep	Central Committee of KKE takes to the mountains and proclaims 'Positional War' strategy

Oct 8	KKE and EAM press banned
Dec 24	KKE sets up provisional government; Markos figurehead PM; 25th Democratic Army fails to take Konitsa
1948 Feb	'Greek revolution must be stopped immediately' (Stalin)
Jun 15	Operation Coronis; Democratic Army defeated on Mt Grammos
Jul 28	Yugoslavia expelled from Cominform; Markos replaced by Supreme War Council, dominated by Zakhariadis
Dec 11	DA captures Karpenissi and holds it for 18 days
1949 Jan 25	Papagos appointed commander of Government Army Operation Pidgeon clears DA from Peloponnese
Jul 10	Tito formally closes Greek border
Aug 10	Operation Torch launched on Mt Gramnos (captured 27th)
Oct	'Temporary halt' proclaimed by Communists: end of Civil War
1950 Mar	Election won by EPEK (Plastiras and Tsaldaros); no overall majority; Archbishop Makarios becomes Ethnarch of Greek Cypriot people
1951 Jul	Papagos founds Greek Rally
Sep 9	Elections under modified PR; Greek Rally wins 36%
Oct	Greece and Turkey enter NATO
1952 Mar	US ambassador advises 'simple majority voting'
Nov 16	Election: Greek Rally 49.22% 247 seats; EPEK 34%, 51 seats; EDA 0 seats
1953 Feb 28	Greek–Turkish–Yugoslav Treaty
Oct 12	US–Greek Military Agreement
1954 May 31	Tito visits Athens
Jun	British leave Canal Zone and (Jul) say Cyprus will 'never' be independent
Aug 9	Greece, Yugoslavia and Turkey sign treaty of mutual alliance at Bled
1955 Apr	EOKA begins attacks on British installations
Aug 20	Britain, Greece and Turkey hold Conference in London to discuss Cyprus
Sep 6	Anti-Greek riots in Istanbul and Izmir; 25th Sir John Harding appointed Governor of Cyprus
Oct 4	Papagos dies; replaced by Karamanlis
Nov	State of emergency in Cyprus
1956	Karamanlis founds ERE (National Radical Union) to replace Greek Rally
Feb	Election: ERE 47.3%; Opposition wins 44%, but divided; Karamanlis forms government
Mar 9	Makarios exiled to Seychelles; 12th Greece asks for Cyprus question to be put before UN General Assembly

1957 Feb	Sixth Plenum of KKE criticizes 'errors' during Civil War; 26th UN General Assembly calls for 'peaceful, democratic solution' in Cyprus; 28th Makarios released
Oct	Zakhariadis expelled from KKE; 27th Sir Hugh Foot appointed governor of Cyprus
Dec 15	Greek resolution on Cyprus fails to get ⅔ majority
1958 Jan 20	USSR threatens Greece with economic sanctions if NATO missiles installed
Mar	Karamanlis resigns
May	Election: ERE 41% (171 seats); Liberals 36; EDA 25% (79)
Jun 19	British 'Partnership Plan' rejected by Makarios and Karamanlis
1959 Feb 19	Greece, Turkey and Britain agree on independence for Cyprus
Mar	Makarios and Grivas return to Cyprus
June 14	US agrees to supply Greece with nuclear information and missiles; 25th USSR proposes nuclear-free zone in Balkans
Sep	Formation of Centre Union
1960 Jan 18	London Conference on Cyprus breaks down
Jun 24	Balkan Alliance of Aug 1954 dissolved
Jul 1	Britain and Cyprus agree on bases
Aug 16	Cyprus becomes republic
1961 Feb 16	Cyprus votes to join Commonwealth
Oct 29	Parliamentary Election: ERE wins with 50.8% of the vote. Papandreou's Centre Union wins 30%, but he claims fraud, and calls for 'relentless struggle'
1963 May	Gregory Lambrakis ('Z') assassinated in Salonika
June 11	Karamanlis resigns over royal visit to Britain
Jul 9	Queen Frederika attacked by London crowd
Nov 3	Election: Centre Union largest party with 42.04% Papandreou refuses to rule with EDA
Dec 24	Papandreou resigns
1964 Jan 15	Cyprus Constitutional Conference meets without conclusion
Feb 16	Election: Centre Union wins majority with 52.7% Papandreou forms ministry
Mar	King Paul dies; replaced by Constantine II
Aug 8	Turkish planes attack Cyprus after communal violence against Turkish population; 17th Greece withdraws from NATO
1965 Jan 1	Income tax reduced by 10%
May	'Aspida conspiracy' precipitates crisis
Jul 15	Papandreou resigns after King refuses to dismiss disloyal defence minister
Sep 17	Stefanopoulos becomes PM, supported by 45 CU 'apostates'

1967 Mar 16	Result of 'Aspida' trial; 15 officers convicted
Apr 21	The 'Colonels' stage a Coup' against the civilian government
Sep	Constantine signs decrees retiring Royalist officers
Nov 19	Colonels forced to withdraw Greek troops from Cyprus
Dec 13	King Constantine fails in attempt at counter-coup and leaves Greece
1968 Jan 12	Andreas Papandreou announces the formation of the Pan Hellenic Liberation Movement [PAK] to co-ordinate opposition to the regime; 23rd US resumes diplomatic relations with Greece, and resumes arms sales [Oct]
Nov 1	George Papandreou funeral turns into a demonstration against the Junta; 15th New Constitution proclaimed by Colonels. It is declared illegal by the Opposition
1969 Dec	Greece withdraws from the Council of Europe after criticism of the Junta's human rights record
1970 Sep	US announces that it is resuming sales of heavy military equipment to the Junta
1971 Jul	US cuts military assistance to Greece until constitutional government is restored.
Aug	Papadopoulos reshuffles government to increase personal power
1972 Mar	Papadopoulos becomes Regent
Sep	US Sixth Fleet given port facilities under 'Home Port Agreement'
1973 Jun 1	Papadopoulos deposes King; proclaims 'Presidential Parliamentary Republic'
Nov	Sit-in at Athens Polytechnic crushed with many dead. Occupation of law faculty of Athens University brutally suppressed; 25th Papadopoulos overthrown in coup led by Brig Dimitrios Ioannides
1974 Jul	An attempt by the Junta to overthrow President Makarios of Cyprus provokes a Turkish invasion of the island. Greek and Turkish forces face each other in Thrace, but the Junta backs off; 24th Collapse of dictatorship; Karamanlis invited to return and is sworn in as President
Aug 14	Turks begin new advance in Cyprus after Geneva Conference fails to find solution
Sep	Papandreou founds the Panhellenic Socialist Party [PASOK] to contest the new elections
Nov	Elections: The New Democracy Party of Karamanlis wins a crushing victory [54%] 69% vote against a restoration of Monarchy.
1975 Mar	Greece decides to close US bases

	Jun	Constantine Tsatsos elected President, but the opposition denounces the new constitution, and refuses to participate
	Aug	Junta leaders sentenced to long prison terms
1976	Jan	Demotiki established as the medium of education
	Feb	Greece to be considered for membership of EC after a 5 year transitional period
	Aug	Confrontation with Turkey over activities of Turkish survey ship *Sismik* in Aegean
1977	May	Tension in the Aegean as Greek forces fire on a Turkish patrol boat
	Nov	Parliamentary Elections New Democracy wins a clear majority [42%], but PASOK becomes the main opposition Party [25%]
1978	Mar	President Karamanlis meets Turkish Premier Bulent Ecevit; little progress is made
1979	May	Greece signs Treaty of Accession to EEC
	Oct	Greek poet Odysseas [sic] Elitis wins Nobel Prize for Literature
1980	May	Constantine Karamanlis elected President
	Jun	PASOK and Communists boycott debate on ratification of EC Treaty
	Oct	Greece reintegrated into NATO command structure
1981	Jan 1	Greece becomes 10th member of EEC
	Oct	Parliamentary Election: Victory for PASOK. Andreas Papandreou forms the first Socialist government in Greek history. Evangelos Averof becomes leader of New Democracy Party
1982	Feb	Andreas Papandreou becomes first Greek PM to visit the Republic of Cyprus
	Jul	Greece and Turkey sign Moratorium on provocative acts
1983	Jul 1	First Greek presidency of EEC
	Sep	Agreement with US over keeping military bases in Greece
	Nov	Independent Turkish state of North Cyprus proclaimed
1984	Apr	Athens to be the European Cultural Capital for 1985
	Sep	Constantine Mitsotakis replaces Averof as head of New Democracy
1985	Mar	Karamanlis resigns presidency. Christos Sartzetakis, is elected his successor, but is not recognised by New Democracy
	June 3	PASOK wins an absolute majority in Election; US State Department advises Americans not to go to Greece because of poor security at Athens airport
	Oct 11	Economic austerity package introduced. Trades Union members expelled from PASOK

Nov	Defence and industrial co-operation agreement with US
1986 Feb 7	Journalists sentenced for libel on president
Mar 7	Papandreou attacks US military aid to Turkey
May 19	Greek Communist Party [KKE Interior] reconstituted as New Hellenic Left Party
Jul	Greek–Turkish naval confrontation in Eastern Mediterranean
Oct	Cabinet reshuffle after PASOK suffers heavy losses in Municipal elections
1987 Feb 7	Turkey rescinds legislation blocking Greek assets in Constantinople (1964)
Mar	Another naval confrontation between Greece and Turkey over mineral rights in the Aegean
Apr	Law passed to confiscate Church lands; Turkey formally applies to join EEC. Greece says that it will block Turkish entry until the Cyprus dispute is solved
Jun	Greece wins the European Basketball Championship
Oct	Rumours of Papandreou's affair with Dimitra Lianni undermines his government
Nov	Economic minister Costas Simitis [a future PM] resigns after Papandreou dilutes his anti-inflation policy
1988 Feb 2	Greece and Turkey sign Davos Agreement establishing 'Hot Line' and cultural contacts
Jun 13	Turkish Premier Turgut Ozal receives cool reception on his visit to Athens
Aug	Papandreou goes to England for two months for medical treatment, and announces impending divorce. The Bank of Crete Scandal begins to unfold
1989 Jun 18	Election victory of New Democracy, which forms a government in Coalition with a small left-wing Party
Sep 27	Papandreou and four colleagues to stand trial over Bank of Crete Affair
Nov 5	New Election after collapse of Coalition. Party leaders agree to an All-Party Caretaker Government until April 1990
1990 Apr 8	New Democracy wins election. Constantine Mitsotakis becomes Premier; 27th Emergency economic package introduced
May 4	Constantine Karamanlis elected President; 21st Full diplomatic relations with Israel established
Jun 6	Greece paralysed by General Strike. Another fellows on 4th
Aug	Government introduces economic austerity measures; Crisis with Albania as thousands of ethnic Greeks flee the country

1991 Jan 9	Education minister resigns after teacher killed in demonstrations against educational reform
Apr 9	34 Greek tourists killed in Istanbul bus atrocity
May 6	Government forced by EC to allow individuals the freedom to invest abroad
Nov 29	Budget for 1992 promises intensification of economic austerity
1992 Jan 10	Greece tells European Union that it will not assent to recognition of the Former Yugoslav Republic of Macedonia [FYROM] if it used the word Macedonia in its name
Feb	Andreas Papandreou acquitted of corruption charges
Apr	Foreign Minister Samaras dismissed in conflict over Macedonian policy
Jul 8	PM Mitsotakis says that he will not sign the EU–Turkish Financial Protocol, or a Greek–Turkish Friendship Pact, before a resolution of the Cyprus question; 31st Greece ratifies Maastricht Treaty strengthening moves towards European unity
Aug–Sep	A series of General Strikes over Privatisation of public transport in Athens and reform of the Social Security system
Oct 3	Purchase of US F16 fighter aircraft announced
Dec 2	Mitsotakis dismisses entire Cabinet after disagreements over economy and Macedonia. Macedonia recognised by several EC States; 10th Athens: a million people demonstrate against recognition of 'Macedonia'
1993 Jan 17	The UN admits Macedonia under the name 'FYROM', and without a flag
Feb	Greece accepts the idea of international arbitration over the Macedonian name and flag
Mar 16	Five Year Convergence Plan for Greece adopted by EC; 18th 24 hour General Strike against privatisation policies
Aug	Visit of Ex-King Constantine
Oct 10	Parliamentary Election: PASOK returned to power with 47% of vote; 26th Mitsotakis resigns as leader of New Democracy
Dec 18	35 Senior military officers resign in protest at reinstatement of 'socialist officers'
1994 Jan 18	Merlina Mercouri accuses Mitsotakis of involvement in 'illegal archaeological diggings'; 28th Investigation of Mitsotakis and his daughter on telephone tapping charges; 24th The former head of National Bank is assassinated for involvement in privatisation programme
Feb	World Bank and IMF announce loans to Macedonia; 16th Greece imposes trade ban on Macedonia

Mar	Death of famous actress, and Minister of Culture, Merlina Mercouri
Apr	Former King Constantine deprived of his citizenship. Royal property confiscated
May	Lifting of controls on capital movements triggers run on the drachma; 19th Day of Remembrance for 'Turkish Genocide' in 1919 [coincides with Turkish Atatürk commemoration day]; Crisis in Greek–Albanian relations following the shooting of two Albanian border guards and the arrest of five ethnic Greeks [known as the Omonia five] Greece threatens to close Albanian border
Jun 24	European Summit meets in Corfu under Greek Presidency; 29th European Court delays judgement on Greek trade ban against Macedonia
Sep 7	The 'Omonia Five' given eight years in prison
Nov 16	The Law of the Sea, comes into effect, allowing the extension of territorial waters to 12 miles. Turkey, fearing that this would undermine her national security, threatens violent action if Greece tries to implement it
1995 Feb 9	Albania releases four of the 'Omonia Five', but on the shooting of an Albanian by Greek border guards [21st] causes a new crisis
Mar 3	EU announces that negotiations for Cyprus's full membership will begin in 1997; 4th Greece lifts its veto on EU-Turkish Customs Union; 6th Turks warn that they will annex Cyprus if the EU tries to make it a full member before an agreement on its status; 9th Constantine Stephanopoulos elected President of the Republic
June 1	Greek parliament ratifies the Law of the Sea Convention. Turkish parliament warns of military action if Greece seeks to implement it [8th]
Jul 2	Riots between Greek and Serb fans at the final of the European Basketball Championships in Athens
Sep 8	Final Agreement on Trans-Balkan Oil Pipeline, to be built by Greece, Bulgaria and Russia; 12th Greece criticizes the continued bombing of Bosnian Serb targets; 14th Greece and FYROM sign an agreement at the UN opening the way to normalisation
Nov 20	Andreas Papandreou admitted to hospital with what proves to be a terminal illness. PASOK leaders cannot agree on a successor
Dec 1	Greece and Bosnia Herzegovina establish diplomatic relations; 6th Greek forces to participate in Bosnia peacekeeping force; 13th European Parliament votes for EU.

	Turkish Customs; 24th Islamic party becomes the largest party in the Turkish parliament [21.3%]; 28th Turkish fisher crashes near Mitylini as Greece and Turkey manoeuvres for air-supremacy in the Eastern Mediterranean
1996 Jan 15	Prime Minister Andreas Papandreou resigns, and is replaced by Constantine Simitis
Feb 1	US official Nicholas Burns says that the US does not recognise either Greek or Turkish sovereignty over thousands of tiny marine rocks and inlets; 1st The Greek Press and opposition attack the government over its failure to make a strong stand in the dispute over rocks and islets; 4th Turkish gunboat fires on Greek fishing boats in Northern Aegean; 5th Greece cancels visit of US official Richard Holbrooke; 5th Turkish Premier Tansit Ciller questions the sovereignty of 3000 tiny islets off the Turkish Coast. US suggests that the 'Islets question' should be decided by the International Court. Britain and Germany prefer it to be solved by direct Greek–Turkish negotiation, which the Greeks resist
Apr 8	Serbia recognises the Republic of Macedonia. Criticism over 'ingratitude' by Serbia after Greek support during the Bosnian crisis; 18th Greek tourists killed in Egyptian terrorist attack on hotel in Cairo
May 6	Greece says that it will continue to block the EU–Turkish Customs Union if it does not get its way over the Islets dispute; 10–15th The Greek President tours US cities to drum up support for his campaign in the Aegean
Jun 5	Turkey suggests that it could dispute the sovereignty of Gavdos off the Island of Crete and 250 miles from Turkey
Jul 19	Greece announces that it will bid for the 2004 Olympics; 15th In return for an EU call for Turkey to respect Greek territorial integrity, Greece lifts its veto over MEDA development programme for 12 Mediterranean countries
Aug	Serious crisis in Cyprus. A Greek-Cypriot demonstrator who tries to cross into the Turkish zone, and another who tries to pull down a Turkish flag, are killed by Turkish forces; 16th The Greek PM attends the demonstrators' funeral. Other leading politicians visit Cyprus
Sep 22	Parliamentary Elections: PASOK retains power. New Democracy plunged into a leadership crisis
Oct 7–9	Greek and Cypriot forces hold joint manoeuvres
Nov 10	Greece proposes mechanism to resolve disputes between NATO members; 8–12th Athens Stock Exchange closed

	down because of fraud allegations; 13th $16 billion armaments programme announced; 28th A General strike against government measures designed to prepare Greece for membership of the Single Europeran Currency
Dec 5-22	Greece paralysed by farmers blocking the transport system
Dec 9	A Turkish business delegation arrives in Athens; 17th Greek Embassies and Consulates all over the world closed down by a strike of the Diplomatic Corps; 22nd Parliament passes the government's economic measures
1997 Jan	US State Department warns Cyprus against acquiring Russian air-defence system, but Greece supports the Cypriot government, 28th New wave of strikes.
Feb	Political unrest in Albania, Serbia and Bulgaria threatens Greek security; 15th Teachers' Strike paralyses schools and universities; 16th The restructuring of Greek and armed forces to allow 'flexible response' to Turkey; 25th EU decides to postpone negotiations for accession of Cyprus
Mar	Chaos in the north as the Albanian state disintegrates; 6th Madeleine Albright disappoints Greece by failing to announce US Cyprus initiate; 21st Costas Karamanlis [41] elected leader of main opposition Party New Democracy
Apr 9	Greece to join multinational force in Albania; 16th; Greek and Turkish officials meet in Malta amidst hopes of a détente
Aug 2-10	The World Track and Field Games held in Athens
Sept 5	Athens wins the right to stage the Olympic Games in 2004
Oct 31	A Greek court orders Germany to pay war reparations to a village whose population was massacred by Nazi troops in World War Two
Nov 1	Greece and Turkey hold rival naval exercises off Cyprus.
Nov 4	At a Balkan Summit in Crete, Greece, Turkey, Albania, Bulgaria and Macedonia pledge to work together for peace in the region
Nov 10	Turkey holds practise air strikes in North Cyprus
Nov 11-12	American envoy Richard Holbrooke chairs abortive talks on the future of Cyprus
Nov 23	In Salonika, the first Greek memorial to the seventy thousand Greek Jews who died in the Holocaust is unveiled
Nov 27	Turkey announces it wants to join the European Union,

	but Greece threatens to veto it unless Turkey accepts the jurisdiction of the International Court of Justice in its disputes with Greece
Dec 2	Turkey cancels planned military exercises in the Aegean after an agreement with Greece on the control of air space
Dec 12	Turkey's bid to join the EU is rejected. The Turkish President blames Greek obstruction, and warns Athens that there would be a price to pay
Dec 18	A 24-hour General Strike against government's latest economic reforms
1998 Jan 7	Greece protests at joint Turkish, Israeli and US naval exercises
Jan 8	Greek and Turkish war planes again confront each other over the Aegean
Jan 12	Turkey announces plans to buy forty American F15 fighter aircraft
Jan 10	Turkey accuses a Greek minister of racism after he accuses Ankara of 'Kurdish genocide'
Jan 22	Athens brought to a halt by a one day strike against the government austerity measures
Feb 2	Thousands of Greek farmers block the country's main north-south highway
Feb 3	The US halts all future military assistance to Greece and Turkey
Feb 5	Greek archaeologists announce they have found the cave where the ancient Greek poet Euripides wrote his plays. Shortly afterwards, a 2000-year-old brothel was uncovered in Salonika
Feb 16	Russia says it will honour its contract to supply anti-aircraft missiles to Cyprus
Feb 25	Greek lawyers hold a two-day strike
Feb 27	Greece says it will not meet the economic targets necessary to join the Euro in 1999
Mar 14	EU foreign ministers agree to start membership negotiations with Cyprus after Greece threatens to block the entry of other new EU applicants
Mar 15	Greece joins the European Exchange Rate Mechanism [ERM] after the government announces a package of austerity measures and devalues the drachma by 14%
Mar 19	A new high-speed link between Salonika and the Macedonian capital, Skopje, is announced

Mar 21	Turkish Cypriots break off UN sponsored discussions because the EU has decided to open membership talks with 'Greek' Cyprus
Mar 29	The Greek anarchist group 'Arsonists of Conscience' burn the car of a Turkish diplomat in Athens
Apr 9	A general strike against the new economic reforms causes widespread chaos in Greece
Apr 7	Olympic Airways flights halted by a 24-hour strike against re-structuring plans
Apr 7	The 'November-17th' group carries out a rocket attack in central Athens
Apr 23	The former Greek president, Constantine Karamanlis dies at age 91
May 9	Greece's first democratically elected Orthodox Archbishop is enthroned
May 24	The Greek director Theo Angelopoulos wins the Palm d'Or at Cannes for his film "Eternity and a Day"
June 4	Greece and Turkey agree measures to ease tensions over the sovereignty of islands and airspace
June 4	Eleven countries formally establish the Black Sea Economic Co-operation Group [founded in 1993]
June 9	Greece calls on Britain to return the Elgin Marbles, following revelations that the British Museum damaged them by over-zealous cleaning in the 1930s
June 13	At the EU summit in Cardiff, Greece threatens to veto a proposal to suspend membership talks with Cyprus so that discussions with Turkey can be reopened
June 15	A 24-hour teachers strike against the introduction of new examinations for graduate teachers
June 17	Four Greek F-16 fighter-bombers visit a new Greek-Cypriot airbase. Next day Turkey sends six similar warplanes to Turkish Cyprus
June 21	Workers at the Ionian Bank in Greece end their six-week strike against privatisation
June 25	The first official visit by a Greek head of state to Cyprus. A month later [25th Jul] the Turkish President pays first official visit to North Cyprus
Jul 10	Turkey threatens to deploy missiles of its own in North Cyprus if the Greek-Cypriot government persists with its plan to put missiles on the island

Jul 15	Britain agrees to return the Castor marbles to Turkey, four years after they were discovered in the wreckage off the coast of Kent
Jul 25	United States protests after the Greek Foreign Minister says that President Clinton's promise to seek a settlement in Cyprus was an election lie
Jul 27	In Athens, 'Arsonists for Social Cohesion' burn foreign owned cars
Aug 7	Forest fires rage throughout Greece, many of them deliberately set
Aug 12	Turkey accuses Greece of seeking a limited armed conflict to damage Turkey politically
Sep 6	Greece repeats its support for the Cypriot decision by to install Russian missiles.
Sep 14	Greenpeace activists arrested for trying to stop waste dumping by the Greek state metal company, Larco
Sep 27	Greece attacks the recent military agreements between Israel and Turkey
Oct 4	Greece, Bulgaria and Romania appeal for an immediate cease-fire in Kosovo but Greece opposes military action
Oct 9	Greece announces the purchase of missile defence systems worth over two billion dollars as part of its programme to modernise its armed forces
Oct 9	The European Commission says it will prosecute Greece for its failure to protect the egg-laying sites of the Mediterranean sea turtle on the beaches of Zakynthos
Oct 13	Greece and France reject a proposal to cut EU farm subsidies
Oct 18	Despite conservative gains in local elections, the Prime Minister says he will continue the austerity policies to enable Greece to enter the Single European Currency
Oct 20	Thousands of Greek and Cypriot troops take part in joint military exercises
Oct 22	Russia delays the delivery of missiles to Cyprus following protests from Turkey
Oct 22	Turkey welcomes an EU aid package designed to circumvent the Greek veto
Oct 29	Costas Simitis re-shuffles his cabinet to counter the unpopularity of government austerity measures
Nov 19	Turkey sends six fighter planes to north Cyprus as a part

	of a joint military exercise with the Turkish Cypriots
Nov 23	The heir to the British throne, Prince Charles, begins a three-day official visit to Greece
Nov 27	Greek and Cypriot leaders discuss the crisis over deployment of missiles in Cyprus
Nov 30	A fresh wave of strikes against the government's tough proposals for the 1999 budget
Dec 1	The U.N. refugee agency criticises the maltreatment of asylum seekers in Greece
Dec 22	Parliament passes the government's austerity budget for 1999
Dec 22	The first visit of the Greek Foreign Minister to Skopje marred by disputes over the existence of a Slav minority in Greece
Dec 29	Cyprus says that it will not deploy Russian missiles on the island, sending them instead to Crete. The Greek and Cypriot governments come under intense press criticism for their climb-down
1999 Jan 1	Costas Simitis says he will stick to his programme to prepare Greece for the Single Currency
Jan 15	Students throwing stones and petrol bombs clash with riot police in Athens, block roads across the country, and occupy hundreds of schools in protest against education reforms
Feb 9	The EU Annual League of Wealth names Ipeiros as the poorest place in the EU. All 13 Greek regions fall into the poorest category
Feb 10	Turkey says it will respond to the threat of Russian-made missiles on Crete
Feb 18	Three cabinet ministers resign over mishandling the affair of Kurdish dissident, Abdullah Ocalan
Feb 27	The US reports that arms sales to Greece were frozen earlier his month on suspicion that Greece had provided Russia with secret NATO aircraft jamming codes
Mar 22	An explosion in Athens causes extensive damage to the American Citibank, the latest of two hundred terrorist attacks in Greece during the previous year
Mar 23	Greece refuses to take part in NATO military action against Yugoslavia, but allows NATO to use its bases on Greek soil

Mar 24	NATO air attacks on Yugoslavia begin
Mar 26	In Athens, thousands demonstrate against NATO's strikes on Yugoslavia
Apr 3	Greece says Belgrade's ethnic cleansing in Kosovo threatens the stability of the whole region
Apr 6	The Yugoslav Defence Minister and the head of the Yugoslav state armaments company visit Athens
Apr 22	The first cargo of Russian anti-aircraft missiles arrives in Crete
Apr 28	The Intercontinental Hotel in Athens is bombed in protest against NATO's action against Yugoslavia
Apr 30	Greece says it will buy fifty American F-16 fighter planes as part of a new a two billion dollar rearmament programme
May 1	Protesters burn United States flags and an effigy of President Clinton outside the American embassy in Athens
May 7	An explosion damages the Dutch embassy in Athens
May 12	Greece calls for the bombing of Yugoslavia to stop and pledges aid to Serbia
May 29	Albanian police shoot the hijackers of a Greek bus who have taken its passengers over the border
June 12	NATO troops enter Kosovo
Aug 17	After a massive earthquake in western Turkey, Greece is among the first countries to send relief workers and food
Sep 7	A powerful earthquake strikes the Athens region
Sep 23	Greece and Turkey set up a joint disaster-response team
Nov 20	During a visit to Greece marked by violent anti-US protests, President Clinton admits that the US was wrong to back the military junta in 1967
Dec 12	Greece agrees to drop her veto on Turkey joining the European Union after Turkey makes concessions on Cyprus entering the EU and submitting disputes to the international Court
Dec 14	The United Nations says that a second round of indirect talks between Greek and Turkish Cypriots will soon be announced
Dec 14	Greece and Macedonia sign an agreement on military co-operation, and Greece pledges support for Macedonia's integration into NATO and European institutions
Jan 2000	Greece removes passport controls for most European Union countries

Selected reading on Greek History

Part I

ANDREWES, A. *Greek Society* (Harmondsworth, Penguin, 1975)

ARRIAN *The Campaigns of Alexander the Great* (Harmondsworth, Penguin, rev. ed., 1971)

BOARDMAN, J., GRIFFIN, J. & MURRAY, O. *Greece and the Hellenistic World* (1988); first published in *The Oxford History of the Classical World* (Oxford, Oxford University Press, 1986)

BOARDMAN, J. *Greek Art* (London, Thames and Hudson, 2nd ed., 1985)

BROWN, P. *The World of Late Antiquity* (London, Thames and Hudson, 1971)

BUCKLER, J. *The Theban Hegemony 371–362* (Cambridge, Mass., 1980)

BURN, A. R. *Persia and the Greeks* (London, Duckworth, 2nd ed., 1984)

DAVIES, J. K. *Democracy and Classical Greece* (London, Fontana, 1978)

FINLEY, M. I. *The World of Odysseus* (London, Chatto and Windus, 2nd ed., 1977)

FORREST, W. G. *The Emergence of Greek Democracy* (London, Weidenfeld and Nicholson, 1966)

HERODOTUS *The Persian War* (Harmondsworth, Penguin, rev. ed., 1972)

JEFFREY, L. H. *Archaic Greece* (London, Methuen, 1976)

KITZINGER, E. *Byzantine Art in the Making* (London, Faber, 1977)

LANE FOX, R. *Alexander the Great* (Harmondsworth, Penguin, new ed., 1986)

MEIGGS, R. *The Athenian Empire* (Oxford, Clarendon Press, 1972)

MURRAY, O. *Early Greece* (London, Fontana, 1980)

OSTROGORSKY, G. *History of the Byzantine State* (Oxford, Blackwell, new ed., 1981)

ROBERTSON, M. *Shorter History of Greek Art* (Cambridge, Cambridge University Press, 1985)

STE CROIX G. E. M. de *The Origins of the Peloponnesian War* (London, Duckworth, 1972)

SHERWIN-WHITE, A. N. *Roman Foreign Policy in the Greek East* (London, Duckworth, 1984)

THUCYDIDES *The Peloponnesian War* (Harmondsworth, Penguin, rev. ed., 1972)

309

WALBANK, F. W. *The Hellenistic World* (London, Fontana, 1981)

WHITTING, P. D., ed. *Byzantium, an introduction* (Oxford, Blackwell, new ed., 1981)

XENOPHON *A History of My Times* (Harmondsworth, Penguin, rev. ed., 1978)

Part II

ANDERSON, M. S. *The Eastern Question 1774–1923* (London, Macmillan, 1966)

CAMPBELL, J. & SHERRARD, P. *Modern Greece* (London, 1968)

CLOGG, R. *A History of Modern Greece* (Cambridge, CUP, 1986)

CLOGG, R., ed. *The Struggle for Greek Independence* (London, Macmillan, 1973)

DAKIN, D. *The Unification of Greece* (London, 1972)

EUDES, D. *The Kapitanios: Partisans and Civil War in Greece 1943–49* (London, NLB, 1972)

HONDROS, J. *Occupation and Resistance: The Greek Agony 1941–44* (New York, 1983)

HITCHENS, C. *Cyprus* (London, Quartet, 1984)

KOUVETARIS, Y. & DOBRATZ, B. *A Profile of Modern Greece* (Oxford, Clarendon Press, 1987)

LLEWELLYN SMITH, M. *Ionian Vision: Greece in Asia Minor 1919–22* (London, Allen Lane, 1973)

ST CLAIR, W. *That Greece might still be Free: The Philhellenes* (Oxford, 1972)

STAVRIANOS, L. S. *Greece: American Dilemmas and Opportunity* (Chicago, 1952)

TSOUCALAS, C. *The Greek Tragedy* (Harmondsworth, Penguin, 1969)

WOODHOUSE, C. M. *Apple of Discord* (London, Hutchinson, 1948)

WOODHOUSE, C. M. *The Struggle for Greece 1941–49* (London, 1976)

ZAKYNTHINOS, D. A. *The Making of Modern Greece: From Byzantium to Independence* (Oxford, Blackwell, 1976)

Historical Gazetteer

Aigina (Aegina) A triangular island in the Saronic Gulf, and at one time an important rival of Athens, Aigina's navy made a crucial contribution to the defeat of the Persians at Salamis in 480 BC. Capital of Greece under Capodistrias between 1827–29. **136, 137, 171**

Akrotiri A Minoan town buried beneath pumice following the eruption of the volcano on Thera (see below). Excavations, started by the Greek archaeologist Spiros Marinatos, who was killed on the site in 1967, have revealed streets and houses with doors, windows, pottery and very fine wall paintings still intact. The town seems to have been initially destroyed by an earthquake before the eruption; **6, 184, 185, 224**

Amphipolis An Athenian trading colony on the river Strymon at the north of the Aegean. Thucydides, the historian, was exiled for losing the city to the Spartans and it was outside its gates in 421 BC that the Spartan Brasidas defeated the Athenian demagogue Kleon, both generals dying in the battle. **59**

Ancient Battles

ACTIUM (*Akarnania*), 31BC: Octavian defeated Mark Antony and Cleopatra, who fled to Egypt where they both committed suicide. Octavian was left the undisputed ruler of the Roman world and under the name of Augustus became the first Roman Emperor. **105, 128**

AEGOSPOTAMI 404 BC: The final defeat of Athens in the Peloponnesian War when the Spartan commander Lysander caught the Athenian fleet beached in the Kherronesos. **67**

AMPHIPOLIS, 421 BC: (see above). **59**

ARGINOUSSAI, (*Asia Minor*), 406 BC: An Athenian naval victory over the Spartans. On the fleet's return the Athenian generals were condemned to death for failing to save some of the sailors. **66, 67, 71**

CUNAXA (*Mesopotamia*), 401 BC: An attack on the Persian king Artaxerxes by his brother Cyrus who was killed in the battle and whose 10,000 Greek mercenaries Xenophon was able to extricate from Persian territory. **65**

GAUGAMELA (*Mesopotamia*), 331 BC: The final victory of Alexander the Great over the Persian king Darius III. **90**

GRANIKOS (*Asia Minor*), 334 BC: Alexander's first victory over the Persians. **88**

HYDASPES (*Punjab*), 326 BC: Alexander's victory over king Poros. **92**

ISSOS (*Cilicia*), 333 BC: Major defeat of the Persian king Darius III by Alexander the Great. **90**

KHAIRONEIA (*Boiotia*), 338 BC: Philip II's victory over the Thebans and Athenians brought Greece under Macedonian suzerainty. **78–80, 83, 90**

KYNOSKEPHALAI (*Macedonia*), 197 BC: The Roman general Flamininus defeated Philip V of Macedonia and in the following year proclaimed the freedom of Greece. **102**

KYZIKOS (*Hellespont*), 410 BC: A naval engagement during the Peloponnesian War in which the Athenians, with the return of Alkibiades as general, defeated the Spartans, whose offer of peace terms was rejected. **65**

LADE (*Asia Minor*), 494 BC: A naval battle where the rebellious Ionian Greeks were defeated by the Persians. **29**

LEUKTRA (*Boiotia*), 371 BC: The Thebans, led by Epameinondas and Pelopidas, defeated Kleombrotos and destroyed the myth of Spartan invincibility. **73**

MANTINEIA (*Peloponnese*), 418 BC: The Spartans defeated Athens and Argos, forcing a treaty of neutrality on the latter so that the Argives took no part in the Peloponnesian War. **59, 74**

MANTINEIA (*Peloponnese*), 362 BC: The Thebans defeated the Spartans, thus confirming their superiority; but the Theban leader Epameinondas was fatally wounded. **59, 74**

MARATHON (*Attica*), 490 BC: The Athenians defeated the Persian punitive expedition sent by King Darius I. **30–5**

MYKALE (*Asia Minor*), 479 BC: A Greek victory over the Persians which was thought to have taken place on the same day as Plataia (see below). **40**

PHARSALOS (*Thessaly*), 48 BC: Julius Caesar defeated Pompey, who fled to Egypt where he was murdered. **105**

PHILIPPI (*Macedonia*), 42 BC: Octavian and Mark Antony defeated the assassins of Julius Caesar, Brutus and Cassius, who both committed suicide. **105**

PLATAIA (*Boiotia*), 379 BC: The 'Hellenic League' under the leadership of the Spartan Pausanias defeated the Persians commanded by Mardonios and ended Xerxes' plans for the conquest of Greece. **19, 31, 39–40**

PYDNA (*Macedonia*), 167 BC: Rome defeated Macedonia and divided the kingdom into four republics. **103**

PYLOS (*west coast of the Peloponnese*), 425 BC: Kleon captured 120 Spartiatai, who were trapped on the island of Sphakteria during the Peloponnesian War. **8, 58**

SALAMIS (*island off Athens*), 480 BC: The 'Hellenic League' defeated Xerxes' fleet in the narrow waters separating the island and the mainland. **38–9**

SELLASIA (*outside Sparta*), 222 BC: The Macedonian king Antigonas Doson defeated the radical Spartan king Kleomenes, who fled to Egypt. **99**

THERMOPYLAI (narrow pass in Boiotia), 480 BC: After a valiant effort to halt the Persian invasion of Greece the Spartan king Leonidas was killed along with all his Spartans in a last stand. **37–8, 159**

Arkanes A Minoan site on Crete, where, in what was possibly a shrine, evidence of a human sacrifice was found. **5**

Argos After the collapse of Mycenae, *c.* 1100 BC, Argos aspired to the control of the Peloponnese but was constantly held in check by Sparta. In 418 BC the Argives, along with the Athenians and others, were defeated by Sparta at Mantineia (see above). In 362 BC Argos gained revenge when she helped Thebes destroy Spartan power in the Peloponnese. It was in Argos that the adventurer Pyrrhos was killed in 272 BC when he was hit by a roof tile. **54, 59, 60, 97, 137, 159**

Asprochaliko A cave, about 58 km south of Lake Ioannina (Janina), where Palaeolithic stratified deposits were found in 1965. **1**

Athens (ancient Athenai) The capital and largest city of Greece. The Acropolis ('the High City') was first occupied during the Neolithic (New Stone Age). During the Bronze Age a 'Cyclopeian Wall' (see Mycenae) was built on the Acropolis and there is evidence of the worship of an earth goddess, the prototype of Athena. At the time of the Dorian invasions Athens was one of the few Greek sites which revealed continuous occupation. After the Geometric period Attica emerged as unified with the city (an eighth-century date is more probable than the traditional date of the union under Theseus in 1300 BC). After a time of social conflict democracy was established in the sixth century and Athens became one of the leading city-states in Greece. Success against the Persians enabled her to establish a maritime empire and a major building programme (a temple to Athena, the Parthenon, the Erechtheion and the Propylaia) was undertaken on the Acropolis to replace the buildings destroyed by the Persian sack. After the defeat by Sparta and her allies in 404 BC the Athenians never regained their former power but the city remained an important cultural centre throughout antiquity: until the restrictions imposed upon pagan learning by the Christian emperor Justinian in the sixth century AD Athens was the leading university city in the Mediterranean.

Under the Byzantines Athens decayed and dwindled, playing virtually no role in the affairs of the Empire. After the fall of Constantinople in 1204 a Duchy was established at Athens but the westerners did little to improve affairs there. In 1456 the Turks seized the Acropolis and Athens was annexed to the Ottoman Empire. Throughout the Middle Ages it was an insignificant village (although the Parthenon remained an important citadel and was damaged in 1687 during the Turko–Venetian war). It changed hands several times during the War of Independence and did not become the capital of Greece until 1833. Many public buildings were constructed in the nineteenth century but the city remained very small until recent times. It was the centre of revolutionary movements in 1843, 1862, 1909, 1922, 1944 and 1967. After 1922 the large numbers of poor immigrants from Asia Minor founded suburbs like Nea Smyrna. During the Second World War, the Hotel Grande Bretagne in Sindagma (Constitution) Square housed successively Greek, British and German HQs. Winston Churchill narrowly escaped a bomb placed in its basement in December 1944, when the city was severely damaged in street fighting between left-wing forces and the government army supported by the British. Since the war Athens has drawn over three million people from the countryside and now contains over 40% of the country's population. In recent years the quality of Athenian life has been put under great strain by various developments: the population has been further swelled by the arrival of large numbers of ethnic Greek refugees from the former Soviet Union. It has become a base for Middle Eastern terrorists, and a target for the violent activities of various dissident groups hostile to the government of the day. The rapid growth in car ownership has made the city one of the worst places in the world for the toxic smog produced by car exhaust fumes, known to Athenians as the *nefos*. **106, 174–7, 235, 248**

Averoff (Battleship), moored at Phaleron. Presented to Greek navy in 1910. Played major role in securing command of the sea during Balkan Wars of 1912–13. Moored off Constantinople in 1920. Brought Greek government-in-exile home in October 1944. **190, 234**

Ayia Triadha (Hagia Triada) A small Minoan palace (named after a Venetian church at the location) just two miles from Phaistos. **5**

Corfu see Kerkira

Corinth (Korinthos) The ancient city was a major seapower, establishing important colonies, e.g. the island of Kerkira (Corfu) and Syracuse in Sicily, and mercantile contacts throughout the Mediterranean. Most of the Greek city was destroyed by the Roman general Mummius in 146 BC and most of the remains that can be seen today belong to the Roman period. **13–14, 54–6, 68, 71, 104, 106, 160**

Corinth Canal Made Piraeus a major Mediterranean port after 1893. **181**

Delos The island sacred to Apollo, where Leto was said to have given him birth after finding refuge from Hera, who was enraged by her husband Zeus's infidelity. In 478 BC the island became the treasury for the league Athens formed to gain revenge on Persia. In the Roman period it became the major slave market of the Mediterranean, and it was claimed that as many as 10,000 slaves could be sold in a day. The site today has many fine examples of ancient houses, decorated with floor mosaics, which the wealthy Roman merchants built for themselves. **42–3, 47, 104**

Delphi The most important oracular sanctuary in ancient Greece. According to the myth the god Apollo defeated the serpent Pytho and took over the oracle, which was announced by a priestess, the Pythia. It became the richest sanctuary, receiving gifts from all the Greek city-states, and even non-Greeks, like King Croesus of Lydia, consulted it. There were several struggles between the local city-states for political control of Delphi and in 338 BC Philip II of Macedon used the pretext of settling a dispute to destroy the power of Thebes and bring Greece under his control. During the Roman period the oracle lost prestige and after Julian, the last pagan emperor, the Pythia no longer functioned and the sanctuary was closed. Much of the site still survives today and richly repays a visit. **21, 22, 36–7, 77**

Dhimini (Dimeni) A prehistoric settlement in Thessaly which has given its name to a period of the Neolithic (New Stone Age). **2**

Epidauros An ancient sanctuary to the healing god Asklepios; now a fine archaeological site boasting the best-preserved of all Greek theatres, which dates from the fourth century BC. Greek independence formally proclaimed here in 1822. **74**

Eretria A city-state on the island of Euboia destroyed by the Persians in 490 BC in revenge for the help the city had sent to the Ionians in 499. **27–31**

Evvia (Euboia, Euboea) A long narrow island off the mainland of Greece. In antiquity its two most important towns were Eretria and Khalkis. During the fifth century BC it was one of Athens' most important possessions. In 1210 it was seized by the Venetians (see Khalkis). **28, 30, 44, 126**

Gournia A Minoan 'town' on Crete. Excavation by the Americans, 1901–4, has revealed hundreds of houses built on to narrow streets and connecting stairways, as well as a palace dominating the highest point. **4**

Herakleion (Candia) Important Venetian fortress which fell to the Turks in 1669 after 20-year siege. Scene of fierce resistance to German invasion in 1941. **34–5, 137, 224, 225, 256**

Hydra Maintained a semi-independent status during Turkish rule. In the eighteenth century became a significant shipbuilding and mercantile centre. Its shipowners played an important role in the War of Independence. **146, 147**

Ioannina (Jannena, Janina) A town established during the Byzantine period on a rocky promontory overlooking Lake Ioannina (Limini Pambotis). Between 1788 and 1822 it was the capital of quasi-independent state of Ali Pasha, who was assassinated on an island in the Lake in 1822. Captured by Greece in 1913 during Balkan War. In 1941 the large and long-standing Jewish population disappeared. **153–4, 158, 226**

Kalyvrita In nearby monastery of Agia Lavra Archbishop Germanos proclaimed Greek independence. Scene of one of the worst massacres perpetrated by occupying forces during the Second World War (Dec. 1943). **226**

Karpenissi Souliot leader Markos Botsaris killed near here in 1823. Only town to be captured by the Democratic Army in the Civil War. **241**

Kastritsa A Palaeolithic settlement at the south end of Lake Ioannina, discovered by the British School of Archaeology at Athens in 1966. **1**

Kavalla Birthplace of Mohammed Ali, whose son Ibrahim was offered the Peloponnese in return for putting down Greek Revolt. Became part of Greece in 1913. Large Jewish population deported in 1941. **199, 226**

Kerkira (Corfu, ancient Kerkyra, Corcyra) The second largest of the Ionian islands. In the eighth century BC a colony was founded here by the Corinthians and Kerkira developed a powerful navy, but her strength was dissipated in a series of civil wars between democrats and oligarchs in the fifth century BC. It later became the hub of Venetian naval power in the Adriatic. Kerkira town, massively fortified by the Venetians, withstood seven Turkish assaults. Although the Venetians tried to impose their language on the inhabitants, the island played an important role in preserving Greek culture and maintaining links with Western Europe. During the Revolutionary and Napoleonic Wars it was ruled by the Russians, the French and finally the British, whose administration continued until 1864. In the First World War it was occupied by the Entente and became a haven for the defeated Serbian Army. It was seized by Italy in 1923, but reverted to Greece in 1949. In June 1994 the island became the focus of world attention as the location for the European Summit chaired by Andreas Papandreou in his role as president of the European Union. **55, 128, 137–8, 149, 212, 231**

Khalandriani (Chalandriani) A settlement of the Cycladic era in the north of the island of Syros. **3**

Khalkidike (Chalcidice) A peninsula to the east of the Thermaic Gulf in the north of the Aegean. It acquired its name from the number of colonies established there by the city of Khalkis in Euboia. Its eastern promontory became the site for a series of Byzantine monasteries below the mountain of Athos. The Orthodox Church maintains many of the monasteries

and still today no females (animals included apart from chickens) are allowed to set foot on Athos. In 1979 it was the site of the first conference of New Democracy, when Karamanlis introduced the principle of elected leadership and resigned to stand for the presidency. **55, 59, 258**

Khalkis (Chalkis, Negroponte) In the Classical period an important city-state on the island of Euboia. A centre of Venetian influence in the Middle Ages. Captured by the Turks in 1470; a Venetian attempt to recapture it in 1688 was thwarted by malaria. **136**

Khios (Chios) A large island off the coast of Turkey. Famed for its climate and fertility it was prosperous during the Classical period, claiming as its own, amongst others, Homer, the historian Theopompos and the sophist Theokritos. It became the centre of Genoese rule over Samos, Lemnos, Lesbos, Thassos and Samothrace, 1346–1566. In 1822 a massacre of its inhabitants did much to rally European support for independence. **137, 158, 170**

Klidi Palaeolithic site in the Vikos Gorge, near Konitsa in the northwest. **1**

Knossos The largest Minoan site on Crete, consisting of a palace and surrounding villas. Excavations were begun in 1900 by Sir Arthur Evans, and since 1967 further work has been carried out by the British School. The first palace seems to have been built *c.* 1950–00 BC and was destroyed by an earthquake *c.* 1700. After the destruction the palace was rebuilt and it is mainly this building which survives today as a result of Evans' controversial reconstruction. Around 1450 BC the palace was destroyed by some natural disaster and the site was reoccupied by Mycenaean Greeks from the mainland until about 1380. **5, 6, 8**

Larissa Under Turkish rule from 1389–1881. Briefly recaptured by the Turks in war of 1897. **185**

Lavrion (Laurion) The site of silver mines in Attica. A fresh seam of silver found at Laurion in 483 BC enabled the Athenians to increase the size of their fleet so that Athens became the leading naval power in Greece. **6, 36, 62**

Litochoron Scene of bomb outrage sanctioned by KKE on eve of 1946 election. **239**

Mallia A Minoan site, centred around a large palace, on the north coast of Crete. Excavations by the French School of Archaeology have revealed palace construction phases like those at Knossos and Phaistos: the first palace from *c.* 1900 to *c.* 1700 BC and the rebuilt second palace destroyed *c.* 1450. **5**

Melos (Milos) The most south-westerly of the Cycladic islands (see Phylokopi). Dorian settlers, the islanders refused to join Athens' Empire and were either killed or sold into slavery in 416 BC. Thucydides in his *History of the Peloponnesian War* used the occasion to expose the Athenians' misuse of power. **43–5**

Methoni, Methone (Modon, ancient Pedasos) A fortress town mentioned in Homer. It was strategically important as a naval base and port. Known, with Korone (Coron), as 'the eyes of Venice'. Bridgehead and supply base

for Ibrahim Pasha's invasion in 1825, and for the French expedition against Ibrahim in 1828. **164**

Missolonghi Long defiance of the Turks made it a symbol of Greek nationalism in Western Europe, particularly after Lord Byron's death here in 1824. Its fall in 1826 helped to mobilize European public opinion for the Greek cause. **159, 160, 165, 168, 171**

Mistra (Mystra) A Frankish and Byzantine fortress town overlooking the plain of Sparta. It became a Byzantine cultural centre, governed by a Despot, and many of its fine churches have been restored. It fell to the Turks in 1460. Recaptured by the Venetians between 1687–1715. Burned and pillaged by the Russian Orlov expedition (1770), by the Albanians (1780), and by Ibrahim Pasha (1825). **116, 125, 164**

Monemvasia A Byzantine fortress built on a high, rocky promontory which can only be approached by a single entrance from the mainland. The Church of Ayia Sophia, founded by the emperor Andronikos II in the fourteenth century, was restored in 1958. It was captured by the Turks in 1540. Briefly regained by Venice between 1690–1715. **116, 127, 129, 136, 155, 156**

Mount Grammos Site of two defeats inflicted upon the Democratic Army in 1948 by Greek government forces. **240, 241**

Mudros (Island of Lemnos) Taken over as supply base for the Gallipoli campaign in 1915. Turkish Armistice signed aboard British warship in 1918. **198, 202**

Mycenae (Mykinai) Known traditionally as Agamemnon's capital and first excavated by Heinrich Schliemann in 1874. The city seems to have acted as an administrative centre from 1650–1100 BC and was fortified with 'Cyclopian Walls', large polygonal stones fitted together (such was their size that Greeks during the Classical period thought they must have been built by the giants, the Cyclops). Mycenae's name has been given to the dominant Greek civilisation (recognized as Greek by the decipherment of the writing Linear B) which is found throughout Greece and the islands in the late Bronze Age. Sometime before 1200 BC a disaster overwhelmed the Greek mainland and this was followed by a second attack *c.* 1100, known as the 'Dorian Invasions', which brought a final end to Mycenaean Civilization. The stories of family treacheries and tragedies which beset the Homeric dynasty of Mycenae provided the basis for many of the plots of Classical drama. **5, 7–9, 11, 12**

Mytilene The main city-state on the island of Lesbos. In 427 BC the citizens rebelled against the Athenians who, when they had overwhelmed the islanders' resistance, determined to kill all the males and sell the women and children into slavery. Thucydides records a debate in which the Athenians changed their minds and sent a ship which just managed to arrive in the nick of time and prevent the executions being carried out. **240, 241**

Nauplion As Napoli di Romania, Venetian administrative centre of Peloponnese from 1388–1540 and from 1686–1715, and heavily fortified by

them. In the War of Independence the Turkish garrison held out until 1822, when it fell to Kolokotronis. The town became a centre of the Greek independence movement and temporary capital between 1829–33. Many fine neoclassical buildings date from this period. It was the site of Capodistrias' assassination in 1831, and of the landing of King Otho in 1833. **136, 137, 156, 162, 164, 167, 176**

Naupaktos (Lepanto) In 455 BC the Athenians settled here some Messenian helots who had rebelled against the Spartans. It became an important Turkish naval base and garrison for Janissaries. Scene of great naval battle in 1571. **99, 126**

Naxos Famed for its marble, the largest of the Cycladic islands. It was here that the legendary Theseus abandoned Ariadne after their escape from Crete. Though allegedly of Athenian stock the Naxians became unwilling members of the Athenian empire after a revolt was crushed in 472 BC. In AD 1207 Marco Sanudi seized the island and founded a Venetian duchy which finally succumbed to the Turks in the sixteenth century. Giacomo IV, the last Duke, fought at the battle of Lepanto. **3, 46**

Olympia A beautiful sanctuary site where the Olympic games were held. Every four years the Greeks proclaimed a truce while they competed with each other in a series of games: chariot racing, wrestling and athletics. The games were finally abolished by the Christian emperors in the fourth century AD but the sanctuary site has been well preserved by the flooding of the river Kladeos, which buried the stadium, the temples and other buildings under several feet of silt. **34, 51, 52, 74, 79**

Parga Sold by the British to Ali of Janina in 1817, and remained in Turkish hands until 1913. **153**

Paros One of the Cycladic islands, famous in antiquity for its marble. Colonized by the Ionians, Paros became a member of the Delian league in the fifth century BC. After 1204 the island was part of the Venetian Duchy of Naxos until it was taken by the Turks in 1537. **3, 36, 129, 148**

Patras Captured by the Turks in 1460. Burnt by them in 1821, and subsequently rebuilt as a spacious nineteenth-century city. British troops landed in October 1944. **234**

Pella Philip II's capital of Macedonia where Alexander the Great was born. Excavations begun in 1957 have revealed a fine series of pebble mosaics done in a classical style. **77**

Potidaia (Poteidaia) A colony founded by Corinth c. 600 BC in the Khalkidike. Potidaia's determination to resist Athenian power in 432 BC was given by Thucydides as one of the causes of the Peloponnesian War. **55–6**

Petralona Cave In the Khalkidiki, 61 km from Thessaloniki, where the remains of Neanderthal Man, dating back 500,000 years, have been found. **1**

Phaistos A Minoan palace, on a superb site in the south of Crete, excavated by the Italian School of Archaeology at Athens after 1900. The first palace, like that at Knossos, was destroyed c. 1700 BC and was replaced by a grander building which was devastated c. 1450. Unlike Knossos the palace has not been restored. **5**

Phylakopi A prehistoric site on the island of Melos, with phases of settlement from the Cycladic period down to the Mycenaean era. **3**

Pylos (Navarino) At old Pylos to the north of the island of Sphakteria are some Mycenaean remains which are probably the port for the 'Palace of Nestor', a Bronze Age archaeological site (c. 1300–1200 BC) excavated near Khora. Linear B tablets (the earliest Greek writing) were discovered at the palace on the very day Italy invaded Albania in 1939. During the Peloponnesian War the Athenian Kleon captured 120 Spartan citizens (who were never supposed to surrender) on the island of Sphakteria in 425 BC. The bay was the site of the decisive naval battle of 1827, when Ibrahim Pasha's combined Turkish and Egyptian fleets were destroyed by Admiral Codrington's British, French and Russian force. **8, 58, 126, 137, 148, 156, 164, 170, 172**

Rhodes During antiquity an island famed for its navy and a colossal statue which bestrode the entrance to the harbour of Lindos. It was ruled from 1306–1522 by the knights of St John of Jerusalem, who engaged in massive construction but also in piracy. Captured by Suleiman the Magnificent in 1522 and ruled by the Turks until 1912, and then by the Italians until 1948. **9, 101, 127, 128, 158, 189, 212**

Salonika (Thessaloniki) The second city of Greece and the capital of the north. Founded by Kassander in 316 BC and named after his wife Thessalonikeia, a half-sister of Alexander the Great, the city soon became important because of its geographical position at the head of the Thermaic Gulf. In 146 BC the Romans made it the capital of the Province of Macedonia and Pompey used it as his base during the civil war against Julius Caesar. In antiquity the city's population included a large Italian and Jewish element and it was visited by St Paul. In the fourth century AD the Roman emperor Galerius lived there and during the Byzantine period it was the Empire's second city after Constantinople, until it was sacked by the Saracens in 904. In 1204 the city became the capital of the Latin kingdom of Boniface of Montferrat. In 1246 it returned to Byzantine suzerainty but during the fourteenth century the city changed hands many times until, devastated and depopulated, it eventually fell to the Ottoman Turks in 1430. In 1821 the Turks forestalled attempts to join the Greek Revolt by massacring thousands of its inhabitants. At the end of the nineteenth century, after the construction of a rail link with Austria and Germany, it became a major port, developed mainly by French investment. In 1909 it was the centre of a rebellion against the Sultan led by Mustafa Kemal (Atatürk). In 1912 it was occupied by Greek forces only hours ahead of the advancing Bulgarian army. In 1913 it was the scene of King George I's assassination. In 1916 a large Anglo–French force, later disparagingly nicknamed the 'Gardeners of Salonika', was landed against the wishes of King Constantine, and the city became a centre of the Venizelist rebellion against him. In 1917 much of the city was destroyed by fire. The large Jewish population disappeared after the German occupation in 1941. In 1963 it witnessed the assassination of Left-wing deputy, Gregory Lambrakis ('Z'). After the former Yugoslav Republic of Macedonia's declaration of independence in 1993, the city has become the centre of national fears that this was seen to pose to Greek interests. Huge demonstrations were held to protest against the perceived usurpation of the name *Macedonia*, and against an article in the new Republic's constitution which implied a claim to the city and its hinterland. In 1994 the Greek government closed the port to the former Yugoslav Republic, for which it was a vital trading outlet, in order to force it to change its name, flag and Constitution. **144, 147, 185, 187, 198, 218, 226**

Sesklo A Neolithic site 20 km west of Volos, the chief port of Thessaly. Excavations have revealed a palace, and other remains may go back as far as the seventh millennium BC. **2**

Sparti (Sparta) A Dorian settlement which developed a unique constitution traditionally based upon the reforms of Lykourgos in the ninth century BC (although such an early date is unlikely). The city of Sparta consisted of four villages which were undefended by any wall as the Spartans put their security in their ability to beat any other city-state in pitched battle. Spartan society was basically divided into three groups, the Spartiatai, who were citizens, the *perioikoi* ('dwellers around'), who were conquered Dorians, and the helots, who included an enslaved people of Lakonia as well as the conquered Messenians. All male Spartiatai spent most of their lives in military training so they could sustain their dominance both at home and abroad. Although Sparta was able to defeat Athens in 404 BC, the Spartans, because of their narrow regime, were unsuited to provide any unity within Greece and their power was smashed by Thebes after 371. Ancient authors were fascinated by Sparta's conservative political and social structure but Sparta itself contributed little to Greek culture and has left virtually no material inheritance. **17–19, 57–73**

Syros (see Khalandriani) Despite capture by the Turks in 1537, the island remained a centre of Catholic Christianity. After 1821 its port, Ermopoli, grew from nothing to become Greece's chief port, developed largely by immigrants from the Ottoman Empire. It was eclipsed by Piraeus after the Corinth Canal was opened in 1893. **3**

Thebes (Thebai) The dominant city-state of Boiotia which had an important part in Greek myth: for example, Thebes was the scene of the Oedipus story. As an inveterate enemy of her neighbour Athens, Thebes had helped Sparta win the Peloponnesian War. However, it was not long before the Thebans themselves resisted Spartan dominance and in 371 BC their newly-trained hoplites destroyed the myth of Spartan invincibility. Thebes' own power was ephemeral and, along with her erstwhile enemy Athens, the city was defeated by Philip II of Macedonia in 338 BC. After Philip's death an unsuccessful rebellion was ruthlessly punished by Alexander the Great and the city razed to the ground. **8, 31, 56, 68, 71–8, 159**

Thera (Thira, Santorini) The most southerly of the Cycladic islands. The island was a huge volcano, the centre of which disappeared when it erupted with devastating force in 1500 BC, burying the Bronze Age site of Akrotiri. During the rule of the Egyptian Ptolemys it was a naval base. After 1207 it was included in the Duchy of Naxos (see above). **6–7**

Tiryns A Mycenaean site which occupies a low rocky outcrop in the plain of Argos. It seems to have always been secondary to Mycenae or Argos, and although it was reoccupied after the devastation of 1100 BC, it never regained any importance and was finally destroyed by Argos in 468 BC. **8**

Varkisa Seaside villa owned by the politician Kanellopoulos in which an agreement was signed ending the fighting between Left and Right in 1945. **235–7**

Vergina Identified with the Macedonian site of Aigai, it was here in 1977 that M. Andronikos discovered the intact tomb of Philip II. **81**

Zakro A Minoan site with a palace on the east coast of Crete, first investigated at the beginning of the century but only thoroughly excavated by N. Platon after 1962. Part of the Late Minoan I palace is now in the sea and the whole site seems to have suffered a severe catastrophe *c.* 1500 BC. **5**

Index

Interlink Bestselling Travel Publications

The Traveller's History Series

The Traveller's History series is designed for travellers who want more historical background on the country they are visiting than can be found in a tour guide. Each volume offers a complete and authoritative history of the country from the earliest times up to the present day. A Gazetteer cross-referenced to the main text pinpoints the historical importance of sights and towns. Illustrated with maps and line drawings, this literate and lively series makes ideal before-you-go reading, and is just as handy tucked into suitcase or backpack.

A Traveller's History of Australia	$14.95 pb
A Traveller's History of the Caribbean	$14.95 pb
A Traveller's History of China	$14.95 pb
A Traveller's History of England	$14.95 pb
A Traveller's History of France	$14.95 pb
A Traveller's History of Greece	$14.95 pb
A Traveller's History of India	$14.95 pb
A Traveller's History of Ireland	$14.95 pb
A Traveller's History of Italy	$14.95 pb
A Traveller's History of Japan	$14.95 pb
A Traveller's History of London	$14.95 pb
A Traveller's History of North Africa	$15.95 pb
A Traveller's History of Paris	$14.95 pb
A Traveller's History of Russia	$14.95 pb
A Traveller's History of Scotland	$14.95 pb
A Traveller's History of Spain	$14.95 pb
A Traveller's History of Turkey	$14.95 pb
A Traveller's History of the U.S.A.	$14.95 pb

The Traveller's Wine Guides

Illustrated with specially commissioned photographs (wine usually seems to be made in attractive surroundings) as well as maps, the books in this series describe the wine-producing regions of each country, recommend itineraries, list wineries, describe the local cuisines, suggest wine bars and restaurants, and provide a mass of practical information—much of which is not readily available elsewhere.

A Traveller's Wine Guide to France	$19.95 pb
A Traveller's Wine Guide to Germany	$17.95 pb
A Traveller's Wine Guide to Italy	$17.95 pb
A Traveller's Wine Guide to Spain	$17.95 pb

The Independent Walker Series

This unique series is designed for visitors who enjoy walking and getting off the beaten track. In addition to their value as general guides, each volume is peerless as a walker's guide, allowing travellers to see all of the great sites, enjoy the incomparable beauty of the countryside, and maintain a high level of physical fitness while travelling through the popular tourist destinations. Each guide includes:

• Practical information on thirty-five extraordinary short walks (all planned as day hikes and are between 2 and 9 miles), including: how to get there, where to stay, trail distance, walking time, difficulty rating, explicit trail directions and a vivid general description of the trail and local sights.

• Numerous itineraries: The Grand Tour which embraces all thirty-five walks; regional itineraries; and thematic itineraries.

• One planning map for the itineraries and thirty-five detailed trail maps.

• Trail notes broken down into an easy-to-follow checklist format.

• A "Walks-at-a-Glance" section which provides capsule summaries of all the walks.

• Black and white photographs.

• Before-you-go helpful hints.

The Independent Walker's Guide to France	$14.95 pb
The Independent Walker's Guide to Great Britain	$14.95 pb
The Independent Walker's Guide to Italy	$14.95 pb
The Independent Walker's Guide to Ireland	$14.95 pb

Wild Guides

An unrivalled series of illustrated guidebooks to the wild places far from home and work: the long walks, mountain hideaways, woods, moors, sea coasts and remote islands where travellers can still find a refuge from the modern world.

"The Wild Guides will be enjoyed by everyone who hopes to find unspoiled places."
—The Times (London)

Wild Britain	$19.95 pb
Wild France	$19.95 pb
Wild Ireland	$19.95 pb
Wild Italy	$19.95 pb
Wild Spain	$19.95 pb

Cities of the Imagination

A new and innovative series offering in-depth cultural, historical and literary guides to the great cities of the world. More than ordinary guidebooks, they introduce the visitor or armchair traveller to each city's unique present-day identity and its links with the past.

Buenos Aires: A Cultural and Literary Companion	$15.00 pb
Edinburgh: A Cultural and Literary Companion	$15.00 pb
Madrid: A Cultural and Literary Companion	$15.00 pb
Mexico City: A Cultural and Literary Companion	$15.00 pb
Oxford: A Cultural and Literary Companion	$15.00 pb
Rome: A Cultural and Literary Companion	$15.00 pb
Venice: A Cultural and Literary Companion	$15.00 pb

The Spectrum Guides

Each title in the series includes over 200 full-color photographs and provides a comprehensive and detailed description of the country together with all the essential data that tourists, business visitors or students are likely to require.

Spectrum Guide to Ethiopia	$22.95 pb
Spectrum Guide to India	$22.95 pb
Spectrum Guide to Jordan	$22.95 pb
Spectrum Guide to Maldives	$22.95 pb
Spectrum Guide to Mauritius	$19.95 pb
Spectrum Guide to Nepal	$22.95 pb
Spectrum Guide to Pakistan	$22.95 pb
Spectrum Guide to Tanzania	$22.95 pb
Spectrum Guide to Uganda	$19.95 pb
Spectrum Guide to the United Arab Emirates	$21.95 pb

The In Focus Guides

This new series of country guides is designed for travellers and students who want to understand the wider picture and build up an overall knowledge of a country. Each In Focus guide is a lively and thought-provoking introduction to the country's people, politics and culture.

To order or request our complete catalog,
please call us at **1-800-238-LINK** or write to:
Interlink Publishing • 46 Crosby Street, Northampton, MA 01060
www.interlinkbooks.com